RUINS AND FRAGMENTS

RUINS
AND
FRAGMENTS
TALES OF LOSS AND REDISCOVERY

ROBERT HARBISON

REAKTION BOOKS

Published by Reaktion Books Ltd
33 Great Sutton Street
London EC1V 0DX, UK

www.reaktionbooks.co.uk

First published 2015
Copyright © Robert Harbison 2015

Printed and bound in Great Britain
by TJ International, Padstow, Cornwall

A catalogue record for this book is available from the British Library

ISBN 978 1 78023 447 2

Contents

In memory of happy times at
Hill Top on the North York Moors

Prologue

WHAT IS IT IN THE AIR of the present that makes us suspicious of works or histories that are too smooth, too continuous? That makes us feel fragmentariness has a kind of meaning in itself before there's any content to fill it? Is it that urban experience is inherently discontinuous and fragmented, or that the only truths we can believe are partial ones? Certainly much interesting work of the last century makes us feel that we've got part of something, not the whole – Carlo Scarpa finding a ruin in a seemingly complete building at Castelvecchio in Verona, inventing an archaeological dig where no one had seen any fracture before, or Ezra Pound discovering a discontinuous ruin in Eliot's lengthier draft of his *Waste Land*, removing sections and shortening others to leave it resembling an incomplete inscription, remnant of something once longer and more intelligible.

The story begins with dramatically shorn off ancient fragments, of the Pergamon frieze and Aeschylus' plays, but we find them stuck to other things that in one sense have nothing to do with them, a grimy location in England or a rubbish dump in Egypt, but their later history is now part of them and makes these ragged scraps more riveting than the others who stayed behind in their proper places. Likewise we wouldn't trade Wang Bing's ruined Chinese factories for all the wealth of Shanghai, or the ruined lives in Douglas's Newcraighall or Agee's Alabama for more intact ones. It was intended that the first chapter should treat inadvertent fragments, the second constructed ones, but the two bounce off and rebound on each other. Deprived lives can be ruinous for the writers who expose themselves to them.

The first chapter ends with collectors of scraps and builders from bits who salvage something from the common ruin that surrounds them, tattered Venetian brocade or marble rubble in Athens or old boards in Essex or passersby in Moscow and Kiev. The next chapter takes on the great early twentieth-century monuments to a fragmentary view: *Ulysses*, *Battleship Potemkin*, Vertov's *Enthusiasm* and Benjamin's *Arcades* – literature, film and literature as film – in the optimistic moment when the breaking up of the old certainties and loosening of form into ceaseless movement tempted writers and filmmakers to epic scale and exuberance. There are bleaker but no less ambitious versions in Eliot's and Stevens's lyric epics which predict apocalyptic collapse or Buddhist withdrawal as the likely terminus for the fragmented vision. Museums of the early twentieth century translate this way of seeing into another realm and construct a discontinuous history out of purchases themselves disruptive of the places they hail from, the collections finally graveyards disguised as historical sequence.

The chapter about modernist architecture and ruin begins with Le Corbusier and considers his villas of the 1920s as ruin-like in their bareness and their startling rearrangement of the conventional parts of the dwelling. Seen through the filter of modernism certain landscapes (Dungeness), prehistoric sites (Skara Brae) and Japanese works of art (Zen gardens) all have the same properties and bring together ruin and modernity. Brutalism, an offshoot of Corbusian clarity, restores the strong textures which had been banished, from which a resemblance to historical depth can arise, and new work can then share the numinous quality of ruin. Then comes actual modernist ruin at Cardross, followed by modernists coming to terms with war-damaged ruins, results largely unforeseen in Döllgast's Munich and Chipperfield's Berlin.

Now three writers devoted to the fragment or the patchwork made of small pieces, who contrive monumental works out of scraps, seen as transcendental achievement by their readers and as failure by themselves. So Coleridge, Montaigne and Robert Burton are further ruined lives that leave behind great incomplete constructions over which their followers have climbed happily for centuries. For Coleridge ruin comes prior to achievement: he already knows he must give up before he gets the courage to begin, and his most gripping passages are fitted round the edges of other people's pages in marginalia that scale the greatest heights disguised as commentary on someone else's text. Montaigne tried withdrawing from the world, but it did not work as expected and he was left inventing a new way of fending off melancholy by writing short pieces that followed the meanderings of his mental life. Burton too thought writing could come between him and melancholy, which partly explains how his work can be both so long and so un-unified.

The next chapter treats two unrepeatable fictions, more unlike other books than practically any known, both of which show very persuasively that confusion is a truer, deeper representation of reality than easy sense or intelligibility. In *Tristram Shandy* the order of the simplest events is so scrambled according to the haphazard order of subjective experience that straightening it out seems much more impossible than putting the broken pieces of a shattered pot back in order. Not that we want the ruined sequence restored; we know that would be banal and pointless.

Finnegans Wake is a far more demonic puzzle, teasing us with the idea of a narrative or narratives buried somewhere under all these layers of confusion like compost laid down by lots of intervening cultures. Like other instances scattered through this book, Joyce seems in search of a pre-literate level of consciousness more authentic than anything since language got corrupted, but the only way to get there is through a mist of words.

The last two chapters are a pair, Destruction and Reconstruction. Destruction tackles the seemingly perverse phenomenon of creating ruin deliberately, starting with Cubism, which doesn't actually destroy the canvases but the conventions of painting and the integrity of the image. Both Picasso and Braque set about making their subjects un-recognizable and in various ways unpalatable, because there is a new truth in that. Schwitters goes a step further, welcoming into the picture defaced and ruined bits of the world, scraps he picks up in the street or finds in his pockets. In the Merzbau he practises collage on an architectural scale in defiance of rational principles of building.

Gordon Matta-Clark is a pivotal figure in this book for his attacks on actual buildings, which he destroys in order to save them, or rather to find something in them of which they were unaware. He makes it possible to appreciate the radicalism of John Soane more fully than we could before Matta-Clark showed us how. Soane's attacks on structural complacency are shrouded by the fragments from his collection that pepper the walls, but they run very deep. Next come more literal and serious efforts of extermination at the hands of Byzantine, Puritan and Soviet iconoclasts, who only in the last case pay any artistic dividends. Graffiti are another pivotal phenomenon, defacement to some eyes, art to others, creating or drawing attention to urban squalor, offering a kind of critique or just doing damage. The iconoclasts won't accept that art is a protected realm no matter what it says. The issues are vaguely similar with graffiti: to welcome them you need to overlook social or ideological intents, or at least become more tolerant of them. Via Tony Harrison's poem set in a graffiti-laden graveyard we find ourselves contemplating the ultimate ruin, a corpse (or a whole lot of them), found here or on the battlefield. Deaths in the *Iliad* are constant and troubling, and the poem's distance from us invests it with some of the properties of a ruin, which experts assure us is just the soil the *Iliad* and all other epics sprang from. Other treatments of war, and Berlin in 1945, bring us to the great urban ruin of our era – Detroit, a memorial to a ruinous industry.

The final chapter sets out to treat the contrary of ruin, reconstruction, but this is easier said than done. All the best cases seem ambiguous, Shakespeare's Globe, Williamsburg in Virginia, Warsaw Old Town – each of them in some way doubtful, not that nothing by that name ever existed, but this simulacrum isn't it, whatever its virtues as entertainment. Then a wonderfully paradoxical group, ruins which can be resurrected to look a lot like they did in the first place – Ephesus, Angkor and Athens; Brooklyn, Ryedale and Bangkok. A wide field for a tremendous variety of fantasies to play in. The chapter ends with something less ambitious and more successful, in their own modest terms: Alan Sorrell's drawings of archaeological sites with all the clouds, smoke, rutted tracks, rustic folk, donkeys and dogs that go with them.

1

Rough Edges

IN 1962 A LARGE CHUNK of a Hellenistic frieze from Pergamon in Anatolia turned up in Worksop, a decayed industrial town in Nottinghamshire. A less likely place for this discovery is hard to imagine. The fragment is a battered male torso of heroic proportions resting on one knee – the knee itself missing – which turns violently leftward and thrusts out its thigh, most of which is elsewhere, part of a different marble slab now in Berlin. The marble lump in Worksop is dirty and ruined and scribbled with graffiti. It is kept in a back corridor of a former library building, now host to the world's largest jumble sale. It is mounted on a plywood frame, but mounted incorrectly: the sheered-off edge of its left buttock should be vertical, not sloping leftward, which would make the twist of the muscled back much more dynamic, careening backward. But there is such energy in the turn of the ruined head and the clench of his badly damaged hindquarters. Even in this roughly broken-off chunk the unorthodox power of the whole 120-metre frieze comes through.

The Pergamon frieze is astonishing in its more than human scale, in its writhing forms fighting free of the wall that notionally contains them, in the terrible violence of the battle it depicts between monsters and godlike men or human-style gods. There's biting and scratching and torching living flesh. Every substance depicted is contorted – the clothes, the hair, muscles, scales, fur, fins. Heroic nude forms are twisted and trampled by heartless clothed figures and intertwined with enormous serpents showing mouthfuls of sharp teeth. It is nightmarish and fascinating and very hard to disentangle.

Above all, the frieze is ruined and fragmentary, many of the faces erased or half erased, a few figures labelled with names scratched into the stone, but many more impossible to identify precisely, stranded among large stretches that are completely missing.

The frieze dates from the second century BC, but disappeared in Byzantine times, broken up and used as building material in fortifications or buried in later foundations or turned into lime on building sites. In 1864–5 a German engineer building roads in Anatolia saw a few stones that made him think the altar mentioned as a wonder of the world by a single ancient source might lie buried here. It was a dozen years before he could convince anyone to support the excavations and only in 1880 could the altar begin to be reconstructed in Berlin, which is where everything he found ended up.

So the Worksop fragment is only the furthest reach of the dispersal of the Pergamon altar, and the rest of the story will yield plenty of

A fragment of the Pergamon frieze from Asia Minor at home in its current location, Worksop, Nottinghamshire.

A section of the Battle of the Gods and Giants from Pergamon now in Berlin, showing a cast of the Worksop fragment integrated with the other surviving remains.

incongruities too. But how did this drab Midlands town come by a large remnant of the Battle between the Gods and the Giants from the capital of an empire in Asia Minor of the second century BC? The fragment had been in plain view, built into the wall of an ordinary brick house, since at least the early twentieth century, when the house's resident, a local historian, knew very well it was a piece of classical sculpture, but not exactly which one. He died in 1908 and even that much of the piece's history was soon forgotten, so that in 1960 a new owner, bothered by damp he thought was caused by the fragment, extracted the marble and tried to flog it unsuccessfully to a cemetery mason to be turned into marble chips, and then to an art school for sculpture students to practise on.

This is where Mr Straw comes in. Recently the town has been in the national news for a special kind of house museum, Mr Straw's House. Mr Straw was the son of a local grocer who never married and hardly left Worksop after an early brush with art school in London. Called back to Worksop by his father's death he settled with his brother in his parents' house and lived a life so ordinary that the house has become a byword for unremarkable detritus. To a casual observer it looks as if nothing was ever thrown away. So although no single item strays outside what one might expect to find in an ordinary early twentieth-century home, the steady accumulation of insignificant detail finally comes to seem remarkable. And so the National Trust has put a lot of energy into keeping this house the way it was, in its nondescript street full of others like itself.

Mr Straw sat on the Library Committee of Worksop Council, which is how he came to save the Pergamon torso, at first parked in the Highway Department depot, until he again agitated to have it properly displayed, but now the Parks Department wanted to know more about what they were getting, and this insistence led to the British Museum and the recognition of the fragment's true identity.

The torso is still in Worksop but isn't really at home there. The story of its travails since it left Ottoman territory has been pieced together since 1962 and forms a weird footnote to the strange fate of the Pergamon altar in general.

In 1635 the Earl of Arundel, the first great English collector of classical sculpture, sent his chaplain, William Petty, prospecting for antique remains in Greece and Asia Minor. Among the fruits of this expedition were 200 ancient fragments, including a few pieces of the Pergamon frieze. One of these showed a hand holding a thunderbolt, now lost, which must have belonged to the figure of Zeus, suggesting that the arm presently attached to the god in the frieze is an incorrect restoration. Anyway, the largest of Petty's fragments was the chunk now in Worksop, which Arundel displayed in his Thames-side garden in London. Worksop Manor also belonged to him, so the torso must have come there with the mistreated cast-offs of the collection, and after the fire of 1761 it found its way to a townsperson who decorated his house with it.

Now the figure has reassumed its place in the larger frieze. A plaster cast taken from it confronts one of the most horrifying giants on the south segment, the so called Steer-giant. So the Worksop figure must be a god, not a giant. But this is disputed; most writers call him a giant. Gods in the frieze tend to stand straight up; giants are often sunken onto or even into the earth, the most outlandish case being Ge or Gaia, an oversized being who half emerges from the ground in time to watch Athena dragging her favourite son by the hair while he is poisoned by one of the huge snakes.

The tormented history of the frieze includes an appearance in the Book of Revelation, whose author identified the monument as the Seat of Satan, possibly hastening its medieval demise. American fundamentalists have revived the old, disparaging name in no ironic spirit, connecting the sculptures from Pergamon with Satan and, via its relocation in Berlin, with Hitler, and finally with Barack Obama, who visited the museum and was, they say, inspired by the pagan seat in planning a temporary construction for his inauguration as President.

The altar had arrived in Berlin piecemeal in the 1880s, fruit of German excavations in Ottoman Turkey, 1878–86, in conscious emulation of Elgin's removal of the Parthenon frieze to London and the British Museum. The later transfer functioned similarly as firming up ideas of nationhood and empire.

At the end of the Second World War, and just before the postwar carve-up of Berlin, Russian troops came upon sections of the Pergamon frieze which had been reburied in the earth, in tunnels near the zoo, to protect them from bombing, and carted them off to Leningrad where according to different accounts they were displayed in a museum (and inspired Russian novelists and poets) or locked away in storage. There are savage ironies in the looting of this unwieldy monument. First of all, a subliminal link with the fall of Berlin, because the frieze shows vivid scenes of battle, not comfortably tranquillized but carrying a strong hint of apocalypse, a war that could barely be contained and didn't look as if it were over.

The reconstructed monument was removed from a ruined city in a ruined Germany, both of them about to be politically fragmented all over again. The sculptures have generally been interpreted as part of a victory monument, but portray a world in ruins, and have also inspired counter interpretations that take sides against the victors and even detect in the stones an early work of proletarian art, a subversive work that in its sense of struggle against great odds could form a model for the overblown murals of Socialist Realism to come, which might also turn on the masters and bite the hand that fed them.

A long novel in the form of a lecture

Peter Weiss's immense historico-political novel *The Aesthetics of Resistance* opens with a long description of a ruined but alarmingly vivid work composed of bodies that lunge outward, reach blindly, burst open. His prose comes in large unwieldy blocks which contest the space of the page with the reader. It is at least a good page and half filled with this plastic stuff of language that involves the reader in a special brand of struggle before we are sure that this takes place in a museum and that it is all a museum display. The first proper names are names of characters whose fierce attention climbs over these sculptures like primitive creatures just waking to a kind of consciousness. Maybe the strange backward-facing way of introducing the subject is trying to recreate the encounter of three uneducated teenagers with a very daunting work of art, an antiquity, fragmentary and ruined, but all the more intimidating as a cultural symbol for all that. Its ruin is part of its exclusiveness and makes it harder to know all you need to know in order to 'appreciate' this work, that is to own it and stop being frightened by it.

Jacob Burckhardt was one of the first to make a rich aesthetic appreciation of the Pergamon frieze. His initial comment remains the freshest example of its kind, exhilarating even for someone who knows the work well, in its unfettered seizing of the work's movement, energy and force, and its complete disregard of all the historical baggage of the monument's own original time and place, its connection with tyrants and dead armies. Burckhardt welcomes the frieze as a whole new epoch of classical art, utterly unclassical, whose truest kin are Rubens and seventeenth-century Baroque. He conjures up an enemy of the work, the whole tribe of conventional art historians who cannot think themselves past the cold classicism of Winckelmann. Apparently the battle over the frieze didn't take place the way Burckhardt predicted – the unruliness of the sculpture was welcomed by all kinds of observers; the dead hand of Winckelmann didn't detain them after all.

But there's still a vast distance between Burckhardt's and Weiss's appreciation of the Pergamon frieze, for it is the frieze that transfixes and perplexes the three teenagers at the beginning of the mammoth novel. Works of art are scattered through the book at intervals, as stopping places or stumbling blocks, creating problems of digestion, throwing up foreign substances that the book wants to ingest but can't pretend will ever blend smoothly with the impoverished lives around them. Pergamon is the first and for a long time the furthest away in time and space, both the most powerful and the most difficult of these, which include Bruegel's crowds and Millet's peasants, Kafka's victims (*The Castle* a proletarian novel, reclaimed here) and Géricault's corpses.

Pergamon is first because it is the most difficult, and if it could be successful would be the most satisfying, reclamation. Weiss gradually uncovers his vision of the frieze as a depiction of the class struggle, commissioned by rulers, told by artist-employees who subvert the message by using the slaves who haul the heavy blocks of marble as models, and suffered by workers who are afraid to look too hard at it, but get the point that there are gods (their rulers) and beasts (themselves). Two demonstrations go forward in tandem or entangled: that great art can be inverted or subverted away from its original dictatorial intentions, and that workers can transform themselves by the effort of taking intellectual possession of works of art. This project requires turning a dingy kitchen in Berlin into something more like a lecture hall or seminar room, which doesn't sound appetizing but results in the richest interpretation so far of a work of ancient art.

Richest in spite or because of being seriously fractured between appreciative description, dramatic visualization of the process of production, and imagined encounters with the work by unlikely modern types, which amounts to imagining an extraordinarily widened range of ways the work can be. They can't be completely integrated with each other, and are left deliberately in tension, forming a kind of dramatized analysis.

The missing hero

One crucial figure is missing entirely from the frieze in its present ruined state, Hercules, on whom the gods' chances depend. Only if they can convince a human being to join them can they defeat an earlier, stronger species, the giants, whom they want to replace. So

Hercules is the most crucial element in the current action, but that panel of the frieze is entirely lost, except that we know where it would fall because his name survives and one paw of his lion-cloak. The three boys in Weiss's novel have heard the story and so are keen to find Hercules, but of course they cannot because he isn't there. The story gets an even stronger hold on them through this absence. From somewhere comes an interpretation of the Labours of Hercules as the hero's penance for having gone over to the gods, a series of attempts to undo the tyranny of the victors. So Hercules becomes the idea of a hero who will lead the working class to victory, and throughout the book characters keep finding false-Hercules(es) who seem momentarily to be that saviour.

The New World reports itself to the Old

I'm fascinated by physical dispersal that causes important artefacts to come to rest in odd locations like driftwood on a beach, shorn of explanatory context. Maybe Weiss's novel and the Russian one reputedly inspired by Pergamon's brief sojourn in Russia partly discredit the pious idea that these bits of stone need to be reunited with the soil they rose out of to bear worthwhile fruit. Maybe Bernardino de Sahagún and Guaman Poma, two preservers of the native cultures of Mexico and Peru, would have had less startling impact if their great works had found their proper home in Madrid as intended, instead of ending as strange orphans in Florence and Copenhagen respectively.

In any event, the survival of subversive works in unsuitable places is often stirring, surviving to be discovered and appreciated many years after the time for them to fulfil their creators' intentions has passed. Sahagún's *Historia General de las Cosas de Nueva España*, a gargantuan study of native language and culture in sixteenth-century Mexico, is an outstanding instance of empathetic entry into the consciousness of a deeply foreign and subjugated people. It was energetically suppressed by the Spanish ruler to whom it was addressed and disappeared for two centuries until the hand-coloured original was discovered in the national library in Florence in the eighteenth century.

The precarious process of transmission makes the fragility and contingency of the great work inescapably real. It happens that Sahagún's and Guaman Poma's manuscripts (a parallel recovery of native culture in Peru) are both treasure troves of images that record a host of rituals and everyday activities otherwise lost beyond recall. Our fascination comes into clearer focus: the unique copy stands for the unrepeatable human individual, and the miraculous survival stands for other, even less likely ways of outwitting death.

Garbage dumps as cultural depths

Seven of Aeschylus' plays survive more or less intact; fragments and mentions of other missing works bring the total up to 73. All the fragmentary survivals of lost plays of Aeschylus are collected into one handy little Loeb volume. These scraps took two main routes to get here – being quoted by an ancient author for another purpose entirely, usually a writer we would otherwise never read, or surviving on semirotted papyrus, from the rubbish heaps of the vanished Egyptian town of Oxyrhynchus above all. Both routes are fascinating in their own ways, but the papyrus path bristles with more bewitching contingencies.

Fragments of a satyr play by Aeschylus on papyrus discovered in a garbage dump in Egypt, now in the Sackler Library, Oxford.

These papyrus fragments are not neat selections chosen to make a point, but scraps so little regarded that they may have something else written on top of them or lie next to a bit of garbage that bored a hole in them as it decomposed. I always want to know more than anyone will tell me about how the new verses or sentences were found, what they were stuck to, or interleaved with, and what could be guessed about the transcriber and his purposes.

Aeschylus resurfaced for me in a recent resurrection of his most famous plays, translated by Tony Harrison and staged by Peter Hall. The strangest features of this production were an all-male cast and a set of expressionless masks with open mouths and staring eyes. Sometimes it was difficult to tell who was speaking, and then one had to watch for movements in the actors' throats or catch glimpses of their tongues glittering inside the mouth-slots. By such simple means the players became something not quite human, propelled by forces speaking through them, using them as mediums. Thus the action transcended individual concerns or desires and ordinary actors could convey the grandeur of myth, evoking in the audience something like religious awe.

The Aeschylean fragments conjure up awe a little like this, arising from the feeling that we are mostly in the dark about how the lost plays presented their subjects, only able to catch occasional glimmerings of what this might have been. The patches of illumination seem the more intense because of the surrounding darkness, created by our uncertainty about which parts of a familiar story would find a place in the vanished fabric. Such drastic incompleteness occasionally gives the remnants hallucinatory strength.

There's always the possibility that more lines will be found, as did apparently happen at least once when Italian archaeologists dug up further fragments of the same leaf that the British team had already deciphered and published a part of. And a Sophoclean fragment (from *Epigonei*) became legible for the first time in 2005 via the latest infrared technology. Real historians, like the editor of the brilliant Aeschylean Loeb of 2008, view such detail as a form of distraction that contributes nothing to our understanding of what Aeschylus is saying.

But for me the circumstances of the city abandoned because its system of canals had fallen into disrepair, far enough from the Nile to escape the corrupting effect on papyrus of the annual inundation, are crucial in making real to us our distance from these texts. Likewise the succeeding stages of the recovery, carried out every winter from 1896 by hundreds of Egyptian workers, supervised by a pair of British classical scholars, who dig up tight-packed layers of papyrus mixed with earth, which are sifted, partly cleaned and shipped off to Oxford, where every summer they are more thoroughly cleaned, sorted, translated and compared to what already exists.

The resulting discoveries are wonderful but still, of course, fragmentary. A few of the most famous missing texts are found in tantalizingly partial form; other icebergs show their first tips, and what is found only brings home in more complete detail how much is lost.

Only a small portion of the finds have been published in the wonderfully complete annual volumes sponsored by the Egypt Exploration Society, and only a tenth of the deciphered material is literary anyway. In 1896 the British were the virtual rulers of Egypt, and perhaps the anomaly of shipping anything valuable back to Oxford seemed then less difficult to justify than it does now. It isn't the Elgin Marbles all over again, because this really is rubbish, not irreplaceable works of art, but *valuable* rubbish to those who realize what's lurking underneath the dirty surface. By now 70-odd volumes of annual reports have appeared, looking very respectable in their grey linen spines, each of them carrying its hefty superstructure of scholarly translations, notes and appendices. Almost three-quarters of all literary papyri discovered so far come from Oxyrhynchus; what began as a trawl in a garbage dump has become a great cultural edifice.

The long devotion to the unwanted detritus of this vanished Egyptian city by the two British classicists Grenfell and Hunt is a thrilling instance of seeing the value of insignificant fragments that will of necessity remain painfully incomplete. Tony Harrison, one of the most imaginative students of the classical texts, was so intrigued by the phenomenon of Oxyrhynchus that he wrote a play about it, *The Trackers of Oxyrhynchus* (1990), which brings Apollo and a troop of satyrs to the Hunt and Grenfell dig. These hallucinations of ancient creatures take possession of the Edwardian archaeologists and act out their buried secrets.

There is something wickedly apt in how hard it can be to track down Tony Harrison's transmogrifications of classical material, especially his films, that come at contemporary politics via Greek myth. For the moment texts are available, that is all, unless you count the reminiscences of those who saw the films themselves years ago, recounted in the midst of something else, like the ancient pedants illustrating some point of grammar with a momentary glimpse of a missing play by Aeschylus. *Trackers* is Hunt's translation of *Ichneutae*, the only surviving satyr play by Sophocles, which was dug up along with an ancient life of Euripides and other literary treasures on 13 January 1906. It is fascinating to watch Hunt dealing gingerly with this rogue work by the great tragedian, finding in it an attractive light-heartedness, subduing its linguistic liberties ('less coarse than Euripides but not always above reproach') in lengthy notes. The virtual disappearance of satyr plays arises from centuries of editorial decisions, a cleansing of Greek drama that Harrison's *Trackers* bullishly reverses.

Sometimes the fragments of Aeschylus are so ruined that barely any whole words remain and the Loeb editor is reduced to guessing who might be speaking them and in what context, then reaching for suitable vase paintings to conjure up some kind of action on stage. After the fragments of *Ichneutae* have turned up, Hunt can say that Welcker's earlier guess that a play with such a title might be about the wanderings of Europa is completely wrong. There must be many similar wrong guesses hiding in the latest commentary on the fragments.

This is no cause for despair, far from it. Much of the speculation about which vanished plays went with which to form those trilogies and tetralogies favoured by the Greeks, and many of the attempts to mark out which parts of the well-known stories figured in each of the connected plays, could easily be knocked down by any new evidence that came along. But the rambling edifice built on unprovable hypotheses, the huge undergrowth or tangle of not-exactly-known Aeschylus, has amplified the territory of the securely known into something much richer and more mysterious.

No one has thought of a site-museum at Oxyrhynchus; guidebooks don't include it and tourists aren't encouraged to visit. The very idea probably sounds about as feasible as holiday tours of large landfills of household rubbish. Oddly enough, there has been a successful

The world's largest landfill site, Jardim Gramacho, on the outskirts of Rio de Janeiro, as it appeared in a feature-length documentary, *Waste Land* (2010).

feature film about the world's largest rubbish tip: Jardim Gramacho on the outskirts of Rio, made just as it was about to close. Even venerable dumps like Monte Testaccio in Rome, a hill consisting entirely of clay storage jars discarded in ancient times, are not regarded as interesting enough to open them to the public. The history of this site is probably more complicated than we realize, judging by the picturesque paths carved in the pile of shards you can make out through the locked gates, suggesting that this ruin had its heyday, now past.

Oxyrhynchus may be a special case, but ruined texts aren't usually things people need to see with their own eyes, much less in the spots where they were discovered. The Loeb volume doesn't include a single photograph of a papyrus fragment. Maybe it would be different if, like the comedies of Menander, Aeschylus survived only in ruins. When we go further back, we find more ambiguous cases, like *Gilgamesh*, the Sumerian epic which exists in a state of even greater disrepair than the main Greek texts.

In fact in the last few years translations of *Gilgamesh* have regressed from clarity to obscurity, becoming more archaic, less continuous and more fragmented. The semi-ruined clay tablets on which the oldest version is incised have surfaced as the main divisions of the tale even in a Penguin version for the general reader. Gaps in the text aren't glossed over or filled seamlessly in as they were 45 years ago (in an earlier Penguin), and we are even encouraged to savour the damage of the centuries and the resulting incompleteness as depicted in the translator's little drawings of the flawed lumps, where every mark of the gouging tool on the clay is faithfully recorded. This is a different, discontinuous *Gilgamesh* that keeps reminding you it is a wreck salvaged from piles of less interesting debris.

There are probably readers who feel that Andrew George, responsible for this more tactile and deconstructed version of *Gilgamesh*, has strayed too close to the cliff face, reminding us too vividly what a labour it has been to extract a poem from the rubble of a vanished culture.

The issues are different but similar with bigger ruins, whole buildings for which there's no question of moving them to more convenient locations for inspection. We've grown very used to ruins in state care cleared of extraneous debris, which make the plan of the building easier to pick out and smooth our passage from room to room, space to space. Ground which has no building on it is levelled and grassed or gravelled.

It is a cleansed and purified version, and why not? . . . except that as with a rouged corpse there has been an attempt to conceal what a bad state the patient is really in. All is trim, and in some peculiar way remains in working order, meaning that every remaining element is informative and clearly distinct. The approach is a scientist's not a poet's, conveying the maximum amount of information with the least interference. Yet one has only to read any full response to a ruin, like Ruskin on Torcello, to realize that 'extraneous' is not always such an easy line to draw.

With rich old surfaces it's hard to know where cleaning should stop. A vogue for brightening early Italian paintings left Sassettas in the National Gallery in London so ruined in their starkness that they now look unfinished. Sometimes one can even think that the only ruins allowed to keep their full flavour are ones so despised or huge that no one can be bothered to tidy them, like, above all, abandoned factories and other large industrial buildings enjoying a precarious half-life under threat of demolition.

West of the Tracks

Wang Bing had just finished a film course when he began his lengthy study of a chain of factories laid out along a railway line on the outskirts of Shenyang in northeast China. The tracks became a fortuitous organizing principle, tracks like all those in the history of film which have provided an image of movement analogous to that of film itself. So the resulting film, finally pared down to nine hours of documentary footage about the decline, closure and disassembly of these factories, followed by the achingly gradual deconstruction and disinhabiting of the shanty dwellings of the last workers and their unemployed descendants, opens with a wonderful train journey through a working landscape now buried under a shroud of snow. Great sensory variety unrolls in front of us, constantly shifting, dropping behind before we've really taken it in, yet already deserted, abandoned.

Wang's film is called *West of the Tracks* in English, a literal translation of the name of the bedraggled working-class district where it all takes place. So it's a name as well as a description for a kind of nowhere in which you can't feel the nearness of a large city, a place cut off. I doubt if Wang knew from the start that he would devote three years of his life (1999–2002) to this subject and that the resulting film would dwell so insistently in one place. Only in retrospect can we talk about how well edited the result appears, how logical, how complete. As it goes along, *West of the Tracks* simply impresses us by how close it has gotten to the material, which is the experience of heavy, repetitive labour and its aftermath.

From the beginning we are watching processes which are about to cease: the last delivery of unwieldy lead sheets or sacks of red dust, the last smelting of impure copper in vats which crack and spew their contents across the workfloor, the last meeting in the dingy break room, the last showers in the foggy baths. If we didn't see it functioning, we'd say the factory shed, open on one long side to the tracks, framed by rickety walkways still usable but not looking it, was already a ruin. Because Wang stuck around so unreasonably long we end up seeing one unexpected stage of dereliction after another. They are industrial spaces perpetually on the verge of ruin, or dysfunction, the prelude

Ruined factories strung along the tracks in Wang Bing's nine-hour documentary *West of the Tracks* (2003).

to ruin. They are being taken apart by big and little, official and wildcat scavengers, even as a few workers squeeze the last drops of production out of them. So they are dying piecemeal, and resemble living beings crawled over and pecked at by smaller agents of decay.

The large spaces are almost invariably sublime; the small ones crammed with workers' lockers and their lunch arrangements are more poignant. A speaker recounts the stages of the shutdown. He's lying stretched out on a narrow bench and we can't get a good look at him. Then he sits up, according to some unforeseen rhythm in his narrative. But prostrate seems the default position here.

The factories and mills threaten to expire many times before they die; little reprieves that mean nothing constantly recur. But one day the end finally comes and we know we can no longer trundle up and down on listless trains watching parts subtracted from the familiar buildings one by one. What will *we* do, we wonder, when we no longer have the stimulus of travel or the grandeur of the big sheds? Where will we go, for the film still has many hours to run?

Until now we haven't seen how the workers live, but I guess we think we could imagine it. These particular factories are so visually rewarding because there's so little that's new about them: all the parts and processes look old and outmoded, like a lesson in the history of the industry. We've read somewhere that they were first constructed under the Japanese occupation and we can almost believe that much of the original fabric survives. Even the components being assembled or polished today look like relics or leftovers from processes long obsolete. Different kinds of patina, meaning different signs of use or passage, are everywhere.

Now we find all this repeated on a more intimate scale in every dwelling. All the interiors are dim. The light makes a selection of tones for us, reduced to a few shades the way Vermeer might do it. Surfaces are rich with age, print of hands, fog of cooking, papers taped to walls then taken down. There isn't room to spread things out in space; they crowd in on each other like lives multiplied. But much of the time we can't really make out the detail. And we are busy figuring out who is who and how they use the space. We notice that people lounge on their bed platforms in the daytime, because there are no chairs, or any room for them.

We venture out and find the street silted up in human debris piled against the houses, leaving narrow lanes between them to pass through. Some of the debris is fuel, but much remains indecipherable. As the seasons wear on and the threat of eviction comes nearer, different sorts of gear begin to appear along the lane and against the houses, as if the buildings are turning themselves inside out or coughing up their contents. Here too nothing ever looks shiny or new, but well thumbed and not easily distinguished from trash.

The process is more painful in the lane full of dwellings, but similar to what we saw along the tracks bordered by factories. These piles are not manufactured goods discarded by a whole economy shaking itself and sloughing off what it has no use for, but represent intimate selves which the owners no longer recognize. A few of them make a half-hearted attempt to sell the debris in the street and a few bedraggled buyers appear to haggle over the price.

Again as with earlier shutdowns, there are many stages, and nothing happens simply or smoothly. Family members have disappeared, single men are left out in the new allocation, and a few holdouts dig in their heels. Gradually the lane is taken apart. Some residents remove their own roofs, in search of what? They seem to be made of mud, old plaster, cardboard, a tile or two and rotten wood. Everyone is carting old window frames and doors to the new place. These seem purely in the nature of relics; it is hard to imagine them reused. Maybe they are firewood; there's a great deal of knocking furniture to pieces and then piling the bits, but it doesn't look as if they're being saved, just condensed.

The snow comes down again to bring it to a close and make you feel it's over. The seasons make regular appearances, and not helpful ones, like another enemy who will pile on rain, heat or cold just when life's becoming too much to bear. These changes are Wang's way of applying an outside measure to his closed little world. We watch the verges of the tracks get bushy, turn brown, then grow white again, and we envy the natural world for knowing where it's going. We never see any of the new houses people are moving to; when they load up their carts or pile into someone else's truck, that is the last we will see of them.

We will never follow any of them, with one exception, Old Du, the lowest of the low, who is connected with the railway but not employed by it, suffered to scavenge along the tracks and to live there with his autistic son in an abandoned hut. Suffered until one day he's thrown in jail for doing what he's always done. His son goes to pieces and Du spills the beans on parts of his past he's always concealed. He disappears and a year later turns up in a leather jacket. He has a new house, with bare cement walls but watertight, and a mobile phone. His son is there too, uncommunicative as ever.

These were boom years for China, when it became the fastest growing economy in the world. Against the background of the biggest economic boom in history appears a nine-hour epic on grainy video film like surplus or discarded material which charts the physical and human decline and finally the comprehensive ruin of the old Chinese industry, a powerful counter-narrative to everything that one has read or will read about China. The boom constitutes the essential context of the film, and yet any moralized or politicized element is deeply buried here. If rage propels the maker, it has been thoroughly transmuted by the time it reaches us, and his passion is filtered through days and months of patient observation.

Ruined lives

There's an honourable history of attempts to tell the story of human ruin, meaning the story of the downtrodden, which includes Gospel parables, Zola's novels, Orwell's reportage and Peter Weiss's heroic entry into the consciousness of working-class opponents of Hitler, which revives worn out disputes others thought buried long ago. One of Weiss's methods for bringing the old arguments back to life is to conflate them with some of the hoariest monuments in the history of European art, which are forced by the power of his descriptions to take part in current struggles, meaning those of the late 1930s, the time in which his book begins. But this is one of those works in which time is constantly shifting or conflated. There's always the writer's present, 40 years after the events he's describing, and the consciousness of the protagonist's father, almost completely stuck in 1916–19, two moments framing the book's present.

We're forging a new consciousness, but we do it by picking around in the bones of various pasts, which sometimes feel like obstacles deliberately erected just to show how hard it is to enter the mind of anyone from another class. At first *The Aesthetics of Resistance* is so entirely focused on the mental life of the working class and the attempt to appropriate the great art of the past (most of it aristocratic or bourgeois in origin and tone), that it is extremely poignant to remember that Weiss was thoroughly bourgeois himself. So the stridency of his book often seems a strange form of self-flagellation, and now and then a kind of hypocrisy.

At about the same time the first parts of Weiss's novel were appearing, the Scots film-maker Bill Douglas made three films about his childhood in a depressed mining village. The place where Douglas grew up was not far from the centre of Edinburgh on the map, but infinitely far in any way that mattered. The titles of the three parts, 'My Childhood', 'My Ain Folk', 'My Way Home', seem to make the connection explicit, but the works themselves turn normal notions of what an autobiography is on their heads. In a superficial way the settings of Douglas's films are clearly recognizable, the impoverished world of *West of the Tracks* all over again, 50 years earlier, but outside history in their bareness.

The mode of vision is utterly different. The world of Wang's film is above all full, clogged with a lot of superfluous stuff; Douglas's is empty, defined by what is missing or has been taken away, first of all, parents and any sort of love or welcome. It is a still and silent place; deprivation has removed the child's will or ability to speak. Wang's world is almost completely communal, not that of a novel that follows individuals. Douglas's is almost pre-social, even pre-individual. It's a place so archaic that most of our ways of making sense of reality aren't there yet. The word 'father' is occasionally bandied about, but the boy has no idea what that is. He learns very painfully that his brother's father isn't his, which also means (it dawns on us) that his brother isn't entirely his brother, maybe isn't his brother at all.

Douglas's ways of conveying such depths of deprivation are very beautiful at the same time that they uncover a nearly intolerable absence. The boy is permanently smudged with coal dust picked up on the piled-up mountain of mine-waste where we meet him first. His ancient grey jumper is eaten away in holes of a Rorschach-like pattern. He's been living with one grandmother and then another. The first one is like a geological feature, seen mainly from behind in a chair before the fire; the second is maudlin when drunk and cruel when sober, retracting offered treats before he has time to accept them.

Deprived of words and warmth the boy fastens on the visible world. We share his confusion about grown-ups and their purposes, and often see them conferring without being able to hear what they're saying. The film's intensity of vision is the boy's way of coping; he stares at the world he doesn't understand and it imprints itself according to an unconscious surrealism. Ecstatic moments like climbing the footbridge over the tracks to lose one's solidity in the steam of a passing train are rare, but in some sense are constant, a searing intensity is always cropping up, fruit of looking that is the substitute for speech. The unheard-of intensity of these films springs from the grownup Douglas's ability to deprive himself in the present of all the help he didn't have in the past, to work out, like a scientist of childhood, what made those years so terrible and potentially fertile.

All the appliances of the dwelling, even the doors and windows, and finally the walls themselves, look as if they've had violence practised on them, as if they too have been victims of unprovoked attacks. Not that anyone feels sorry for them; there's no time for that, for pitying any thing or beast, which is plainest when cats or pet birds are bashed to death without a thought. So there's nothing decorative or picturesque about the shabbiness here; it's too much like a wound, too continuous with the boy's own sullen endurance of his lot.

From a certain perspective the earliest episodes will always have primacy, will remain the richest though not the happiest, like the amazing sequence of putting a cup on a bare table, filling it with boiling water, letting it run over and then dumping it on the floor. What is this all about, we wonder? He takes the warm, empty cup and places it between Granny's palms in a shot where nothing is visible but her nerveless hands and his nimble ones. It takes place in silence of course, and we aren't looking at people's expressions, because there aren't any.

Douglas's trilogy is the story of a protagonist's development, but its best achievement was to burn into your consciousness the feeling that this was a life ruined before it got going, that a start in life so bleak would snuff out any urge to break free. The boy is offered various chances, usually flawed it is true, and can't accept them. This seems a pattern which won't be broken, and then improbably, in Egypt, it is. Which is what we've been waiting for, so we think, but mysteriously the interest now goes out of the situation, or rather the anguish, and from then on it seems to matter less.

It has been said that Bill Douglas's treatment of childhood isn't really filmic at all, but a series of disjunct, still images that function as unassimilated fragments. The missing interstices would take more time than what remains. The strength of the films comes in part from these refusals and omissions. Douglas will not ease our passage by including analytic comprehension the child couldn't have managed. So the result cannot be any sort of social critique, can't contribute to a view of the plight of miners or enter political debates about poverty, this in spite of rendering so vividly the helpless experience of deprivation.

'Fortune' magazine examines its conscience

In this there's an unexpected parallel to another attempt to inhabit the most backward, ruined lives in the whole country, this time in the American South in the depths of the Great Depression. This began as a journalistic assignment, not an almost metaphysical plumbing of one's own damaged origins like Douglas's. The plan to find a sharecropper family in one of the poorest Southern states and to convey what their life was like, seen in closest proximity, could have ended in a standard sort of sociological reportage. James Agee's roots in the South made him a likely candidate to undertake this. The result was meant to be a single article that would run in a high-class business magazine not known for radical sympathies or poetical excursions. The idea would have been more at home in the WPA Writers' Programme, but Agee may have hoped to jump that boundary to reach a different, wider audience. He travelled with Walker Evans, a photographer who had worked as one of the WPA's documentary team recording poverty in a crusading spirit.

For eight weeks in the summer of 1936 the two of them lived with three families deep in rural Alabama. Agee must have been caught off guard by how profoundly the experience affected him. Before long it was a question of a book not an article, or even three books. Agee projected a multi-part, biblical-sounding epic about the downtrodden, of which the book he wrote was only the beginning. In fact it already has the dishevelled, multi-faceted structure he foresaw for the more gargantuan whole. He forged a powerful romantic identification with the poor families, whom he saw as more authentic inhabitants of an American place than educated people like him.

This identification is based above all on Agee's lonely inspections of the detritus of their rural lives, most memorably recorded in an inventory of a ramshackle wooden house, carried out when its inhabitants have all gone to town, leaving the way clear for him to open their cupboards and rifle through their drawers, meticulously writing out everything he finds. He views this as something like a sexual violation, which he can only redeem by reverence, transmuting it into verbal ecstasy like a form of prayer.

Elsewhere too, the book's most intense moments occur when Agee is alone, writing under an oil lamp late at night, the only person still awake in the whole rural South, who therefore embodies it and even gives it birth. At these moments the book approaches a wordlessness like that of 'My Childhood' or 'My Ain Folk'. The final form of Agee's and Evans's book, *Let Us Now Praise Famous Men*, a strange and in some way furiously inapposite title, put a sheaf of Evans's photographs, uncaptioned and unexplained, in front of Agee's text, the two parts juxtaposed not integrated, set against each other in a special inarticulacy. So throughout the verbally extravagant text there is always the sensation of words crucially missing and withheld, of a text that wants to burst on you without preparatory explanation. The ideal, to which it stays true a surprising amount of the time, is immersion in an overpowering welter of detail, and that is how he renders lives beautiful in their ruin, and because they are ruined. Like Douglas's films therefore, the book exists entirely outside social critique or political commentary.

Like Douglas, Agee holds himself to the most stringent notions of authenticity, yet produces results that are mythical in their purity and separation from the world of everyday description and connected sequence. Douglas went back to the mining village where he grew up to film his story. He waited six years before starting the final section so the boy who played the part would be the right age to represent him grown up. Now his village of Newcraighall isn't there any more, the tenements swept away in a later housing scheme, the miners' institute consumed by fire (2009), the whole place now dwarfed by a discount warehouse, but decorated with a plaque telling that the films were shot there.

Fifty years later other journalists went back to Agee's Alabama and found 128 descendants of his sharecroppers, who live in pretty much the same conditions Agee found their parents and grandparents in. The young girl in whom Agee and Evans saw the greatest promise bore her first child at fifteen and killed herself with rat poison at 45, Agee's age when he died of drink and tobacco. Perhaps Douglas's was in some sense a ruined life too, but who can fathom what draws writers or film-makers to ruinous subjects that suit them distressingly well.

Looking into a tenant farmer's kitchen in Alabama, Walker Evans, 1936.

When Agee begins searching through the sharecropper's house he finds it full of broken things, still treasured though ruined: plates and toys which cannot be mended but haven't been thrown out because their possessors can't afford to replace them or wouldn't know how to. To the owners they are embarrassments; to Agee, unbearably poignant, another form of embarrassment. He feels he shouldn't be seeing them, yet they give him the most intimate sense of these lives he would like to share, identities he hopes momentarily to assume.

Lilies from dunghills

Maybe this helps explain why certain ruined landscapes exercise such a strong attraction. Deptford Creek, which enters the Thames just west of Greenwich, is one of these, modest enough in scale to be practically invisible when you're on top of it, swallowed by the city, yet a molten world of mud where tides are more vividly present than in the giant river itself. Deptford Creek at low water presents a twisting landscape of glistening mud-lava which looks treacherous and unstable, which has turned hefty boats upside down and is partway through taking them to pieces before swallowing them completely.

The Creek's immediate surroundings are a museum of disuse, presided over by an old lifting bridge now welded into a single position and reduced to a rusty diagram of activity. It's been pushed out of the way by a barer, recent substitute. At the base of the bridge someone has made a little display of the most curious objects dredged from the river, mounting them on pilings like the pedestals in a gallery.

Most surprising of all the items salvaged from the Creek are 400 shopping trolleys that continue to be deposited there from a supermarket a little way upstream. Lying flat and thrusting out their awkwardly angled legs they resemble failed wading birds. Maybe a rebellious streak makes us prefer the dereliction of Creekside and the offering of worn-out devices the water exposes as it recedes to the shiny but flimsy regeneration now springing up in Deptford. There's something magical in the proximity of this underworld of filth to the life of the High Street and the surrounding council flats.

Deptford Creek has also attracted a couple of the most inventive recent buildings in London to its edges, partly because the land was cheap or a gift, partly for this surprise of newness right up against irremediable decay. I suppose it could be cleaned up; not far away the Creek has been made to run between concrete retaining walls, but for the moment its beauty lies in its intractability, and Herzog & de Meuron's Laban Centre for contemporary dance profits hugely from the contrast between its own ethereal substance and the squalor of the creek. It doesn't seem far-fetched to imagine the school as a flower spawned by the dunghill, the school which looks like a refined version of the utilitarian warehouses it replaces. Its architecture is founded on the idea that cities thrive when remembering their unbeautiful roots in dirty industry and pungent compost of past lives. Deptford Creek seems realer than but not entirely separate from the cleaner later activities that have grown up around it. Though it is pitifully disused now, it's probably the main reason that there was a distinct settlement here in the first place. In the sharecropper's house Agee feels he's reaching back to an earlier, truer phase of human development; at Deptford Creek we inhale a strong gust of London before it was London, and come close to some of the underlying forces that brought the city into existence.

The search for authenticity in disregarded, hence ruined things can take odd turns. And one can detect something like primitive forces of nature at work in what are or were once simply manufactured goods. There's a conceptual artist turned collector named Seth Siegelaub who's become fascinated with textile patterns and assembled a bunch of woven scraps in which his interest is evidently not just aesthetic. Recently, when a selection of them was shown in London, the cloth samples were laid out in horizontal cases like landscapes. The most mesmerizing were the most ruined, which sometimes looked as if they lay partly underwater, so that the patterns were blurred by distance or an intervening fluid. They were worn in patches, and velvety top layers of Venetian brocades gave only a smudged impression of baroque curves. Weaving even when fresh provides only an approximate translation of the underlying drawing and, worn away, turns it into a vague memory. Inexplicably, the partial destruction of what the fabrics were trying to say makes them into archaic objects that suggest a pre-literate phase one longs to return to. Ruin has changed them into little microcosms of a lost naturalness.

Deptford Creek, London, at low tide with the Laban Centre for Contemporary Dance (Herzog & de Meuron, 2000–2003) on the left bank.

We can't explain the fascination of these fragments by understanding how they got this way, reconstructing the sequence of use and neglect like a whole novel of Balzac with its roller coaster of triumphs and defeats. Maybe it's the human drama they give hints of that makes them seem so rich, but it's more likely to be their way of escaping domestic life and becoming forces of nature in miniature.

The pavements made by Dimitris Pikionis on the Acropolis and another nearby hill in Athens exist on a more expansive scale but share key features with Siegelaub's woven scraps. These constructions are primarily paths, though broken by platforms, steps and promontories, which are ways of not keeping to the path. They play a continual game of regularity and irregularity; particularly at the edge there's a calculated roughness. The most interesting feature of these works, which don't look like works at all to many of those who tread on them, is what they are made of.

Most of the components are marble debris, odd slivers and slices. The designer has taken what he finds: he doesn't shape his ruined pieces but chooses groups and combinations, harmonies and conflicts. The

Paving by Dimitris Pikionis on Philopappou hill, Athens, made from classical rubble found nearby.

result is bricolage, a whole made out of elements that all had previous lives now mostly forgotten, with a special feature: they were all found here, so they haven't left their native soil but have been joined to it more intimately, as if returning to it. And yet, for someone who is paying attention, this is decisively a work made, not found. Sometimes the patterns underfoot are like abstract art, sometimes like partial plans of vanished buildings, as if something lies just beneath the surface, which is of course usually the case in Athens, though not so visibly.

We walk along enjoying the wildness of Pikionis's dishevelled composition, and we arrive at his rustic little church of St Demetrios. Confined within its narrow bounds is a pavement wilder and more primitive than those outside. The architect is always playing the natural against the contrived, but inside, where architecture provides the frame, his patterns are more unruly. Outside, where unshaped rocks and trees supply the background noise, he contributes order. Even there, reality sometimes appears to reverse itself and we feel as if we're walking on a natural marble mulch that classical architecture grew out of.

The reconstructors of the Parthenon would hate to have their work likened to bricolage, a mode still mainly disreputable, with its suggestions of impoverished makeshift. But they too are combining things that don't really match, authentic remnants long fallen from their places on frieze or pediment, now laboriously re-identified, and modern replicas of missing pieces which are needed to prop up the authentic bits so they can be remounted. The result is a hodgepodge, not relaxed and surprising like Pikionis's, but stiff and a little unsightly, marred by class distinctions between the real thing and a kind of falsehood which is just filler, barely tolerated. The Pikionis treatment, more artistic than scientific, would never be allowed to touch anything as venerable as the Parthenon, a relic too serious and important to let an aesthetic vision tinker with it.

No more than shacks

Even within the world of bricolage there are sharp class distinctions. The new Pevsner guide to Essex calls the houses at Jaywick Sands 'no more than shacks really', and starting from Frinton we had to fight resistance from church ladies to go there at all. Nineteenth-century authors venturing into the slums of East London gave their books titles like *In Darkest England*. Jaywick began as an outpost of the East End, a couple of rungs further down the social scale than resorts like Southend, and much wilder. Jaywick has its own East End (actually west), a more ruined bit called Brooklands where the streets are named after different makes of British cars, many of them now obsolete. These little roads, no more than tracks really, run away from the sea below its level, and are still liable to flooding. The names are sometimes explained by an original population of Ford workers from Dagenham who are said to have built the first chalets from car packing cases. Then we are told that bombed-out East Enders moved into their chalets during the war and never went back, so that the lack of services, like plumbing, which you expect in permanent dwellings, became a more acute kind of problem.

In the last few years Jaywick has been labelled the most deprived municipality in Britain, and has attracted documentary filmmakers to study its plight. Since 2006 Brooklands has been under threat of demolition and comprehensive redevelopment. Apparently the present population of the little toy roads full of potholes and the little toy houses sporting rotting window frames is divided between retirees who remember summers spent here fondly and young refugees from London fighting addiction and depression, who hope they won't be here long.

On a bright day in October I saw none of this, just varieties of picturesque decay, extensions in unmatching materials that began to lean, garden walls robbed of bricks at the corners, render stained by sagging gutters. Much of it looked older than it was, as if forced to live in a speeded-up nature film. Houses got more neglected the further you ventured from the beachfront road. Up there, a few were proudly painted and decorated with folk art or Gaudí garden walls of clinkers and shells.

For me Jaywick remains an epitome of making do and incorporating whatever comes to hand into a collage where the elements don't function as intended, but approach the task aslant or sideways, sometimes forming a porch out of doors or a door out of gates, and

A house at Jaywick Sands, Essex, partly assembled from found fragments.

throwing in a decorative flourish at an awkward moment. In that perspective the car names are at least a little fanciful; that won't be how the early inhabitants got there. No room was made for cars, so it's lucky parking-wise that so many chalets are burned out or otherwise abandoned. If cars can ever be said to blend harmoniously, they almost do here, being battered and few.

Perhaps the names are yet more signs of hopes unfulfilled, dreams of modernity that never materialized, like the hopeful imitations of houses with gables and extra storeys and projecting porches, all at five-eighths normal size. It still represents an unruly outburst of ingenuity but it was never true for long and has since recoiled on its users.

A disassembly line for the self

Searching for a new method for the new medium of film, Dziga Vertov (or 'spinning top', not his real name) hit on something like bricolage. He regarded the city as a lot of found material whose dynamic energy could only be conveyed fully by film, through its inhuman flexibility, cutting ceaselessly from one subject to a seemingly unrelated one.

Vertov never acknowledged a debt to Surrealism, but he repeats continually juxtapositions so incongruous they provoke a gasp or a laugh, like the woman throwing water on her face followed by someone hosing down an ornate streetlamp base. Even after all these years Vertov's *Man with a Movie Camera* is still a series of shocks. The eye can just about cope with the jumps from fragment to fragment, but the mind cannot.

It doesn't seem natural to keep careful track of the sequence of images; maybe it isn't even possible, at least that is how the film makes you feel. It turns the lives of individuals into a blur of action and process. The telephone is represented by a long row of operators connecting and disconnecting hundreds of calls without pausing for breath. Smoking is depicted through smiling girls packing cigarettes at superhuman speed, the process broken into many stages, none left out, but speeded up so it's like a magic trick.

The labour of the girl-machines is exhilarating but not really heroic. If the film had a hero it would be the machine, which keeps popping up in various guises, especially as forms of transport, trains and trams

Trams as emblems of constant motion in Dziga Vertov's *Man with a Movie Camera* (1929).

above all. The passing of trams in crowded streets is the most dreamlike bit of motion in the whole 68 minutes, which is a poem about motion as far as something so jittery can be just one thing.

Near the end the cameraman's tripod, the nearest thing to a single overarching presence in the film, does a little dance by itself. Now a leather case slides up alongside, and we expect the tripod to jump in, ending the film, but the camera jumps out and attaches itself to the tripod and walks around a little, stretching its legs.

Like most episodes in this ultra-lively work, this is fleeting yet unnerving. Vertov's is the most de-individualized vision ever and at this moment we seem to stare into a future in which the new Soviet Man will be indistinguishable from the machines the director is so fond of. The strange new medium takes apart the life of a city like the disassembling of a mechanism and recombines it in a fractured continuity which moves too fast for human senses to keep up with. The concentration on process and devaluing of any person's specialness creates situations in which strange things happen to the truth. Spectators are intercut with sportsmen jumping, clearing hurdles or kicking balls, but are we really seeing what they see and respond to? Is the game even the same game from one frame to another, or does the ball come down after its long flight on another field? Lives are interchangeable like building materials, *are* building materials, out of which you can cobble a film or a society.

2

Fragmented Wholes

ULYSSES IS THE SUPREMELY FRAGMENTED modernist text. But it doesn't declare itself that way from the start. In the opening pages we could almost be living in a Yeats poem, in a tower by the sea. Yet the controlling myths already begin to unravel, and appear in dismembered form. A character named Buck, like a mythical creature from a boisterous old story, enacts parodies of hoary rituals, spouting sonorous words borrowed from incongruous sources. He's a disruptive comic force, set off against Stephen Dedalus, not a middle-aged wizard in this book, but a young and withdrawn would-be writer we are probably expected to remember from the author's previous work.

Dedalus functions like a cultural medium who turns the simplest features of the Irish landscape into enormous symbols, like the illiterate crone who supplies them with milk, whom he elevates into Mother Ireland, an alchemy both preposterous and grand. We see right through it (she mistakes Haines's educated English speech for her native Gaelic, from which she's completely cut off), yet something makes us want to believe, and Joyce's rhetoric gives us a powerful push.

So Dedalus is the conduit through which the exotic makes its way into Dublin, in moments like the parade of the Church's most dangerous heresiarchs that passes through his head when sparring touchily with Haines, or the Moorish dance of Arabic numerals set in motion as he looks over a backward schoolboy's copybook. So far these are private ecstasies, overheard by the reader, but they alert us very early to the way entire universes open out in consciousness without warning, a sign that this tale set in a provincial backwater recognizes no limit on where it can go or take the reader.

Joyce likes turning trivial fragments, random scraps of reality, into weighty symbols by causing them to recur unexpectedly, hence uncannily. A little cloud obscures the sun briefly and causes Stephen to see the bay in front of him as the bowl of green bile beside his mother's sickbed. Forty pages further on in another part of Dublin the same cloud makes Bloom think of the Dead Sea, 'the grey sunken cunt of the world'. The first time there's a bowl-like landscape to suggest the negative vision; the second time there isn't, but the ground has been prepared, and we are ready to see the harmless cloud as death-laden all over again.

Rubbish blowing about the streets can serve the same purpose. There's a throwaway announcing the second coming of a particular evangelist that keeps turning up, the ultimate demonstration of the writer's power to give shape to experience via coincidences that are parody versions of a plan for the universe, the more dispensable the better, because exposing our need for such structures more starkly. There are the men who travel round the city in an endless, pointless loop because they're paid to carry signboards advertising H.E.L.Y.S., who cross the paths of more substantial characters at irregular intervals. There's the ship 'arriving from Bridgwater with bricks' that we meet several times by chance – chance a sign of authenticity and non-contrivance for the compliant reader.

Most invasive of all, there's the mental detritus that fills characters' minds, above all Bloom's and consequently ours, like 'What is a home without Plumtree's Potted Meat?' It's Bloom's business to pay attention to ads; they are what send him ceaselessly round the city, another version of circling in one spot, and this legitimizes the view of modern urban life as awash with verbal flotsam and jetsam.

As the book progresses, its parts are more and more defined by peculiar literary techniques, even by peculiar typography or layout. There are whole episodes made of shreds, like the headline chapter that destroys continuity by inserting comic descriptions of what follows next, printed large and bold like tags on newspaper pages, or episode ten called 'Wandering Rocks' that follows the intersecting paths of a selection of the atoms that make up the population of the streets, which Joyce famously coordinated using a stopwatch.

The highwater mark of verbal debris comes near the end and very late in the day (episode sixteen in the cab shelter), when the characters are tired, and so it seems appropriate that language should be tired too, unable to stop a flood of clichés from pouring in. There's a perverse brio in Joyce's collage of exhausted verbiage, a knowing art made from rubbish. The episode that follows is equally impossible, broken into question and answer form, no way to tell a story, and forced into mock scientific lingo to boot. Bloom and Dedalus are finally alone together – what the whole book has been driving toward – and they are prevented from communicating by this absurd device. It is another tour de force, continually staggering in its ingenuity, and to our surprise its dislocated, inhuman wit is unbearably poignant. Bloom and Dedalus are denied the humble privileges of ordinary citizens and turned into planetary bodies like the heroes who become constellations at the end of Greek myths.

This is followed by Molly's monologue, which attracts far more attention than the apotheosis of Bloom and Dedalus and reaches the mythic by an entirely different route. It must sometimes be seen as a forecast of where Joyce would go next, turning from the alarmingly centrifugal structure of *Ulysses*, a novel taking itself to pieces, to the ultimate centripetal work, *Finnegans Wake*, which ends where it began, as if it were an undifferentiated substance, even a single sentence preposterously extended, a long, rich, murmuring muddle in which you never know exactly where you are or where you are headed.

A quick-cutting camera

Eisenstein's *Battleship Potemkin*, an early instance in a new, non-literary medium, retains a few delusive features of a book, like chapter divisions and an epigraph.

> The spirit of mutiny swept the land. A tremendous, mysterious process was taking place in countless hearts: the individual personality became dissolved in the mass, and the mass itself became dissolved in the revolutionary élan.

This epigraph by Trotsky (later replaced) expresses in terms angled toward ideology one of the modernist principles the film shares with *Ulysses*, a breakdown of individuality and its submersion in the crowd on one hand and mechanical process on the other. Not long after, Vertov boasted that he'd made a film without actors, intertitles or three other features borrowed from literature and theatre.

But *Battleship Potemkin* uses intertitles in a modernist spirit, as agents of fragmentation, and goes beyond any previous work in any medium in its demolition of sequential structure. Besides this, the film's lack of stars had shown Vertov the way and was already the main obstacle preventing wide distribution in the Soviet Union. Eisenstein has replaced attachment to an easily recognized individual with a dynamic and disorienting presentation of space.

The most powerful early scenes are below deck, especially the space full of hammocks in which sailors are asleep. These hammocks are a lot of diagonals cutting across each other, the ultimate Constructivist interior sliced into dangerous shards, every one of which contains a twisted human form. The space becomes more confusing, not less, as we move in closer, and inert figures wake and writhe into activity. The conversation which follows, carried out without anyone leaving the hammocks, must be one of the most spatially complex interactions ever staged, sparked off when a junior officer blunders down a ladder, bangs his head, and lashes out at the nearest body, conveniently turned away so that it's not a person but an abstract back.

The film pays lip service to the slowly building revolt, but seems more interested in such alienated spaces as the view from below of figures passing over an open grille on deck, or the aerial diagram of their swarming movements seen from the next higher level. When the fight finally comes, it's a flurry of movement, strangely unviolent, including a lot of climbing and descending of the open stairways the ship is full of.

Battleship Potemkin takes a tiny episode and makes it a great historical pivot. The crucial step in this widening is the move from the ship to Odessa, where a series of crowds represent big, barely conscious forces. The first crowd is seen from above as it snakes along a curving breakwater. The second rushes down a long flight of narrow steps that were empty a second before. The third crowd is the famous one, a confusion of individuals descending wide steps toward the harbour. This was Eisenstein's great discovery, to stage the real battle on an urban site like a sloping mountainside, where the whole action would have the shape of a long, slow fall into an abyss.

It seems to go on forever, and to repeat itself like anxieties in a dream. We reach the bottom, or think our way there, but then we're at the top again and treated to a new horror, the baby carriage jolting downward by its own momentum, or the mother running back to collect a dead child, bringing things to a halt for a moment before the machine starts up again, mowing down the crop of bodies that still remain on the steps. It's both the most concentrated and the most shattered sequence. The most famous frame in the film, the silent scream of a woman whose smashed spectacles are drenched in blood, appears and vanishes in the blink of an eye, yet has somehow burnt itself onto the world's retina. How could Eisenstein be sure we would notice? It reminds us of Joyce burying key moments deep in the interior of *Finnegans Wake* where it seems possible no one else will ever come.

The great novelty of Vertov's *Enthusiasm* which appears just five years after *Potemkin*, is the accompanying soundtrack. As you might expect from this self-reflexive maker, the early minutes of the film are *about* sound, sounds separated from their sources in reality and thus turned into isolated fragments. Before we see anything we hear something, a low, unintelligible garble that shuts itself off almost as soon as begun. When images start appearing toward the end of the credits, they take up the question of sound more selfconsciously: a girl's face, then the girl dons headphones and begins listening intently to the random sounds we've begun to hear – a cuckoo, a metronome, odd bursts from an orchestra.

For someone very used to the idea of film soundtracks, the most striking feature of this pioneer instance is its scoring of wild sound into something distinct from a passively admitted background of sound. In *Enthusiasm* natural sound is formed into the equivalent of an orchestral score. Vertov wrote out a storyboard of sound which survives as a few sheets taped together horizontally like a piece of film, with tiered lines resembling musical notation.

The film now switches to the conductor of an orchestra tapping his baton, comparable to the focus on the cameraman in *Man with a Movie Camera*. Apparently at some point along the way sound and image got far enough out of synch that the taps came along a few seconds after the image of a man tapping. In 1972 image and soundtrack were laboriously resynchronized in Vienna, which revealed a number of places where frames had been lost (or cut by the censor?), leaving sounds that had nothing to go with them.

Resynchronizing the sound seems entirely rational, and yet . . . Vertov sometimes gets wonderful comic effects from deliberate clashes between what we hear and what we see, like the conflations between starstruck worshippers and woozy drunkards, two kinds of blurred consciousness. Believers coming out of deep reverential bows bleed into derelicts being pulled to their feet still comatose. The gurgling sound of vodka leaving the bottle is carried over onto the serious person kissing an icon's feet.

Almost exactly halfway through the film, the principal transition, from religion-bashing to industrial production, begins creakily, with a winding gear cranking up. It's shown at a raking angle, cut off at the chest as if it were a portrait and intercut with a single large miner, first male, then female, who delivers a promise to overfill the plan, fiercely but mechanically, part of an awkward sequence like a lumbering shifting of gears, formally dynamic, technically primitive.

Shock battalions are leading an attack; they parade across the screen against the background of a crooked banner held taut by a

Emblems of socialist progress from Vertov's *Enthusiasm* of 1931, which incorporated a pioneering soundtrack of fractured wild sound.

couple of workers. Martial music plays faintly offstage, mixed with cheers and overlaid by factory whistles, jets of steam and hammer blows near at hand. Sometimes we see the event that produces the noise; just as often not. Short, encouraging phrases are barked out and industrial processes gather speed; longer speeches of a whole line or two are played against no image at all. There's something childishly pleasing about music and cheers produced by unseen actors urging smelting and forging forward in irregular bursts.

The best parts are often those with human background noise and no visible human presence, hoppers of ore on a circular conveyor belt, dangling buckets passing overhead in both directions at once with big gaps between. They're wonderful because it's the most liberated kind of movement, and because the machinery is unfresh, patinated by crust laid down over years of use. Part of the joy lies in the utopian vision of an automated world of work going forward magically, without workers. Vertov confuses the properties of machines with those of organisms, animating objects and sucking the souls out of creatures. The mechanism of film itself lends credence to this effect, because the film-maker is so entirely absent from his orchestration of the work of others.

Workers are not absent from the most beautiful sequence of all, a speeded-up ballet of pulling out great ribbons of white-hot pipe that are swallowed up and then pulled out again. This process stands out in its magical fluidity; most of the others are staccato, broken, pushing against the grain; here for once there's no sense of struggle. It also stands out because the process has no end and no result: here are not shock workers but artists, a conclusion that will only survive in the new Soviet world if it slips past unnoticed.

The book as a city

Walter Benjamin's *Arcades Project* (a name of almost pure convenience: we need to call it something) is gigantic but unfinished, probably unfinishable, assembled by the juxtaposition of fragments into a whole which has been described as nearer to film than any previous work made of words. Debate continues over how close to its intended final form this ruined object had come by 1940, when its compiler took his own life while trying to get the manuscript out of occupied France. The manuscript he apparently valued more than his life subsequently disappeared, so we don't know how nearly identical it was to the one left behind in Paris to be hidden by Georges Bataille in the Bibliothèque Nationale where it was written.

When finally published in the nearest state to completeness (German edition 1982, English translation 1999) the work looks like a normal book, but incorporates plans, sketches, synopses, broken-off pieces published separately as articles in periodicals and then – the bulk of the whole – all Benjamin's notes, hundreds or thousands of extracts from a weird assortment of witnesses, novelists, sanitation engineers, historians, impresarios, criminals, poets, journalists . . . At first this looks like an early or at least intermediate stage of development, with lots of scraps of paper semi-regularized by printing them continuously, forcing them into proximity and making them look more like a single fabric than they really are.

In an obvious and literal way, this is the ultimate discontinuous work in which the fruits of extensive reading and thinking remain in the raw state in which the searcher found them, a cacophonous uproar with edges unsmoothed and variations of tone and style jangling continually. There are thematic divisions but these look more like preliminary sorting devices than settled structural features. The German editor, Rolf Tiedemann, decided to put two different short synopses, or *exposés* as they are called, at the beginning, rather than throwing the reader (who soon finds that normal *reading* won't work with this book) into the maelstrom undefended. But the proportions are unnerving, the props so puny, the sea of detail which engulfs the reader just after, so vast.

More than once Benjamin says that his method is montage, which might send us running to 'The Work of Art in the Age of Mechanical Reproduction', the famous essay in which he treats film along with other twentieth-century art forms. So maybe this work aims at a new kind of form, and the appearance of literary normality is seriously misleading. The *exposés* are headed 'Paris, capital of the nineteenth century', and somewhere Benjamin says that he wants to expose the past to the light of the present, or to characterize it in ways coming from outside itself and unheard of until now.

His subject is the first modern city and the invention of modernity itself, but it's essential that the discussion remains obsessively rooted in one particular place. It's also tremendously telling that Benjamin researched and wrote it while living in Paris. This seems a crucial feature of the enterprise in spite of the fact that the Paris he pursued was no longer there, and many of the features that fascinated him most, like the *cheval de renfort*, the extra horse pulled along behind the tram on steep routes, had completely disappeared. Likewise, the names he picked out often memorialized lost features, like all the *puits* (wells) that turn up in names scattered across Paris but are no more.

He expresses a perverse pleasure in pulling words away from their moorings in reality: names of Metro stops taken from nearby streets above ground have, Benjamin says, become 'misshapen sewer gods'. They are something else entirely from their everyday selves, down here in a labyrinth concealing not one but a dozen raging bulls, into whose maw countless young dressmakers and clerks are fed every morning. On the one hand the city can only be represented truthfully by a vast landscape of disconnected fragments; on the other hand to the intoxicated *flâneur* all streets are precipitous, leading downward to the same mythic substratum. The city is both a landscape without threshold or boundary, and a ramifying interior furnished in suffocating profusion.

The arcade is the fulfilment of this domestic tendency of the nineteenth century, which fascinates and repels Benjamin in equal measure. It is the archetype of the outdoors as an indoors, or the street as a drawing-room, roofed in in the case of the arcade and stuffed with a phantasmagoria of consumer goods. The arcade, an architectural form now obsolete and in prolonged inglorious decline, was a precocious instance of iron and glass construction, self-evidently rational yet liable to perversion to an ersatz kind of fairyland, where the drive 'against nature' ran wild.

Benjamin zeros in on the rags and rubbish of the century, industrial architecture, machines, department stores, advertisements, the tinsel and hollow shells of bourgeois consumption which fascinate him in their unloveliness and which he also feels almost compelled to mythologize. Hashish gives him the key: the overlap or superposition produced by intoxication makes every idea hanker after its opposite and this suggests a new notion of the truth – truth is simply the rhythm by which statement and counter-statement displace each other in turn. Benjamin cannot adhere consistently to this version of a phantasmagoria of ideas, but it helps explain why someone who calls himself a materialist is so drawn to magical transformations that turn ideas inside out.

His great work, which we wrong to call another book, embodies in its own calculated formlessness the unencompassable vastness and variety of its subject. But the fragments are not inert, content to remain poor bounded things. Benjamin's work is continually striving to transcend the pettiness of its separate components, partly by juxtaposing them with other scraps that wrench our perspective round to some new place, partly by reminding us how much of the original source has been jettisoned but lingers there, giving an idea of vastness like an oval reading room's reminder of all the volumes one hasn't even opened. Benjamin was doubtless both inspired and troubled by the fact that he habitually worked not in the streets but in a room full of books, a space that by lucky chance exemplified the early iron and glass construction he thought so crucial in signalling modernity.

He imagined that an exciting film could be spun from the map of Paris. He fastened on someone's idea that certain worthless securities lead a furtive stygian existence, or that Haussmann, the great reorganizer of Paris and especially of its drainage, allies himself more firmly with divinities below ground than the gods above. Each of these strange thoughts could be elaborated into an argument or an allegory but Benjamin prefers to leave them as suggestive phantoms and to move on, having sowed a fleeting doubt in the reader's mind: could *this* actually be *that*? Is it possible to interpret sordid business deals as mythic transformations, or industrial buildings as spurs to new forms of consciousness?

There's a riveting description of how Maxime Du Camp was inspired to undertake one of the most gigantic and encompassing publications on the subject of Paris, a whole universe of rich detail Benjamin mined and mined again. Du Camp had just been told he needed spectacles, which would take an hour or so to knock up. So instead of spending the interval in the waiting room, he left the doctor's office pondering the process of growing old, and stood on

One of Benjamin's *Passagen*, the Passage de l'Opéra photographed by Charles Marville in 1868. This arcade was torn down in 1925.

the Pont Neuf looking at Paris, which was also ageing and slowly disappearing in the form he had known it, and resolved then and there to make a comprehensive record of the city in the second half of the nineteenth century.

Benjamin does not need to say that he sees himself in this man conceiving a huge project that overlaps with his, in a small and useless scrap of time between ordering and collecting his first spectacles. An unbridgeable distance remains between Benjamin's ambition and the texture of the work. He occasionally dramatizes his task as a perilous climb in which he never turns to look back for fear of dizziness and in order to save a panoramic view of the expanse he is crossing until the whole terrain is revealed. There's a constant tension between our sense of the figure in the reading room buried in his piles of paper and the *flâneur* as a werewolf wandering through the social wilderness.

It is not a work one reads consecutively like a novel, but in snatches like a guidebook. Unlike most guidebooks this unruly map of the nineteenth century holds out the hope at every moment, at every shift of one of its thousand voices to another, of a transcendental fusion in which Pausanias and Balzac are one, and the city beneath our feet is another labyrinth with all the same names in a different but matching space not much further underground, like the tunnels prisoners once labelled with all the familiar names of Paris and then gave out their addresses to each other based on the new arrangement. One only needs to have this perception once; one doesn't really need the movie made from the map of the city, or to align one's walks slavishly with the 'voyage autour de ma chambre' to experience the thrill of simultaneity. Benjamin's arcades are the solidest proof that the scaffolding can be more inviting and more productive, both of further thought about the city and of richer journeys through it, than the completed building.

If Benjamin's *Arcades* can be seen as the scaffolding for an immense work of synoptic history, Eliot's *The Waste Land* might be described as the scaffolding for an ambitious poem about the state of European civilization in the aftermath of the Great War. Scaffolding because many things are sketched or briefly alluded to but not completed, yet rational construction is far from the right model for the form of this poem. It reads like ecstatic hallucination in which a hundred presences crowd into consciousness, sometimes clamouring for attention, sometimes fleeing before one can seize them, a marvellous but upsetting cacophony in a mind that struggles to contain all kinds of echoes of the past as it is pulled back by the prose of a little encounter in the London of the present.

It feels well nigh impossible to digest into a single unified awareness all the mixed flavours from huge expanses of the past and the vivid undignified life of the moment. The poem is full of admissions of failure, every encounter goes wrong, all the literary debris of half-remembered lines just make one feel more helpless, and yet an unequalled cultural high arises from the coming together of all these different registers of experience in a final hubbub glorious and night-marish, a portent of extinction or a final collapse. It's a brief but at the same time improbably extended death-song or final utterance, a summing up for which it is hard to imagine any sequel. It is built almost entirely from ruined cultural forms, from shredded fragments of Dante, Spenser, Shakespeare, biblical narrative, Wagner of course and – to make the death knell as comprehensive and final as possible – snatches of Hindu scripture.

Like many lyrics it probably has its sources in the poet's most intimate experience. Maybe much of it was written on the verge of or coming out from nervous breakdown; certainly some was drafted in a sanatorium in Switzerland. But if these are important facts, they are almost entirely concealed from view in the poem. An early name for *The Waste Land* was 'He Do the Police in Different Voices', which must have meant something very different to Eliot from what it calls up for most readers. The poem is an extended act of ventriloquism, a sequence of different voices that follow each other uncannily, the gaps between sometimes bridged by vaguer, more vatic passages that call the solidity of the rest in question. These intervals are full of mys-terious deaths and magical interventions, music like an elusive being or the sea drowning out human sounds. The earlier title is a quotation from Dickens but sounds like more of the comic business that Pound convinced Eliot to cut back, the pub scene which contains the poem's nearest approach to lewdness being practically the only remnant of this mode. As just one of many voices this music hall lowlife takes its subsidiary place. In the first drafts the poem began with another such episode, setting the tone of the whole.

Pound's improvements gave greater prominence to generalized elements like the present opening 'April is the cruellest month', grand meditations on thwarted growth and cultural sterility, uncannily con-verging ruins of both the natural and human worlds. Like Benjamin's *Arcades, The Waste Land* remains rooted in a particular city, but Pound tried to get Eliot to remove names of particular streets and buildings, which in the forms that remain feel like exiles stranded in Dantean landscapes, moments of clarity in a more pervasive fog. Such abrupt incongruities are one of the poem's most invigorating features, putting a strain on the reader who must find a way to keep the fabric from splitting apart.

Pound could only uncover in the draft something that was already there, but he understood better than Eliot had yet done what the poem was really about. He must have had an easier time at some points than others convincing Eliot that whole sections had to go, or techniques to change. There was more pastiche in the first draft and longer sections of it, so that the literary exercise seemed the point. In the revision, pastiche flashes past and serves a higher purpose.

Pound persuaded Eliot to make the whole more enigmatic, suppressing circumstantial connections between parts and allowing the transitions to become more arbitrary and dreamlike. As in *Ulysses*, connectives originally present are taken away, strengthening the subjective effect of a fragmented consciousness. The vision of a world in ruins becomes the framing image of the poem: the heap of broken images which is all the figure in the desert landscape near the beginning has to fall back on, returns at the end in 'these fragments I have shored against my ruin', a phrase that applies first to all the kaleidoscopic clatter of allusions in the preceding three lines, but also to the entire poem, debris treasured but despaired of as a help in fending off madness, which erupts immediately after.

Despair is not really the state in which the poem begins or ends, though: an experience of ruin, the ruin of old cultural certainties and of personal hopes, yes, but even the final explosion and inversion – bats crawling upside down in caves, towers hanging upside down in air – even that is a kind of religious fulfilment, an apocalyptic transformation. This archetypally modernist work is also a helplessly Romantic one, burning itself up in self-destructive ecstasy.

A Buddhist's dusty answers

Like most religious traditions Buddhism has fragmented and then fragmented again. The various further sub-divisions of the Zen (or Chan) fragment are distinguished by a strong distrust of texts as aids to achieving an enlightenment that will finally be wordless. Some of the great teachers in this tradition are famous for using a sharp blow to the head of a disciple as an answer to a question.

One of the most venerable Zen texts, *The Blue Cliff Record*, collects 100 brief anecdotes, many of which show a sage giving an incomprehensible reply. The original compiler added a gnomic poem to each anecdote, a set of interpretations that created further puzzles. Sixty years later, in the early twelfth century, another monk in the Blue Cliff monastery in Honan province gave a series of talks on the anecdotes and the appended poems, talks eventually digested into the scrappy form in which the text is now preserved.

There are still one hundred sections, each with a brief introduction by monk two, followed by the old anecdote. In Chinese versions, monk two's disruptive comments are integrated with the ancient text, making a ping-pong match of opposing views, a stately voice alternating with a disrespectful echo. This was too much for the American translators, who printed the cheeky comments as footnotes, so that one can read the original text intact before allowing the commentary to undermine it.

Next comes a more extended commentary by monk two which, contrary to the main drift of Zen teaching, does actually explain confusing features of the primary anecdote and fleshes out the lives of the Chinese sages who appear there. Then come the oblique comments in poetical form of monk one, once again interleaved with crossgrained responses by monk two, this time in verse form. The English translation distinguishes the comments by a different typeface or a quarantine of special punctuation. The final section is another commentary by monk two, explaining monk one's more gnomic utterance. Again this issues from a different part of his brain from his abrupt and contradictive contributions to the poem.

The alternation of voices and techniques makes for such a bumpy ride that it's hard to imagine anyone reading straight through the finally enormous result. Undoubtedly you need to ponder the 100 anecdotes one by one over years of study. The printed collection wasn't meant as and doesn't conveniently function as a work of literature. And yet . . . not many years after the second compilation one of the favourite students of monk two burned the blocks from which it had been printed to stop aestheticized responses which he thought were making *The Blue Cliff Record* an obstruction rather than a guide on the path to enlightenment.

Burning a book is just a more violent, less articulate form of disruptive comment. And aptly enough the *Record* itself already points the way in the fourth anecdote where a questing monk signals his awakening by rushing out of the lecture hall and setting fire to the huge wad of commentaries he's been dragging round the country. There are lots of other examples: the workman in a temple who produces a counter-poem to a senior monk's effort, in which he negates the monk's beautiful images one by one, clearing the ground until there's nothing there. The old abbot is so impressed by the boldness of the demolition that he makes 'workman Lu' his successor. Woodcutters and old peasant women selling cakes, who are closer to enlightenment than the intellectuals, are scattered through the text. But maybe we shouldn't take them literally as signals of social upheaval but simply as admonitions, like the frequent dictum that one must learn to concentrate without thinking. The greatest teachers are often credited with the power 'to cut off the tongues of the whole world', that is, to end people's enthusiasm for speech, and to stun them into silence. In the period the anecdotes hail from, Chan sages sometimes forbade their disciples to record their lectures; in a famous instance a young monk got round this by writing out the sage's words on his clothes, which were made of paper.

Zen teaching methods can read like translations into the realm of conduct of tactics Eliot follows in *The Waste Land* to jar the reader awake or to suggest extreme states of mental fragmentation. The Zen contradictions have a further end in discouraging rational thought on the way to a new kind of concentration that denies the validity of ordinary reality. We unthinkingly suppose that Eliot's poem has its end in a certain kind of representation, not in trying to change consciousness, but why are we so sure of this?

Sand gardens

There's a sixteenth-century Zen Buddhist garden in Japan that only began to attract a lot of Western interest in the 1930s, that is to say after modernism had changed attitudes toward emptiness and asymmetry for Europeans. Thus, after a certain date this strange work struck many Western observers as uniquely sublime.

The dry garden at Ryoan-ji consists of fifteen rocks distributed in five groups across a rectangular field of coarse sand, surrounded on three sides by a rustic wall that shuts out the world and on the fourth by a narrow veranda from which you view the garden, raised several feet above it. You cannot enter, but only contemplate it. There are no plants, unless you count the moss growing at the feet of some of the stones, or the trees looking over the wall from outside, which barely enter your field of vision and which you might notice for the first time looking at photographs afterward. There is no water, except that some people count the raked sand as a sea, from which the stones poke up like islands. The rocks are rough and uncarved, quite wild when you focus closely on them, but don't fill much of the space.

It is a place stripped practically bare, much more empty than full. Distances between the groups can seem vast, even cosmic, the dark punctuation of the rocks a heavenly constellation. The sand is more prosaically likened to clouds from which mountain tops poke up. *Ryoan*, in the name of the temple, means 'Dragon Peace'; the rocks are also described as a tigress and her cubs swimming across a river. Maybe all these narratives that translate rocks and sand into something else are weak-minded efforts to get over the discomfort of an assertion of pointlessness that is at the same time inexplicably beautiful.

The wall draws a clear line round the experience and says the random grouping forms a whole, but the parts will always look like fragments. You might come to accept that the fragments make sense or that the disturbance can be tolerated, even enjoyed, but you cannot escape entirely from the feeling that something is out of place.

The most wonderful interpretation of Ryoan-ji known to me occurs rather late in a film by Yasujiro Ozu called *Late Spring* in English. The father (a widower) and the uncle of the main character (a daughter who cannot bring herself to leave the nest) sit for a long time in front of the stones without speaking, and then discuss the question of the daughter's marriage. The distances between the stones correspond to the distance between even the closest human beings. They convey this with a soothing remoteness but without fudging; they are immovable; there are truths we cannot argue with or change. No one says anything

Zen rock and sand garden at Ryoan-ji, Kyoto, late 15th or early 16th century. The eccentric spacing of the fragments has inspired wildly diverse interpretations.

like this, but the camera looks at the two men's backs and then at the rocks standing there, and the stones are momentarily individuals enduring their lots, a fleeting perception from which we soon turn away.

The garden at Ryoan-ji is notable for how thoroughly it omits direct reference to the human presence, for how abstract it remains while using unworked natural objects, rocks in their sensuous wild state. Recently a single obscure human touch has begun to attract attention, a signature or two signatures hidden in plain sight on the back of one of the largest rocks. These scratched words are the personal names of a couple of *kawaramono* ('riverbank dwellers'), outcasts who it is now believed went from despised haulers of rocks and trees to designers of some of the most famous Japanese gardens. Incidentally, *kawaramono* are also credited with the invention of Nō and Kabuki, the first of which is commonly regarded as among the most aristocratic of Japanese art forms.

The spaces between words

Ryoan-ji has inspired a surprising number of poems and musical compositions in English. Maybe the whole idea of the authorship of a garden, and of this one in particular, paradoxically obscured and advertised, is part of what draws makers like John Cage, absent and not absent from his own work. Wallace Stevens's 'Thirteen Ways of Looking at a Blackbird' is not one of the poems which acknowledges a debt to this garden or to Eastern art of any kind. It is not ordinarily seen as a landscape or garden poem, and yet . . . like so many Zen utterances Stevens's poem continually wrong-foots the reader. It consists of thirteen unmatched parts that are so brief and come from such different compass points that it's hard to view them as constituting a whole. The spaces or voids between the parts appear to have more presence than the solids. At Ryoan-ji everything is made from the same narrow range of materials; in Stevens's poem an initial abstraction and austerity give way after a few stanzas to fruity philosophizing, gothic grotesquerie and highly coloured Orientalism before reverting to minimalist landscape, only briefly. After a couple more lurid or surreal scenes the poem ends in two wonderfully empty, Zen moments:

> XII
> The river is moving.
> The blackbird must be flying.

> XIII
> It was evening all afternoon.
> It was snowing
> And it was going to snow.
> The blackbird sat
> In the cedar-limbs.

This poem is Stevens's most thoroughgoing, most nearly doctrinaire experiment with emptiness in the form of a figure-ground game that seems to want to escape literature altogether for something purely spatial. These are impulses often present in this poet's work but usually more concealed, impulses toward a generality about to leave the last vestiges of colour and texture behind and disappear out of sight into some ethereal realm. 'Thirteen Ways' consists of hard-edged fragments bound together by an extremely factitious entity, the idea of a bird or of an absence, black the non-colour. The blackbird can be many things: the singer, and a surrogate for the poet (except that the speaker is always alienated from the bird in one way or another); a bad omen or bringer of trouble (except that we can never take this seriously); a reality principle of some kind, anti-ideal; or contrarily a strong, sensory stimulus that puts human representations to shame.

This poem goes impossibly far in not smoothing the edges of fragments, leaving the reader to pick up the pieces. It marks an edge in Stevens's own practice; I cannot say if it had a progeny outside him, as you could say Ryoan-ji has done. We cannot count 'Thirteen Ways' an Orientalist poem; it departs in too many directions from its Zen self, which we might want to call its central core or principal inspiration, but it won't let us pin it down in minimalist mode. The overall shape or plan is Ryoan-ji-like, but the detail eludes unitary description.

An art-dealer's pastiches

Wallace Stevens is a peculiar kind of modernist, often using materials of an incongruous gorgeousness to produce uneasy wholes. He was a successful businessman as well as a poet, though it is generally assumed that he kept these two spheres apart from each other. In the practice of late nineteenth- and early twentieth-century art dealers there's a process of fragmentation and dispersal that may not be entirely unconnected to the perceptual shift underlying Eliot's and Stevens's most radical poetry. At that time American collectors and museums became able to pay prices for fragments of European medieval and Renaissance buildings that stimulate the piecemeal dispersal of altarpieces, fonts, tombs, portals and window-frames from decayed churches and palaces. Admittedly, hints of the process go back some way before Stefano Bardini, the greatest Florentine dealer of the last years of the nineteenth century. Napoleon brought back religious paintings from Italy and they were secularized in museums. Long before, Roman emperors had plundered Greece: it was something victors had always done. The Earl of Arundel raiding Pergamon in the seventeenth century was a pioneer in acquiring not complete masterpieces but barely intelligible fragments. There are now rooms at the British Museum that you can view as telling either the history of Greek architecture or the history of collecting. The objects collected there are all radically incomplete, some of them even separated from further bits of the same buildings now stored below ground in rooms of inferior status. Roughly speaking, sculptural fragments are preferred, while bulkier, purely architectural elements are demoted to remote and poorly lit spaces.

Stefano Bardini appears at a late stage of this worldwide process of dispersal. His life work was essentially a dispersion of fragments, mainly Florentine but including pieces from all over Italy, to museums and collectors mainly in northern Europe and North America. Bardini was learned and perceptive, a pioneer in appreciation of peripheral art forms like armour and carpets, with a renowned eye for unrecognized quality. He was also a pasticheur who used his expertise to disguise the nature and provenance of the objects he sold. His cleverest creations, doorways loaded with sculpture, pulpits like little temples, fonts straddling two centuries, made imaginary wholes out of fragments, the internal joints of which have now disappeared.

Late in his career, Bardini abruptly fired all his employees and began turning his palatial showrooms into a museum which he would give to the city of Florence, after filling it with a combination of unsold stock and items from his own collection. In the 1880s he had built a huge neo-Renaissance palace on the ruins of a medieval convent where he perfected display techniques which continue to influence Western museums but were devised in the first place to attract buyers. The building feels like a grandiose dwelling but contains a few features which don't fit. Many spaces are top-lit, as if they were courtyards which have been roofed over. Large stone portals take the place of doors between rooms, allowing us to look into several spaces at once, to catch previews of what lies ahead, to get occasional distant views.

By the time the Museo Bardini was turned over to the city in 1922, ideas of display had moved on and Bardini's smouldering blue backgrounds were whitewashed over and the museum's exhibits were forced to obey chronology instead of Bardini's mixture of different

Stefano Bardini's museum in Florence filled with leftover fragments from his career as a dealer.

eras for aesthetic effect. Recently, in keeping with our current obsession with the history of collecting, Bardini's colours and deployments of objects have been restored, a much more complicated historical task than most visitors are ever likely to appreciate. Every piece is trying to look its best, set off clearly distinct from those round it. Maybe there's a war that only experts can see between Bardini's urge to collage fragments into satisfying wholes and his need to isolate each item for sale. It isn't accurate to view him as a faker pure and simple: the individual bits he combines are usually authentic, yet pasted together they become pastiche through and through, even if we can't see it yet.

Of course there is feeble pastiche, like Ancient Rome in Hollywood epics, and inspired pastiche like Piranesi's or some of Bardini's, and given the passage of enough time maybe the first will always turn into the second. But there's a nightmare vision of Bardini's enterprise which can't stop itself from thinking of all the vanished originals – houses, churches, streets – from which his fragments have been ripped, many of them in the general destruction of the old centre of Florence to make the Piazza della Repubblica and the regular streets round about in the years when Florence was the capital of re-united Italy.

In the only form we can easily view his conceptions today, his museum across the river in Oltrarno, the surviving fragments recall Eliot's dissociation of sensibility, substituting analysis or fracture for the old Renaissance immersion in a world seamless and entire.

In spite of his battening on the ruin and destruction of old buildings, Bardini's activity is part of the late nineteenth- and early twentieth-century romance of Florence and the Renaissance, of which Herbert Horne's house-museum is one of the purest expressions. Horne was a transplanted Londoner who made a life-changing visit to Italy in 1889 but had to wait twenty years for the right small Florentine palace to come on the market.

Four antiquarian dealers of the period have left behind personal museums in Florence. Horne's is different from the others, for this connoisseur starts with an authentic Renaissance building and views it as the setting for a careful reconstruction of the right life to fill it, that of a gentleman-scholar of the sixteenth century, the person Herbert Horne supposed he would have been if he'd lived four centuries earlier. Thus he pays as much attention to desks and tables, window-shutters and kitchen implements as he does to paintings and sculpture. So we imagine Horne and his friends eating from old crockery and drinking from old glasses, playing with old ways of lighting fires and regulating the light. It didn't quite happen that way, though it was meant to, for Horne died suddenly at 52 before the carefully assembled equipment for such an existence had been arranged in the spaces.

Medieval New York

Some such effect as Horne strove for is the guiding intention at The Cloisters in New York, except that no one pretends to live there and the interiors slide from chapter houses of monasteries to the great halls of palaces to transepts of large churches, and from France to Spain to Germany in the blink of an eye.

The most fascinating feature of The Cloisters is the attempt to erase the memory of all the Bardinis who supplied the fragments and to naturalize them in a mocked-up fabric in which the sculptural flourishes now take their places. Someday soon if it hasn't happened already, The Cloisters building of 1934–8 will itself become a historical exhibit like Soane's house that holds his collection in London. Then visitors will come to experience the cavernous stair of gigantic stone blocks, the functionless Romanesque tower, the twisting series of imaginary spaces on different levels, and the fragments which fill and embellish the shell will then take a back seat or simply supply punctuation to the journey. This will turn the original intention of this building inside out; it was meant as background which gave the right levels of gloom for displaying medieval, mostly sacred, fragments, helped one forget that they are fragments and created a religious hush. The whole project strives toward an immersive kind of theatre, miles from art history as a scientific discipline.

Part of the genius of Soane's display spaces for his classical fragments is to produce the sensation of inhabiting a ruin without descending to the literal fakery of simulated antiquity. The most complex space, the so-called Dome, in his house is the bleached skeleton of a ruined dome or the scaffolding for one as yet unbuilt, more like what Rodchenko or Schwitters would have devised for such a purpose than the mossy mock-ruins favoured by regular practitioners of the eighteenth-century Picturesque.

The wildest excitement of Soane's most radical spaces comes from the feeling that they would almost welcome destruction. In practically every European country in the years on either side of the First World War convulsive art movements hostile to art of the past appear and threaten to spill out of the gallery into the street, where they hope to wreak havoc. The Italian version of this cultural upheaval, Futurism, was among the most radical, at least rhetorically, but was partly consumed in the War and largely co-opted by Fascism afterward, so it appeared to have come to nothing. What could Herbert Horne have made of Marinetti's rhetorical excesses? We know part of the answer: he forwarded the Futurists' latest attacks on bourgeois complacency to Wyndham Lewis in London. But if he had lived, he would have had to come to terms with their perverse offspring in Mussolini's 'movement' and its cartoon-like misuses of history.

One of the Russian derivatives of Futurism, Constructivism, makes a more worthy opponent. It is the only art movement of the period that runs in tandem for a few years with revolutionary social upheaval in a whole country, so that sculptures and buildings that look like fragmented debris from an explosion are no longer just the fantasies of artists, but give form to pervasive social facts. Change is so sweeping that old categories barely fit: 'sculpture' leaves its pedestal and lodges itself in the corner of the room from which it projects a splintering force that destroys the tranquillity of the interior. 'Buildings' split, teeter or divide themselves with ramps and stairs that are like attacks on stability or permanence; nothing can be allowed to remain the same for two minutes together.

This optimistic self-destructive phase did not survive the counter-revolution which followed in the late Twenties, but enjoyed a surprising second life 40 and 50 years later as 'Deconstruction', which emerged in calmer times or so it seemed. From greater historical distance this phase might no longer seem the dilettantish reprise it did in the '60s and '70s, but a foretaste of disruptions still to come.

3

Modernist Ruin

DURING HIS JOURNEY to the East of 1911, Le Corbusier (not called that yet, of course) made some revealing drawings and photographs of the Acropolis in Athens. They show a world of pure stone, vibrant surfaces crammed with detail that jumps off the page. Although these are anything but featureless blanks, there's a remarkable consistency, everything made of the same material, like a barren landscape without plants, or a Zen garden. There's geometry, and stone and the upper air, and nothing more.

Modernist villas as temple ruins

In some of the purest and most concentrated work of his whole career, the villas of the mid- to late 1920s, Le Corbusier has reduced the constituents of the dwelling to barest essentials, like pebbles worn smooth by the sea or ruins cleansed by time of surface features. The concluding member of this canonical series, the Villa Savoye at Poissy, southwest of Paris, even looks vaguely like a classical temple rearranged over the centuries until the colonnade has sunk to the bottom and the podium climbed on top.

This was the most perfect of these houses, set off in an ideal seclusion, soon spoiled by encroaching neighbours, and falling into ruin after colliding with some of the worst events of the twentieth century. The Jewish owners were shipped off by the German invaders who used the house for storing hay. After the war Mme Savoye couldn't afford to repair the ruin and let it out as a barn to a local farmer. It's in this period that I imagine it inhabited, like the archaic temples in southern Italy depicted by Piranesi, by cows who keep its lawns cropped and find its ramps convenient.

I am unable to locate any pictures of cows at home in Corb's machine but Bernard Tschumi has written that the defaced villa with excrement scrawled on its walls (the Germans poured concrete down the loos as they left) gave him the shock of great architecture all the stronger for being ringed round with danger.

The Villa Savoye was never going to be kept as a ruin, nor was anyone going to live there. In its restored state the building has become a demonstration of architectural properties, unnaturally free of the clutter of passing life. Among the most compelling moments are junctions of oversupplied means of circulation – ramps and spiral stairs doing the same job placed right next to each other. In some of Corb's descriptions it seems that a main motive for turning the house up-side down, with a garden on the roof and a void on the ground, was to instil movement into the inert carcass, movement more tellingly graphed by ramps than stairs, the feature in which the dynamism of the machine appears most clearly.

Japanese beauty in ruins

Junichiro Tanizaki's *In Praise of Shadows* is usually seen as an anti-modernist, anti-Western tract. But Japanese traditional architecture has had a well-documented influence on modernism, and Tanizaki's little book is the most beautiful evocation of the underlying aesthetic of Japanese space, furnishings, food and theatre. Like Corb's this is a minimalist aesthetic, powerfully divergent from his, starting from a dark rather than a white blankness.

The book opens with an insoluble dilemma – how to accommo-date Western technology in Japanese space, particularly electric light, flushing loos and the glittering whiteness that goes with them. Paper walls, wooden toilets and lacquer dishes were never going to survive except in protected environs, the equivalent of the special space the Villa Savoye now occupies.

Before he became a devotee of traditional ways Tanizaki had been a Westernizer who moved to Yokohama to immerse himself more fully in modernity. His particular devotion to tradition is unthinkable without nineteenth-century Romanticism and the ruin-taste that sees the full beauty of cultural forms only when they are lost beyond recall. Traditional buildings perfectly preserved in outdoor museums are petrified ruins of their old selves, like someone under a spell surviving in a world that has forgotten how the old devices work.

There is a view of dry Zen gardens that sees them overcoming the passage of time and the temporariness of existence by undergoing something like death. The Japanese word for dry garden, *karesansui*, apparently includes the sense 'dried out', sacrificing the vividness of full-blooded existence for a kind of invulnerability. The materials, stone and sand, do not change or decay, or change extremely slowly, on cycles longer and grander than those of ordinary seasons. This is not the whole story: Le Corbusier's white forms are meant to be impervious and permanent, receptive to light but not to serious attacks by the weather. The stones at Ryoan-ji, though, have been through a lot before they got here and give signs of a long and not unviolent previous existence. Now they form part of an abstract representation, but still carry traces of the tumults they've left behind. The afterlife of buildings is one of the main subjects of this book; the rocks of Ryoan-ji are all afterlife, living on in a later world that can only guess at the earlier ages embodied in the stones.

For a couple of accidental reasons the oldest domestic ruins in Britain look suspiciously like diagrammatic modernist interiors. The Neolithic village at Skara Brae in Orkney is now a place made entirely of stone in a landscape of sand, cleansed and organized by the disappearance of everything organic, which leaves it looking minimalist by design. The most important subtractions are the roofs: everything now laid bare like laboratory specimens – including the narrow passageways between burrows and the built-in stone furniture and rectangular hearths of upright slabs – was originally topped with more of the mounded-up rubbish the settlement is built on and buttressed by on all sides. Their excavator has described the original style of life at Skara Brae as hopelessly cluttered and filthy. Now it is a place scoured clean and viewed from above and all at once, which thus becomes more abstract and model-like than spaces we can actually enter.

The model-like effect of some of Corb's villas may derive in part from his experience of ruins at places like Pompeii where most of the

Almost a millennium older than similar dwellings at Skara Brae, the farmstead at Knap of Howar on Papa Westray, Orkney, is a similar structure unnaturally clarified by the absence of its roof.

houses are hollow shells without their roofs. From many perspectives and not just the semi-aerial view provided by the platform above the main roof terrace, the Villa Savoye looks like a structure without its roof, which has laid itself bare for inspection, and which is finished off in unexpectedly enterable spaces, giving an entirely different, less conclusive kind of closure. This is a building which doesn't end decisively but unrolls continuously like a film.

These suggestions of inconclusiveness may be even more startling from ground level than from the top looking down. You can look through punctures in the fabric and see the house's innards far within, across intervening voids that suggest an exhilarating incompleteness in the whole construction. All these sensations are repeated in the garden at Ryoan-ji, also enclosed on three sides by a hollow shell, as if part of its conceptual freedom is gained by leaving off the roof. The result is almost as much a building as it is a landscape, but liberated by that crucial omission.

The modernity of the beach

Dungeness is a sand and pebble beach just south of Romney Marsh in Kent, a place where buildings and landscape are confused, where the low houses look like debris washed up, almost as temporary as the trash with which the beach is littered. Derek Jarman's clever garden resembles a lightly organized collection of junk found in the immediate neighbourhood, whose pieces call slightly more attention to themselves than the surrounding flotsam, and whose green elements are kept firmly in check, as at Ryoan-ji.

A shingle beach is more obviously a natural ruin than one of sand; each piece of it shows the ruining effect of the sea and there's even a hierarchy of degradation. Some stones are softer and break down more quickly, but 'quickly' is still too slow for us to watch it happening. It's only lately that human debris decays almost as slowly. Ruined nylon nets eventually look like heads of ghostly hair, and after the sea takes the colour out of plastic, shredded sheets of it can be mistaken for seaweed. The really indigestible debris at Dungeness is manufactured at its nuclear power stations, whose waste isn't organic, resists decay, and forms a permanent ruin no one wants to visit.

Two of the sound mirrors at Dungeness, Kent, advanced technology turned into modernist sculpture.

Among the most interesting pieces of architecture at Dungeness are three sound mirrors built between the wars to pick up and magnify the sound of approaching aircraft before you could see them. They look like Corbusian elemental solids in a favourite modernist material, re-inforced concrete, whose age is always hard to guess. Two of them are spherical bowls tilted at twenty degrees toward planes arriving from France. The third is a curved horizontal screen 200 feet long. Not long after they were built planes became too fast for them and were visible very soon after the mirrors had collected the noise of them. These con-structions are often called an early form of radar, but they look like toys and there's hardly any reminder of their usefulness, just a metal pole poking up in the middle of one, like the gnomon on a sundial. It used to hold a microphone but now makes its dish look like a big, burned-out lightbulb. Any buildings which once accompanied the oversized lumps of concrete have disappeared, and the gravel pit in which they were set has reverted to marsh, a set of conditions that add up to a sort of false antiquity.

Playing at brutality

For a second generation of modernists, concrete's propensity to look ruined before its time came to be welcomed and exploited, first of all by Le Corbusier at the end of his career and then by architects called Brutalist in both admiration and horror. The great monument of this short-lived phase is probably the Yale Art and Architecture Building in New Haven, Connecticut, by Paul Rudolph, completed in 1963. It's a monster of a building, which contrives to look bigger than it actually is by putting together vertical masses that rise through seven storeys without a break or any sign of windows from certain angles. The main entrance is like a tall, narrow cleft in the rock which closes round you as you give yourself up to the experience – sublime but threatening.

Rudolph devised a special finish for the concrete the building is made of, which was poured into ribbed moulds. When the moulds were removed, the ribs were attacked with hammers. The result is an extremely rough surface in which large chunks of aggregate buried inside the concrete are exposed. The violence in the manufacture of these surfaces didn't depart with the workmen; it loomed there

Paul Rudolph's Art and Architecture building at Yale, showing the special finish of ridged concrete surfaces obtained by attacking them with hammers.

continually. Stories abound of the hazard the roughness offered to skin and clothing.

When he designed the building Rudolph was chairman of the architecture department; the architects got the best spaces and the artists were left permanently discontented. This was only the beginning of a contentious and tormented history, which somehow fits the aggressive quality of the building. A piece in the Yale alumni magazine on the twenty-fifth anniversary of its completion praised the school as one of the rare structures that will make a good ruin. It always had that look. In the late 1960s but before the devastating fire of 1969, it appeared grimy and neglected though only a few years old. This was intentional we were told; it was its nature, and its honesty – New Haven was not a pretty place and the building acknowledged that. It welcomed the grime of the city, and the inside was just as tough as the outside. Like Piranesi's ruins it revelled in sensations of rudeness and incompleteness all the way through.

Recently the architecture building has been cleaned and restored, and since then to get the full effect of a Brutalist structure as the modern ruin, you need to turn to a later example instead, like Boston City Hall, by Kallmann, McKinnell & Knowles, completed in 1968, a behemoth on an even larger scale, which was used as the police headquarters in a recent dystopian film (*The Departed*, 2006) that wallowed in urban grime and corruption.

This is a building with a grim and looming underside. Apparently derelicts lodged there when not actively discouraged, in spaces generally unwanted which yet provided a kind of protection. So architecture with its own resemblance to ruin inadvertently brings out lurid signs of social decay.

This effect is by no means unique. The Southbank Centre in London, a more ramifying and less oppressive Brutalist complex, not a bastion of unwieldy bureaucracy but loosely strung institutions devoted to cultural activities, found its darker recesses accommodating a cardboard city of the homeless in the Thatcher years.

Now in the dankest underside on the South Bank the homeless have been replaced by skateboarders, but there are still at least two levels to the experience here, the alpine and the subterranean. It is a mythic landscape of heights and depths, whose grime is sometimes heroic and sometimes alarming, which might pack less punch without the (mostly imaginary) threat. Southbank doesn't appeal to rationalists and was never meant to, but to those who view the city as a sublime ruin.

The story of another of the Brutalist monuments of London is one of the saddest in the whole of modern architecture. For a variety of reasons two very talented British architects, the husband and wife team Alison and Peter Smithson, got to build very little. Some of their most interesting designs, including Coventry Cathedral, Sheffield University and Golden Lane housing in the City of London, remained on paper. Finally the chance came to test their theories about large-scale housing on an isolated site in Tower Hamlets hemmed in by major roads. From the start, conditions were not ideal. The Smithsons' boldest idea about urban dwelling, 'streets in the air', couldn't be fully tested on the confined site; the 'streets' would end before they'd had a chance to go anywhere.

Perhaps this was just as well: the picture of people content to spend their lives well above the ground seems highly fanciful in the Smithson texts of the early '60s. On top of this, the architects' aesthetic choices haven't worn well with the users the project was built for – council tenants who aren't necessarily interested in architectural theories of the decade preceding that in which the buildings are actually built.

For lovers of Brutalist ruin or faux-ruin via concrete – a material which tends to look older than it is – Robin Hood Gardens continues to exercise a grisly fascination, even in its current neglected state, even after unsympathetic changes like cabling run clumsily along the low ceilings of intermediate decks or satellite dishes breaking up the cliff-like elevations of the blocks. Now it is all too obvious that the deliberate crudity (or honesty, or reality) of such buildings is a sophisticated, even paradoxical effect that it probably takes an educated audience to appreciate. Ordinary dwellers don't want to live in something that looks more and more like a ruin.

They are not precisely comparable, but the Barbican development in the City of London becomes increasingly popular with architect-residents as its bumpy, bush-hammered concrete surfaces get grimier, and in spite of its labyrinthine plan, which adds to the look of Piranesi's prisons, the experience of being lost among giant colonnades. Both Robin Hood Gardens and the Barbican are focused on archaic remnants of earlier historical stages, a Gothic church at the Barbican and a mound like a prehistoric burial at Robin Hood Gardens. In fact the tumulus entombs remains of vanished lives, whatever was left of the bulldozed Victorian terraces that preceded the current blocks.

So the Smithsons' new buildings closed their own archaeological site in a curved embrace. The 'curves' are a series of angular bends that give distinct changing views. Thus it turns out that the no-nonsense modernist mode smuggles back the very last attitudes you would have predicted: the hoary, aestheticized taste of the English Picturesque. There are further delicious contradictions between the subtle sculpted forms of the blocks and the rough materials. To the appreciative visitor the canted concrete rail along the balconies seems wonderfully over-expressed, like traces of a great Roman bath now colonized by pygmies. But to council tenants unused to playing such imaginary historical games, the rail just looks illogical and unsightly. Brutalism is an ironical style, and irony always loses some of the audience. It's very sad that Robin Hood Gardens' days are apparently numbered, but it should have been obvious that this mode isn't right for public housing.

Le Corbusier had shocked some of his modernist adherents by breaking away from rectilinear purity of form toward curves and bulges reminiscent of primitive vernacular and even animal anatomy. It wouldn't be true to say that the Smithsons soon got used to playing with hints of archaism and ruin. But we find them specifying variegated surface finishes, bevelled corners and seemingly random building heights in their largest urban project, the Economist towers on a sensitive site in London's clubland. The main cladding material is Portland stone, traditional for public buildings in London since the eighteenth century. But this is Portland stone with a difference, specially chosen to be so shelly that it appears to be disintegrating, as if it is being eaten away by the little creatures entombed in it. The material itself constitutes a graveyard on the most intimate scale, a ruin under the microscope.

True modernist ruins

By a cruel twist of circumstance one of the largest and most imaginative Corbusian buildings in Britain has been forced to become the most notorious modernist ruin. St Peter's Seminary at Cardross, twenty miles northwest of Glasgow, was designed by a team of young architects at Gillespie, Kidd & Coia in the late 1950s and built in the 1960s, occupied in the 1970s, evacuated and reused in the 1980s and left to decay thereafter. Now the roofs have fallen in, there are pools in the main spaces, spalled concrete is crawled over by a lurid lichen of graffiti, and jungle-like growth threatens the structure on all sides.

The design took off from Corb's convent at La Tourette near Lyon, completed in 1960, a design full of quirky features that has been plausibly attributed to Iannis Xenakis, Corb's assistant at the time, rather than Corb himself. In any event, no one thinks La Tourette isn't Corbusian. Cardross has silo-chapels mysteriously lit, a classroom block daringly cantilevered over the library and shaped on its underside like a boat, student cells stepping back over big public spaces to produce a ziggurat, or internally two inverted ziggurats. The big forms survive, obscured by debris, made more Brutalist than they started out by severe weathering pushed further by vandalism.

The building's isolated location, which suited a monastic idea of vocation that the Catholic Church was discarding in the very years the seminary came into use, and which allowed the iconic amplitude of the design, made the buildings difficult to protect and forced them to regress to savagery with terrible speed. The ruin at Cardross provokes a special disbelief: 'modernist ruin' sounds like an impossibility, as if these works would hold their place in the vanguard forever, as if the modernist stripping away of all that historically conditioned detail would buy for them an immortality like that enjoyed by the severest Zen gardens.

More than a century before, Sir John Soane had mounted an attack on certain elements of standard classical iconography, especially the ox skulls that appeared in the friezes of classical buildings. Soane's argument was that the skulls represented leftovers from animal sacrifice, a ritual no longer practised, which when you thought about it was offensively pagan. It's interesting to find him being so literal-minded, yet hard to take him seriously, not that he doesn't want to clear away such clutter, but not perhaps for the reason he suggests. Hasn't the paraphernalia of classical ornament been an anthropological game for a long time, to the extent that it retains any content at all? Isn't the excuse for getting rid of it that it's unthinking, not that it's pagan? At

Modernist ruin at St Peter's Seminary, Cardross, Scotland.

roughly the same moment Philipp Otto Runge is devising quasi-religious imagery derived from plant forms considered as a sort of geometric ideal, which could have seemed more insidiously pagan than the worn-out Greek motifs.

Soane's own results contrive to look as if something's been taken away, as if crucial detail has been erased, leaving a remnant that's hard to interpret, like the product of a culture to which we don't have the key. This is where we might feel a surprising partial overlap with early modernism in architecture. The blankness of these forms and surfaces is mysterious, a void that provokes thought.

Borromini's new clothes

Not long ago, Borromini's little Baroque church of S. Carlino in Rome was thoroughly restored by stripping off all the later accretions and giving the whole interior a final coat of dazzling whiteness. One kind of detail was completely expelled: there were now hardly any variations of tone, and sensations of depth were reduced. Another sort of detail jumped forward: the plastic richness of carved stucco in over-sized palm branches or a putti's wings gained almost hallucinatory power. The main spatial concepts also got much easier to read, so the space as a set of puzzles or an intellectual adventure took over.

I loved this, but have since had doubts. Now the white has begun to look dingy and the perfection to feel soiled. Maybe the whiteness is too much for an actual building to live up to, as opposed to an eternal un-ageing ideal. Maybe it's a radical simplification that only a Corbusian modernist could conceive of imposing on any interior. I seem to remember though that such a purification has happened at least once before. There was a strange interregnum between the last days of Bavarian Rococo and the beginning of Neoclassicism, during which a couple of the buildings of Balthasar Neumann were fitted out in a chilly white like this. There it seems more like a hostile take-over; Borromini lent himself more easily to begin with, but there too there comes a final comeuppance, and this ruin by subtraction doesn't convince us for ever.

Primitivizing the classical, reprimitivizing the primitive

Against the conventional version of classicism as a colourless primitive purity has always stood a subversive classicism of archaic richness whose buildings are loaded with the detritus of myth, the weird unseemly flavours Soane was, at least momentarily, inveighing against. This alternative version stemmed in part from nineteenth-century French draughtsmen repopulating Greek temples with fierce gods and high colour. The recolouring of ancient buildings also comes in intellectualized variants propounded by maverick historians like George Hersey, who reads superstition much more deeply into the fabric of Doric temples until their most innocuous elements are creaturized. Classical myths are also violently primitivized in works like Pasolini's film *Medea* (1969), which takes seriously the resemblance of ancient Greeks to tribal subjects of contemporary anthropologists.

American natives, as met by early European colonists are similarly re-primitivized in another recent film, *Cabeza de Vaca* (1991) by Nicolás Echevarría. In the sixteenth-century conquistador's journal from which this film is adapted, Spaniards marooned among the Indians see themselves as stripped bare: rendered naked by immersion in an alien society with little content. But in the film this overarching nakedness is presented as fantastically colourful. The European captives are gradually loaded with symbolic content and end as ambulatory dramatized myths, far richer than any European equivalent. In the old source-narrative, native life is formidably bare; for months on end the tribe's entire diet consists of a certain berry or type of shellfish and the group teeters on the verge of extinction. Now that extinction is long ago complete, highly coloured depictions of what has been destroyed flourish. Now we collect together all the exceptions – the Europeans like Cabeza de Vaca who saw that there was something worth saving in the subject cultures and tried to preserve it by recording it, producing in the process poignant and beautiful but essentially lifeless ruins.

Finding the ruin within

The painstaking interventions in the fabric of venerable existing monuments by the Venetian architect Carlo Scarpa share something with the idea of re-primitivizing ancient cultures through their myths. At Castelvecchio in Verona Scarpa starts with an apparently intact building and finds a ruin in it, which he then delicately proceeds to display. At first his brief was to update a series of early twentieth-century museum galleries. They had been subjected to an earlier, too-complete restoration whose proudest feat of disguise turned a Napoleonic barracks into a richly decorated Renaissance palace.

So Scarpa's search for the true historical depths of the site began with ruthlessly stripping away the latest layer, which he considered entirely bogus, including pseudo-Renaissance frescoes and painted wooden ceilings which disguised the contradictions beneath the surface and turned works of art displayed against them into furnishings. To Scarpa this historical fantasy of the 1920s had no value; it was simply fake. So not a trace of it remains internally.

Other elements of the earlier 'restoration' were more deeply embedded and harder to remove, like Gothic window frames salvaged from other buildings implanted in the main facade. But Scarpa wanted to make the falsity of these insertions evident, by setting the glazing far inside the frames and making the wall look paper-thin. He also destroyed the symmetry of the faked facade by moving the main entrance from centre to edge, dislodging the regularity of the windows with a few intruders, and adding a chapel-like extension jutting from the long wall.

But the biggest disruption of the monumentality of the long 'palace' wall was Scarpa's demolition of a whole bay where the barracks butted against a high medieval rampart. This is a rare remnant of the old town defences swallowed in the fourteenth century when the fortified ruler's dwelling was built. An old gate in this wall was rediscovered in the upheaval of Scarpa's demolition, a gate that connected the museum's two courtyards. This joint in the buildings is already historically and spatially the most complicated moment in the whole complex, prompting Scarpa to bring more architectural energy to bear on the spot. Having removed the floor he needs to supply a

A modernist architect lays bare discontinuity and ruin in an old building: Carlo Scarpa at Castelvecchio, Verona.

bridge in the gap. Having taken out everything else he's made the roof redundant, so it can become an elaborate canopy for an iconic sculpture that he's decided to locate here on a high plinth.

In Richard Murphy's book about Scarpa at Castelvecchio you can follow the evolution of this space in a series of 30 or 40 drawings. As in other Scarpa designs he seems to pursue the large and the tiny aspects of the problem at the same time. A lot of thought goes into the angling of the big sculpted rider, subject of famous drawings by Ruskin. This figure has been absorbed into the architecture by being placed at once inside and against it.

Its florid detail contrasts violently with the semi-industrial textures of the bridge, stairs and roof that surround it. The site of the demolished bay has become the fullest moment in the structure, not the emptiest. Stripping away a bland surface layer reveals unexpected variety, which Scarpa typically brings out by separating the different layers or periods from each other, leaving a gap, emphasizing the unhealed edges rather than closing the wound.

Scarpa's dissections of historic fabric take place so slowly and so scrupulously that the boldness is somewhat smoothed away in the long process of revision. Even the coarsely boarded concrete of the rider's pedestal and enclosure becomes exquisite in Scarpa's hands, like the rough elements in the old Japanese tea huts.

Scarpa the architect stands revealed most tellingly in his dealings with the works of art that are the museum's reason for being. In his drawings one sees him forming relations with individual pieces, figure sculpture above all. He turns them this way and that, placing them against walls or windows, sometimes disarranging groups that formerly stood closer together or in a single plane in the Romanesque church they were made for.

Scarpa revels in the fragmentary nature of some of the pieces, broken-off limbs of larger wholes, and separates all of them clearly from the place they are in, as fragments in the most obvious sense, which don't belong. None are in their natural homes. All have been selected for qualities that transcend their original function and are now *displayed*, a process which isolates them. In place of the ease of the original context Scarpa has supplied a new appreciation of the sensuous and dramatic possibility they offer the present. So we don't pretend they are anything but stranded fragments, ruins of time, now located in ruined spaces similarly resurrected after long passage and placed at their service. So a dynamic tension arises between the works which have been treated like unrepeatable individuals and settings with their own broken and incomplete histories.

Conserving bomb damage

The Alte Pinakothek in Munich is a much simpler historical artefact than the Castelvecchio in Verona. It has always served the function for which it was built: public display of the Bavarian royal collection of Old Master paintings. The building forms part of an ambitious nineteenth-century redevelopment of the city as a provincial capital. Like most of the other governmental and cultural institutions built in the first phase of this big push, the Alte Pinakothek was designed by Leo von Klenze, a local architect who also played a key part in the cleansing and reorganization of the Athenian Acropolis under the new Bavarian king of independent Greece. But, unlike Klenze's museum for antique sculpture nearby, a porticoed temple in stone, the Alte Pinakothek is an un-temple-like rectangular lump in brick.

In 1944–5 it was seriously damaged by bombing raids which left most of the shell standing but gutted the interior. The ruin sat there for a couple of years, weathering further, and came close to being demolished. Only in 1952 was it finally decided to salvage the old building, and Hans Döllgast, an architect who had already recovered bombed monuments in a discreet minimalist style, was given the job of dealing with the main damage to the fabric, a large cone-shaped rupture in the south facade.

It seems he never considered making all trace of the bombing disappear by replicating Klenze's columns and arcades. He tried out the possibility of closing the large gap in the building's skin with a curtain wall of glass, but returned to the original material, brick, in the end. In an early proposal he leaves the upper storey of the ruptured part un-filled-in, a hollowed-out effect which makes the building look seriously incomplete. The texture of his brickwork contrasts strongly with Klenze's, much harsher, in part because Döllgast's bricks were all salvaged from another ruin created by bombing, the Turkenkaserne, whose debris lay nearby. Döllgast liked the rawness of unrendered brick because it reminded him of effects he admired in ancient ruins. Mysteriously, uncannily, bombing gave the architect a chance to expose the bare bones of architecture.

In the end he didn't keep much of the ragged edge of the blast, which a more fanciful designer might have found a way to do, but the wound still shows, softened in part by concrete lintels and bare mouldings that faintly echo patterned friezes on the old facade. Döllgast has added a row of blank panels, undecorated punctuation from a more primitive classicism than Klenze's. The boldest new element is a set of slim steel posts placed where columns would have fallen on the old facade but running straight through both storeys without a break until they bump into the parapet. These stand forward from the new wall, separate from it.

So it is easy to see why Döllgast's solution was called a 'permanent provisional arrangement' and why demands continued after its completion for the temporary state to be carried to conclusion. The same slighting phrase – 'permanent provisional' – could be taken as expressing a deeply considered philosophical position. Döllgast's restoration doesn't seek to dramatize the damage or make excitement out of destruction. The new materials complement the old and don't stand out from them as starkly as Scarpa's sometimes do. In 1949–50 Döllgast did a simpler restoration of a bombed church in Munich where he allowed himself a more radical cleansing of the old richness. Perhaps he didn't respect the original designers as he did Klenze; perhaps the church was a more compliant client than the whole cultural establishment that interested itself in the museum.

The greatest novelty of Döllgast's work at the Alte Pinakothek, its tentative quality, made it easy for others to come along later and suggest improvements. Döllgast himself changed his mind about the starkness of his solution in the 1970s and proposed elaborations that would have brought it nearer to Klenze. Luckily, by this point no one was listening. The final irony is that this architect's 27-year devotion to this building still goes unrecognized, because it can pass unnoticed except to studious observers, radical yet cautious, uncompromising yet invisible.

Besides the large diagonals of sheared-off wall, of which Döllgast never found ways to preserve more than faint traces, there were many small cracks, gaps and craters in the brickwork, evidence of wartime destruction that he was content to leave, which were gradually made good. Döllgast's wish that memory of the museum as a ruin should be preserved was more and more overridden as time went on. But in spite of everything, his self-effacing work, which isn't exactly restoration, remains a critical assertion that the disasters of war shouldn't be made to disappear entirely from the urban fabric, as if one could pretend they hadn't happened. His rebuilding of the bombed church, cemetery and museum in Munich holds a high place among unromantic appreciations of ruins.

Curating destruction

Hans Döllgast lived through the war; David Chipperfield didn't, and isn't German. So he (and everyone else, for that matter) comes to the Neues Museum project in Berlin from much further away. Most of those involved in deciding what to do with this ruined building won't have remembered it the way it was before the wartime destruction of Berlin. There's a kind of freedom in that, and in having waited so long to deal with the ruin. Chipperfield's solution, probably the most interesting recent treatment of a ruin, would have been unimaginable in the immediate aftermath of destruction.

He has been accused of monumentalizing destruction or dwelling too obsessively on physical effects of the war, but a more reasonable charge might be that of curating ruin and creating a museum of all its stages. By strange or lucky accident almost every conceivable level of survival of the interior structure, decoration and surface finish occurs somewhere in the warren of the Neues Museum.

Many of the objects exhibited are ruined fragments themselves. If they were ever highly coloured, they are so no longer, and their uniformly stony colours gave licence for vivid historicist murals above eye level in many rooms. These scenes survive now in ruined form if they survive at all, and look more like antique remnants than nineteenth-century copies, at least to a cursory glance. The fluted columns holding up segmental arches in reused brick are chewed and mottled by the speeded-up ageing of modern war. So occasionally we feel we are wandering in much older spaces than a nineteenth-century German museum. But in this sequence of rooms nothing ever goes on the same for long, and some of the biggest spaces have more of Chipperfield than they do of the older fabric.

In all the variety, a full conspectus of the stages of decay, one phase is entirely missing: actual decrepitude and squalor. Wonderful care has been taken over all kinds of traces of the past and everything has come out looking in some way pristine. All the inconsistencies of survival are meticulously preserved, showing a reverence for the unaccountable accidents of history that visitors are often moved by, yet everything looks stabilized and frozen at this moment in time by the Medusa-stare of the present. Yet this too will age, and I don't think this approach to ruin allows for that. The pure Chipperfield parts won't always be able to stand so clearly apart from the rest, though it is true that we would have to wait a long time before a visitor could be genuinely unsure which was later, Chipperfield or the nineteenth century.

The Neues Museum isn't only a memorial, but it certainly is a memorial of the war along with whatever else it is. Perhaps it is surprising that Georg Dehio, the inventor of detailed architectural catalogues of the buildings of whole nations, spoke out against slavish

A ruin allowed to display its wounds and feel its age as it meets the architecture of the present: David Chipperfield at Neues Museum, Berlin.

reconstruction of buildings destroyed in the First World War, and that Thomas Mann, the memorializer of defunct regional cultures, poked fun at the 'once-upon-a-time approach' to repairing damaged German cities. Many natives and almost all tourists mistake various architectural replicas in present-day Munich for the real thing. One of the most telling instances is the eighteenth-century Residenztheater, rebuilt after the war according to traditional methods and thus held together by pegs and glue instead of nails, but moved to a new location because the original site was taken up with a theatre in modernist mode which had been the first solution to the gaping hole left by bombs. So two solutions to this ruination exist in parallel, something like the two Vietnam memorials in Washington, an abstract modernist one overlooked by a Norman Rockwell afterthought.

Like Ruskin, Dehio probably realized that he wouldn't be fooled by replicas, and anyway cared too much about what was lost beyond recall, not the look of the thing, not even its patina, but the survival of accumulated experience into the later time. Yet I remember a Rococo interior in Munich that I didn't realize was reconstituted from scratch and which therefore could captivate me completely, who had no memory of the way it once was.

There seems no statute of limitations for memory, and in Germany memorials continue to be built to aspects of the last war which are in danger of being forgotten. Some of the most moving ones try to recapture the most fleeting events of the period, like the distribution of leaflets by the White Rose, commemorated in the scattered paving of a square, or the burning of books, remembered in hidden libraries below street level, or the passage of deportees, marked at wide intervals along their route. The kinship between these two forms, memorials and ruins, is often evident in graveyards and used to be pre-empted by marking graves with ruined columns or collapsing garlands carved in stone from the very start.

The proportions of the Chipperfield project in Berlin will change when his new entry building to the museums on Museum Island is completed, the proportions between old and new, between resuscitated and freshly imagined. In models and mock-ups it appears that the new building will suggest links between existing buildings without insistence and create the sense of a continuum in which the present century takes its place among the others. In the resurrected museum the blank surfaces of the Chipperfield insertions echo the incompleteness of the still ruined fabric. In the new building the same blankness is not the same, no longer just a considered response to surrounding conditions but something more assertive and perhaps an even more powerful comment on the buildings of the past.

The combination of reverence and irreverence toward the past expressed in projects like this would be surprising to anyone who didn't know something about the history of preservation and its uneasy relation to modernism in the visual arts. Modernism and preservation aren't obvious friends, preservation with its origins in antiquarianism and modernism with its urge to scrap all historical styles. Unexpectedly ruin is sometimes just what it takes to get a modernist interested in historical fabric. The architect begins treating the remains analytically, like an archaeological puzzle, and then at some point succumbs and arrives at a romantic result in the end.

The nineteenth-century murals in the Neues Museum, nothing much as works of art, in their incomplete state become witnesses of historical process bigger than architecture, caught up in a narrative that their second-rate painters couldn't foresee. Now framed by Chipperfield's blank surfaces they are salvaged by science not sentiment. At least I think that is what modernism intends to contribute to this exercise in remembering. It remains an unlikely outcome, exhausted historicism rejuvenated by the cleansing oversight of modernism.

Another example of modernist interventions which revivify a ruin that was not that special to start with leaves the observer in even more of a quandary. Astley Castle in Warwickshire is a modest architectural relic, added to and obscured over the centuries like hundreds of other houses scattered over the English shires. It began to stand out from the rest when it was gutted by fire in 1978 and then allowed to moulder further.

Now it has become something much more special by a complicated process including demolition of its most recent parts, stripping back of fragmentary remains from an in-between date to make outdoor rooms two storeys high, and insertion of a new shell in the oldest part to create habitable interiors. The mode of the new building by Witherford Watson Mann Architects recalls Döllgast or the Swedish architect Sigurd Lewerentz in frank handling of basic materials like brick and raw timber, bricks longer than ordinary bricks, timber treated without sealing it, simple materials of slightly unusual form. But this is a more playful building than any of theirs because all the rigour is applied to a thoroughly unnecessary project, the fitting up of an abandoned building as a holiday let.

Another revived ruin that doesn't pretend to make invisible joints between old and new: Witherford Watson Mann at Astley Castle, Warwickshire.

In the eighteenth century landowners who didn't have ruins to hand that could serve as diverting episodes in their grounds sometimes built mock ones, which might be fitted out with fictional provenance: they were said to be all that was left of the castle or priory which preceded the present house on the property. Sometimes the hermitage was periodically inhabited by an actual hermit. Astley Castle is now comfortably furnished, not full of bare monks' cells, and yet it is hard to avoid the thought that its visitors will be playing a version of the game of the hermit, living in a ruin and waking in the night to the standard fears of the heroine of a Gothic novel.

Such thoughts couldn't be further from the architects' intentions, and yet what else can living in a ruin mean? What is the point if it does not put you in touch with the idea of universal decay and make you more aware of your own place in this continuum? The modern insertions are a studied denial of the whole idea of decline, yet everything else is saying something different.

Building castles in the twentieth century

There's a whole history of renovating derelict Scottish castles and fortified houses for current occupation which would doubtless provide us with a rich variety of compromises between house and ruin. It is just as interesting though to look at work by a couple of architects whose interest in ruins turns up unexpectedly in structures they built from scratch. Lutyens had made an old castle into a semi-workable dwelling at Lindisfarne and went on much later to build a castle-like granite hulk, Castle Drogo in Devon, on a virgin site. Building a castle from scratch is perhaps less historically compromised than adding to an existing one, if you can accept that a client could need a castle in the early twentieth century.

Of course it isn't possible to build a real castle in the twentieth century. You could build an imitation of one, and this is probably what the tea merchant who commissioned Castle Drogo started out wanting, a perfect replica. But Lutyens didn't do imitations; instead he did witty variations on themes taken from historical architecture, interpretations that veered more and more toward abstraction rather than literal transcription. Thus at Drogo you get elements like the chapel belfry, a huge lump of stone serving its modest practical task cyclopically, or the stone fins that prolong battlements and suggest speed or movement, such an irresponsible idea you wonder where it came from.

The very idea of a fresh-built castle is more impossible, but in the working out, Lutyens's proposal for a fresh-built cathedral reaches even greater heights of unlikelihood. Castle Drogo got built after all, if not as gigantically as intended, but Lutyens's Catholic cathedral for Liverpool was put into retirement as a ruin before it had risen above ground level. Now the crypt is all that remains of a structure projected as the second largest church in Christendom. It was scaled like the Baths of Caracalla and, like them, built mainly of brick. Blank expanses of brick rose cliff-like, like the largest, most featureless Roman ruins. This choice of material must have been inspired by ancient Roman buildings, whose great red clay flanks give a misleading impression without their coats of render or marble facing.

From further away, and this was a building designed for distant views, Lutyens's cathedral would not have revealed so clearly that its

Detail of brickwork at Sigurd Lewerentz's church of St Mark, Björkhagen, Sweden, which suggests a kinship with ancient ruins.

enormous bulk was arrived at by piling up vast crowds of identical small units of cooked earth, but it remains one of the oddest and boldest strokes of this wildly ambitious project.

At the end of his life the Swedish architect Sigurd Lewerentz turned back to brick in a very different spirit from the classicism of Lutyens's cathedral. Both these architects were unorthodox classicists through large stretches of their careers; both had roots in the local vernacular of their regions, in the English Arts and Crafts, and the traditional forms of rural Sweden. Early in his career Lewerentz took a long Italian journey on which he made many photographs of ancient ruins. Anyone who knows his late brick churches will find startling confirmation in these images. Only a modernist or at least someone capable of modernist perceptions could have chosen these shots. The focus is always close, so that textures jump out at you, but there's also an eye for strong asymmetrical geometry. They show someone in love with old things, savouring the wear and tear of the centuries and the irregularities arising from it. So there's a tension between the rawness of neglected surfaces and a deep underlying order that the human presence has brought. After all this time the old brick feels like a fact of nature, yet we know that it was a made thing in the first place. Thus Lewerentz finds the confidence in his late churches to stray very far from simple consistencies, letting bricks look out at surprisingly infrequent intervals from an enveloping sea of mortar, secure in the binding idea that keeps all the pieces from falling apart. It must have been in some part the freedom of ruins which encouraged him to devise these novel ways of building. It remains an uncanny convergence that at the point where Lewerentz drops all reference to classical style, his buildings establish a strong kinship with ancient ruins.

Keeping some of the past

Many years ago an architect I know decided to live in a ruin, or rather took his conversion of a small industrial building only so far, leaving signs of the space's previous use as a machine shop or meatpacking plant, I forget which, on an expanse of wall made larger by knocking out an intervening floor. He has long outgrown this dwelling and this mode of treating existing conditions like found objects to be turned into unintended works of abstract art, but memories of this space have haunted me ever since. The stains and random marks left behind by former users had been framed and elevated into spurs to contemplation, like the single gnarled prop in a Japanese tea hut or the old fishing lines ('a five haired beard of wisdom') dangling from the jaw of the fish in Elizabeth Bishop's poem.

We live in the midst of ruin without realizing it, until the backing in a cupboard falls away revealing old wallpaper like a pixillated embroidery of flowers and leaves, or we notice that an unsightly lump high on a wall was the mounting for a defunct gas meter. Putting a name to this irritating flaw in the geometrical order of the house makes us try to imagine what life was like when part of this small house was portioned off for another family or for a person whose life went on in a different course from the rest. On certain days things one would like to change, like ceiling tiles later found to conceal damp patches, or doors covered with flimsy board, only recognized as efforts at modernity when the panelled door beneath was let out, become valuable traces of missing lives and their tastes and makeshift arrangements. If only we'd kept the fragments of old wallpaper, brought them out of the cupboard and formed them into a sort of palimpsest in a more prominent place. If only we'd saved this or that feature that now seems precious being gone, but no one could say we change things too quickly, we who were still using paraffin stoves long after other people in the street had stopped.

When our next-door neighbour moved or was moved into a home, her house went from a dilapidated dwelling to a ruin almost overnight. Her tasteful reproductions of Corot, Cézanne and the like, smoke-yellowed as I imagined, had always seemed mildly depressing. Now I kind of long for them because they seem to contain so much of her. But do I really want to organize a little museum of our neighbour Pat? Someone else we vaguely knew has recently had his house turned into a museum. Khadambi's, clad throughout in rich fretwork like a dream-vision of the entire history of human ornament, is no ordinary house but a cave of marvels and should certainly be preserved, but the recent articles about this salvage only made me sad, because I had managed to forget him completely for so long.

4

Interrupted Texts

COLERIDGE'S 'KUBLA KHAN' ranks among the most tantalizing of interrupted texts. It's a visionary rapture that now always comes with a prose explanation attached, an explanation that describes the poem's will-less emergence from a dream-like state in an isolated place at night. 'Kubla Khan; or, a vision in a dream. A Fragment' is its full title, and the prose preface spells out the brutal process which left the poem a broken-off piece of something which should have been (and in a sense, already was) much larger.

Coleridge says he was in the middle of writing out the vision he had unwittingly composed while asleep in his chair when he was 'unfortunately called out by a person on business from Porlock, and detained by him above an hour'. The rest of this agonizing story is well known: Coleridge returns to his pen and finds that the rest of the poem has fled. In the nineteen intervening years he has often tried to coax it back without success. The lonely farmhouse between Linton and Porlock, the exotic and naïve reading (Purchas's *Pilgrimage*) which sets his imagination working, and finally the rude visitor who breaks the writer's seclusion form up into a complete fairy tale of romantic inspiration.

The contents of the poem cast doubt on this story about it. 'Kubla Khan' as it stands, supposedly incomplete, just 54 lines of the original two or three hundred, already contains the motif of the lines lost through something like waking from a dream. If the speaker could recover the playing and singing of the Abyssinian maid he could raise the dome and the caves of ice so vividly in poetry that everyone who heard it would see them, and acknowledge him as the seer who compels onlookers to close their eyes in holy dread. So this short poem which calls itself incomplete is in fact a complete account of the poet as visionary set apart from his hearers. Except of course that this remains a vivid dream, of what the poet might be if he could recall something he has forgotten.

It seems horribly apt that this rupture of a heightened state of inspiration should have befallen Coleridge, leaving the unfinished fragment of a projected work behind. He describes over and over again the personal defects (as he sees them) that prevent him from bringing ambitious plans to fruition. Near the beginning of his career he starts periodicals in search of a form where sustained and elaborate compositions would be out of place. Later he devises a rambling discursive form for a general theory of criticism, which will be autobiographical rather than systematic. This he disguises or dignifies with a Latin title, *Biographia Literaria*. He evidently feels the need (or is pushed by early readers) to supply it with an analytical table of contents, which only discloses for everyone to see the waywardness even of this, one of his most sustained efforts.

Maybe if Coleridge were allowed to be more like Kafka, a writer whose fragmentary incompleteness is telling us about his perception of reality, not just letting slip his personal weaknesses (though perhaps that too), we would acknowledge him as both more compelling and more historically significant than we had thought before. In a number of ways he makes it hard to take this view, by his professions of laziness and his addiction to opium, by a lack of concentrated focus that makes even his most regular productions affairs of abrupt flashes of insight.

Coleridge is widely regarded as the greatest of all critics of Shakespeare, yet he never collected his views in coherent form. He gave several series of public lectures on the subject, lectures whose composition he describes, making them seem more like poems than works of criticism. These lectures have come down in transcriptions made by listeners and in other more or less fragmentary records. After his death some of his most stirring comments were printed as 'Notes' on this or that play, without further indication of where they came from. In fact, many of these comments, sometimes running uninterruptedly for a page or two, were written in the margins of pages in collections of the plays that belonged to Coleridge or his friends.

Coleridge at the margins

How is it possible that revelatory pieces of criticism found themselves hidden at the edges of pages in someone else's books? It is one of the oddest and most thrilling mysteries in the history of literature that this writer concealed so much of himself in this way, so that we cannot really know him without piecing together these fugitive scraps. All these lost or eminently loseable fragments have recently been more diligently collected, extensively annotated and beautifully printed, but all this loving labour might even dull our perception of how fragile Coleridge's own annotation is as a form of expression. Fragile because of its tendentious connection to forgotten writers and to particular forgotten words, because of its unreliable embodiment in pencil scratchings, sometimes retraced by someone else in ink, so that Coleridge's presence is obscured; fragile because of its own brevity and disconnection from everything else but a moment in Coleridge's reading; fragile in its own momentary forgetfulness of everything but the little point of Greek grammar or Christian theology at issue in these few words. Not all of Coleridge's notes involve important writers or important points within them by any means, but the most tedious and minute are important after all, because they fill out the picture of the ups and downs of his attention. The story told by the marginalia is the story of mental life, of Coleridge caught off guard, surprised by someone else's thought or expression, or prodded by a re-encounter to crystallize a general view of one of his favourites, like John Donne, as a poet or thinker.

Once you have had even a taste of how revelatory Coleridge's brief comments can be, all the more startling because sandwiched between much less sweeping notes about the scanning of a line or meaning of a word, you're ready for the astonishing elaboration of the modern edition of Coleridge *Marginalia* in six bulky volumes. The second in the series, which includes marginal comments on 123 books by authors with surnames from C to H outdoes the other volumes. It is almost as thick as it is wide, and hence doesn't look so much like a book as an odd, rectangular solid. Faced with thousands of comments written in or elicited by 500 books, the editor George Whalley falls back on the alphabet as the means of keeping everything

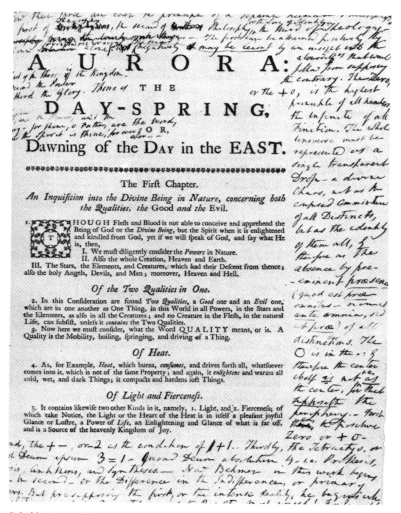

Coleridge's marginal comment swamps Jakob Böhme's text at the beginning of *Aurora*.

in order. So the arrangement isn't chronological or thematic; literary, scientific and theological texts are mixed up with each other; and the English writers on whom Coleridge has the most interesting things to say – Shakespeare, Milton, Donne, Sir Thomas Browne, Bunyan and Defoe – are found in four different volumes. The index volume, which makes it easier to devise other orders for using the volumes than the alphabet, appeared 21 years after the first volume, and comes with a 'brief guide to the index' that fills five pages of very small type.

One easily gets swallowed up by this great monument to the fragment. Coleridge is already a very diverging kind of writer, and the range of his interests is distractingly, even ruinously wide. Now we are confronted with a baffling hierarchy of description and comment before we finally reach Coleridge's own words. First a meticulous physical description of the book he wrote in, an account of how he came by it, or who he borrowed it from and under what circumstances, when he wrote in it (often over an extended period, the different stages hard to disentangle and the comments left in topographical [i.e., page order] not chronological sequence). Then an introduction to the book's author, if like Jakob Böhme someone we aren't likely to know much about, followed by a history of Coleridge's acquaintance with and developing attitude to the writer.

Who can say that any of this is truly extraneous? I for one was pleased to hear that Yeats was also fascinated by the diagrams in the English translation of Böhme when he was assembling his Blake anthology, but ramification has to come to an end eventually or before long a work like this makes you feel that your consciousness is flying apart. There's something centrifugal about the whole conglomerate that can easily throw you entirely clear of the great impacted mass of text.

Of course annotation is like that: it always leads you away from the primary subject. If the new Arden edition of one of Shakespeare's plays contrives to stop you partway through the particular play, either it or you has failed. At the moment I am held up very near the beginning of both *Coriolanus* and *The Merchant of Venice* in wonderfully fat new Ardens of each. I won't be happy if the story ends like this, anywhere short of the whole play.

But with the *Marginalia*, what is the 'whole' we are searching for? Surely it isn't feasible to read all four or five thousand pages. That isn't the way to find the mysterious whole. The alphabetical series of entries isn't an intentional work that the author set out to create, yet all the marginalia together form a unity, though perhaps one it is foolhardy to seek literally to experience.

It is well to remember that the marginalia are not complete, that there are important missing books Coleridge is known to have written in, like Burton's *The Anatomy of Melancholy*, his favourite copy of Milton and the Shakespeare he wrote in most. Some of Whalley's most poignant entries are the nearly blank pages he devotes to these Lost Books. 'Complete' of course is a nonsensical word in this connection. Incompleteness of various kinds is one of the beauties of the form – Coleridge was a notably voracious reader (still awake and responsive at 3 a.m., he notes more than once) – but partly through temperament, partly through the chances every life is subject to, he's at the mercy of circumstance in what books he comes across. That is the main use of the tedious notes of provenance, to show you how accidental Coleridge's reading was.

On top of this, he's deliberately and also helplessly unsystematic in what he notices and comments on. Sparsity of comment might mean he's not reading carefully, but it doesn't need to. There are of course texts he fastens on and worries like an animal with its prey. In cases of the most sustained engagement he gives a sensuous living demonstration of that fusing of intellect and feeling that he is often expounding as the only full understanding of any natural or cultural form whatever. The longest 'marginale' (Whalley's word for a single marginal note) is probably only a few pages. Though a lot can happen in one of Coleridge's pages, certain things simply cannot work themselves out so quickly. But for me, this writer is at his most exciting in these broken forms and has scaled heights of appreciative comprehension here I've never met elsewhere. His best fragments on Donne and Sir Thomas Browne combine the large and the small, the intensely heated and the chillingly abstract – metre, rhythm, breathing, emphasis, tone, thought, wit and the author's philosophical standpoint. In brief comments that come close to jottings he makes you see how indivisible all of these concerns are, in the mind of the poet and in a responsive reader. The real thrill is to watch someone else being so thoroughly understood. Montaigne's depiction of his friendship with Étienne de La Boétie conjures up an enviable and perhaps idealized oneness between two minds and hearts. In Coleridge's highest flights inspired by his favourite texts he reaches beyond the words to this kind of sympathetic union with another human being.

For the reader a certain sensation of being caught unawares seems to be a key part of the experience. We are reading snippets of Donne's letters, intimate ones or more formal exercises in flattery, and, oddly apposite in the present setting where Coleridge is defacing someone else's book, a letter of apology from Donne to a friend who's lent him a book that Donne's young children have got hold of and damaged. First of all, Donne in a rare moment of undress, and then Coleridge so delicate in drawing out complexities of feeling just peeping out of the words of the letter. Later on, no one else has ever been so perceptive or so understanding about the forces acting on an impressive intellect like Donne's as he constructs a piece of elaborate flattery for a social superior in which wit saves a portion of self-respect for the flatterer.

Coleridge's scattered comments on Donne's poetry are among the best responses to particular lines of verse ever, and nearby are these acute appreciations of human dilemmas. The circumstances under which this all takes place are grotesquely peculiar. You are thrown into the middle of a text which isn't actually in front of you in its intactness. You're trying to get your bearings in the unfamiliar discourse and then at the same time to cope with the comment on it by someone who *has* got the whole original and who in his own self-description has an imagination 'like a Surinam toad', a species said to produce infant replicas of itself in abundance from both sides of its body which immediately hop off at right-angles to their parent's course. An imagination setting new, digressive ideas in motion so profusely that it is impossible to keep one's mind on the overall trajectory.

Coleridge's comments on Browne have an unusually concentrated focus. He's sending a copy of a favourite writer to a woman for whom he feels a doomed love, Sara Hutchinson. Who knows what unreasonable hopes he nurses, approaching the loved being through the medium of a book? So here the comments are addressed to one person and have more of 'instructions on how to read the enclosed' than usual. They begin with one of the most beautiful of Coleridge's general headnotes giving an overview of a book or a writer. This contains a delightfully generous and forgiving depiction of Browne the egotist:

> he is a quiet and sublime Enthusiast with a strong tinge of the Fantast, the Humourist constantly mingling with & flashing across the Philosopher, as the darting colours in shot silk play upon the main dye! In short, he has brains in his Head, which is all the more interesting for a *little Twist* in the Brains. – he sometimes reminds the reader of Montaigne

but from no other than the general circumstance of an Egotism common to both, which in Montaigne is too often a mere amusing Gossip, a chit chat story of Whims & Peculiarities that lead to nothing, but which in Sir Thomas Brown's way is always the result of a feeling Heart conjoined with a mind of active curiosity – natural & becoming egotism of a man, who loving other men as himself, gains the habit & the privilege of talking about himself as familiarly as about other men. Fond of the Curious, and a Hunter of Oddities & Strangenesses, while he conceives himself with quaint & humourous Gravity a useful enquirer into physical Truth & fundamental Science, he loved to contemplate & discuss his own Thoughts & Feelings, because he found by comparison with other men's that *they* too were curiosities: & so with a perfectly graceful and interesting Ease he put *them* too into his Museum & Cabinet of Rarities – . In very truth, he was not mistaken – So compleatly does he see every thing in a light of his own, reading Nature neither by Sun, Moon, or Candle-Light, but by the Light of the faery Glory around his own Head, that you might say, that Nature had granted to him in perpetuity a Patent and Monopoly for all his Thoughts. – Read his Hydriotaphia above all – & in addition to the peculiarity, the exclusive *Sir Thomas Browne-ness* of all the Fancies & modes of Illustration wonder at and admire his *entireness* in every subject, which is before him – he is totus in illo – he follows it, he never wanders from it – and he has no occasion to wander – for whatever happens to be his Subject, he metamorphoses all Nature into it. In that Hydriotaphia or Treatise on some Urns dug up in Norfolk – how *earthy*, how redolent of Graves & Sepulchres is every Line – You have now dark mould, now a thigh-bone, now a Skull, then a bit of a mouldered Coffin/ a fragment of an old tombstone with moss in its Hic Jacet – a ghost, or a winding sheet, or the echo of a funeral Psalm wafted on a November Wind – & the gayest thing you shall meet with shall be a silver nail or gilt Anno Domini from a perished Coffin Top. (*Marginalia* 1, pp. 762–4)

It is late when Coleridge is writing this, and time for him to be in bed, so he quotes Browne at a similar moment as a specimen of his manner:

> But the Quincunx of Heaven* (*Hyades or five stars about the Horizon at midnight at that time) runs low, and tis time, we close the five Ports of Knowledge: we are unwilling to spin out our waking Thoughts into the Phantasmes of Sleep, which often continueth praecogitations, making Cables of Cobwebs and wildernesses of handsome Groves. To keep our eyes open longer were to *act* our Antipodes. The Huntsmen are up in America, and they are already past their first Sleep in Persia.

Apparently Browne has got the Earth rotating backwards and his time relations are wrong; Coleridge later thought of a way of correcting this by changing *America* to *Arabia* but that made things worse. He says and others say about him that he regarded books as living beings, and at moments like these above he enters them so fully that he becomes them.

Sometimes Coleridge's enthusiasm for his favourites betrays him or leads at least to outlandish claims, like claiming that Hogarth is Shakespeare's equal in the way he combines comedy and tragedy in the same work, or that *The Pilgrim's Progress* represents the nearest thing to a Protestant *Summa Theologica*. We can't always tell the difference between remarks tossed off casually and positions central to his thinking. Isn't the whole idea of a *Summa* anathema to any truly Protestant mind?

Devoted browsers in the *Marginalia* probably keep returning to the dream of participating somehow in all of Coleridge's main enthusiasms if not of duplicating his reading completely. Can I really believe in some corner of myself that retracing Coleridge's reading and absorbing his responses to it is going to turn me into Coleridge? The depth and physicality of our immersion in his reading has in it something verging on superstition, which recalls those ancient fetishists who thought that getting hold of Epictetus' lantern would make thinking that took place by its light into something special.

So a little excitement at learning that Coleridge's copy of Gilbert White is bound in a piece of one of Mary Wordsworth's old gowns – Gilbert White who brings out a whole new range of Coleridge's attention, his knowledge of the habits of birds, the qualities of spiders' webs and atmospheric effects around twilight. And to hear that Donne's sermons with Coleridge's annotations were sent out to India by Blackwell's with apologies for sending a marked-up copy. What relic-mongering to read these comments differently for knowing this, with what mournful thoughts for all the pencilled words in unknown books rubbed out because they seemed defacements. For there are already plenty of his comments right there in front of us which we are pretty safely never going to read, most shaming of all, the voluminous embroidery on the work of Jakob Böhme, reputed to be the most obscure and difficult of all his comments, certainly as far as I've been able to crack them the furthest reach of Coleridge's thought in a certain direction at least: metaphysics I carelessly call it.

I don't mind leaving the theologians mostly alone; these are interests that with the best will in the world I am not going to share. But Böhme the self-taught mystic I regret, suspecting that he would prove one of Coleridge's most original discoveries. Trying Böhme again, I find Coleridge in the strange enterprise of turning Böhme's mystical allegories into contemporary science, as if the alchemist's animistic chemistry isn't that far from current understanding of physical realities. Here Coleridge leaves me behind – I find this talk of sweet and bitter compass points and love among chemical elements very hard to connect with.

And trying to think myself into what it would be like to view Coleridge's marginalia as defacements, I wonder if an edition larded with lots of facsimiles of pages Coleridge has filled the margins of might add something important. Is the physical form of the marginalia a significant aspect of them? There are interesting examples of defacement as a kind of destruction which from another perspective appear as transformation and the bringing into being of a new form, Duchamp's improvements to the *Mona Lisa* or an Ingres nude, for instance, or Joe Orton's obscene tamperings with library books now regarded as a subversive art form, of which his local library mounts exhibitions.

Coleridge *is* intruding on his chosen texts, but not (as far as I know) actually doctoring them, which is another level of insult, and Coleridge's comments aren't generally jeering or ridiculing the originals – but he still clings onto them, the trellises his own thought now climbs over. We should study the few facsimiles we've got for any meaning in the precise physicality of the pages, hoping to find that it is not entirely incidental how Coleridge's scribbles occupy the pages. Certainly the combination of print and overlaid scrawl can be a serious confusion that leaves you in doubt where exactly the comments belong, unsure at the same time if a complete straightening out is really true to Coleridge's intent.

So a writer's proofs or manuscripts might sometimes be a fuller representation of his intent than the cleaned-up printed book. Some students of *Finnegans Wake* seem to feel this, and there are those who prefer to read *The Waste Land* in facsimiles of the typescript. They want to encounter the poem as it comes into being, enjoying the illusion that they are bringing it out of its raw materials. So a fondness for incomplete works is sometimes a dream of coaxing the fragment into completeness as the creator's deputy.

There's an Anglo-Saxon concept, or it may be epithet, 'word hoard', which might be just a fancy name for memory, or a specialized occurrence of memory in the stored-up vocabulary of the poet, like a personal library, though there's almost a contradiction in that term. Or it might refer to an externalized concretion like a proto-*Finnegans Wake* containing an impossible number of distortions of the very idea of a word.

There is something now in Buffalo, New York, known as 'Joyce's personal library' which turns out to be a disappointment. Joyce's library is in some sense enshrined or hidden in *Finnegans Wake* and hasn't all been found yet; new titles are still coming to light, and you can get some idea of the process from McHugh's *Annotations to Finnegans Wake*. Later editions of this work incorporate newer detections of Joyce's sources, detectable in McHugh because they appear in a lighter typeface. We're getting closer all the time to duplicating Joyce's reading, a less physical but more meaningful form than his actual library.

All the books collected in eviscerated form in the big edition of Coleridge's *Marginalia* don't constitute either his reading or his library, though continually verging on both, because he read many books he didn't annotate and he annotated many he didn't own. Joyce has taken possession of a peculiar assortment of books by burying them in *Finnegans Wake* and Coleridge has imprinted himself on those 500 books by adding words to them threaded round the first author's own.

The marginalia are just the most aggravated instance. The gigantic new collected edition of his work, running to 30-something volumes, finally makes an ideal entity visible on a library shelf that many devotees of this writer must have dreamed of, a vast composite of all the scattered and incomplete forms Coleridge left behind, including notebooks and letters not strictly part of the collected edition but finally appearing in print around the same time and easily assimilated to it, including also lectures, an ephemeral performance art that were never written down by the performer himself but in selective and fragmentary copies by devoted listeners, including also 'table talk', another attempt to fix in permanence oral performances the speaker took little care to preserve. Including other works of maximum import to the writer but abandoned in such ramshackle and undigested form that the disciple left in charge of them thought they would do Coleridge's reputation no good if published. A whole series of unfinished and half-projected works which fit together with and illuminate the seemingly finished ones like the *Biographia Literaria* and the other ephemeral and speckled ones (a way of saying that he mixed borrowed texts with those he'd actually composed) like *The Watchman* and *The Friend*.

Something thrilling about needing to do all the piecing together of the now very dignified-looking fragments; something not thrilling but all of a piece to find that other writers' words are concealed in large chunks among Coleridge's own: Coleridge's plagiarism is like obscure quotations lost deep in *Finnegans Wake* and entirely up to the reader to recognize. Among all the imperfections of this writer's work, his borrowings are the most unsettling. They don't really belong with Duchamp and Joyce as *objets trouvés* swallowed whole and transformed by the borrower. But almost. The deeply damaged quality of the writer and of much if not absolutely all of his work makes Coleridge into a kind of modernist icon. Reading *Finnegans Wake* in the new 'genetic' way you find yourself decomposing it into its constituents, which shows you not just how it got the way it is, but why it has to be like that. With Coleridge, no need for decomposing; you just have to find a way of living happily among all the varieties of ruin this writer has left behind.

The accidental destruction of the Library at Alexandria left Greek culture ruined, a ruin. The dispersal of the libraries of Coleridge or Robert Burton, men immobilized by books, has sometimes been seen as irreparable ruin, though Coleridge's had no physical existence in a single place and Burton willed his to the Bodleian, which you would have thought might keep it safe. But one way or another, it didn't: some of Burton's books were sold because they duplicated items the library already had, others because they were unwanted, still others because no inventory made keeping them seem important.

Keeping anything in overwhelming numbers can seem like hoarding, the very contrary of ruin, and yet . . . the sorted and accessible collection turns into a hoard *and* a ruin when the system by which it is sorted becomes invisible and thus as good as forgotten. The Metropolitcan Museum of Art has secret deposits from its collections scattered over the more remote and dangerous areas of the city, stashes which have recently been shown to include such oddities as sixteenth-century panelling from a Welsh castle that had languished unopened since William Randolph Hearst donated it 60-plus years ago. Obsessive hoarders who fill their rooms with worn-out gear eventually close up the passageways to remoter parts of the house. Perhaps they keep intending to sort the piles, which lose their distinctness from other piles and form what looks more and more like an undifferentiated mass of uselessness. Eventually the margins and edges of objects and locations are swallowed up and movement or productive thought becomes impossible.

A certain negative vision of cities sees them as no more than ruins of former selves, and more dead than alive. Perception like this values cities most for what they can tell you about their past lives, and views new buildings as at best a kind of annotation of the surviving historic fabric, more or less marginal. But plenty of those who believe that the new should seldom be allowed to overbalance the old realize that thoughtful new buildings are the growing tips of the city, and alive in ways the old parts are not.

Why Coleridge hated Montaigne

Coleridge's aversion to everything French might be enough to explain his dislike of Montaigne, but there is much more to it than that. The *Spectator* is another subject that generates surprising heat – Coleridge blames it for corrupting the taste of the young and creating the preference for disconnected form in which subjects are changed too rapidly. Phantasmic fluidity of attention sounds much more a characteristic of Coleridge himself than any eighteenth-century writer. Perhaps the trouble is that he is unhappy with just those qualities in himself that he shares with Montaigne, who by contraries is maddeningly comfortable with this in himself, as with various other weaknesses that come out sounding like badges of humanity.

They share a flickering, unstable attention that delights in straying from the announced topic and finds beginning more interesting than completing. Coleridge had got fixed in his head the idea of comprehensive works on large themes and was always hoping to bring off this Magnum Opus, but left behind instead a lot of fascinating incompatible fragments. Montaigne admitted from the start that his writing was a means of staving off the melancholy that overtook him when his beautiful plan to withdraw from the world to pursue his studies, a plan with plentiful ancient precedent, backfired and left him with a mind full of chimeras and monstrosities. Apparently his first writing was a record of these aberrations designed to make his mind ashamed of itself. As far as I know, a passing mention of texts more intimate than anything we've got is all that survives of this phase.

By the time we can watch him at it, Montaigne has begun to perfect a new form in which he takes himself as a subject, fluid, changeable and more meaningfully unknown than subjects he knows much less about. He doesn't seem embarrassed that his results are fragments of variable extent, most of them extremely short. They all have titles but we don't know if these were spurs to composition in the first place or labels stuck onto them afterwards. For us the titles are strong indicators of a certain kind of form. They jump all over the place, from the sublime to the ridiculous, from petty concerns of domestic life to grand philosophical quests. The sequence is defiantly illogical; the only progression is difference; if the next topic doesn't suit you, the one after will.

It doesn't take long to find out that these titles are seriously misleading. Even the shortest chapters have more than one subject; longer ones have many more than one, and the first topic broached is rarely the one announced in the title. 'On Liars' begins with the subject of memory, which interests Montaigne profoundly. He repeats many times in the *Essays* that he has a poor memory, which causes many social difficulties. Now he twists the discussion round to the advantages of his bad memory: it has saved him from something much worse, ambition. It also encourages intellectual independence: he can't follow in others' footsteps if he can't remember where they go. And finally it makes him a failure as a liar.

Along the way Montaigne has managed to fit in the story of the emperor Darius whose memory was so faulty he had to pay someone to keep reminding him of how much he hated Athens by whispering in his ear 'Remember the Athenians, Sire'. This whole opening sequence is deeply characteristic of this writer – in its preference for an oblique approach, in its inversion of the apparent valency of a phenomenon (a bad condition leads somewhere desirable), in its unexpected arrival at the destination after all. The previous section 'On Idleness' is much shorter and condenses its obliquity more tightly: it fits both straying and return into the first ten lines, which begin 'Just as fallow fields which abound in a thousand kinds of wild and useless plant' and end with the idle mind whose thoughts charge ungovernably about like an unruly horse, a structure like a sentence in an inflected language such as Latin which doesn't have to put the main subject first.

The seeming randomness or scatty variety of Montaigne's titles isn't actually borne out by the text: the reality is much worse, a writer who when he wants to change the topic is capable of saying 'And now to change the topic.' But constant change isn't irresponsibility or faithlessness, but almost the reverse, a kind of integrity in pursuit of the natural rhythms of consciousness. He becomes increasingly aware that his quarry is the self in all its hideous inconsistency. Hence the variability in length of chapters; hence the admission that it's rare for him to read for a whole hour at a stretch (imagine Coleridge admitting this!); hence the threat of smugness in confessing one's faults (and reducing serious moral discussions to chit chat, as Coleridge thought).

But this will help explain how Montaigne – who isn't much concerned with continuity and prefers Seneca and Plutarch because they write in patches or fragments that don't join up, at least not circumstantially – should have produced a book of scraps, or as he calls it 'a pile of ravings', that is so clearly all of a piece. All the more strange that anyone could imagine, as a nineteenth-century German scholar did, that Shakespeare might have written *Hamlet* as a refutation of Montaigne's philosophy or world-view. The idea that Shakespeare's most unruly tragedy is a riposte in a controversy, a polemical reply to someone else's writing, seems a real misunderstanding of the form of the play. *Hamlet* can't be a 'reply' in anything like a literal sense, and Montaigne's work can't be a 'statement' in that sense either. But Shakespeare could at a certain moment not quite consciously be reacting against a general feeling about our position in the world he picked up from Montaigne. This visceral objection could be something like Coleridge's, bristling at smoothness or sophistication that can digest anything and weave it into a continuous discourse that never really breaks down, whatever the world throws at it: war, cruelty, suffering. We know that Montaigne knows these realities but we know this at one remove. He has been a soldier, an experience crucial in shaping his attitudes, but never dramatized and barely discussed. He says he could write about anything, a fly for instance. 'On a fly' would fit right in, but not 'On diseases' or 'On pointless suffering'. His isn't a world that admits the possibility of tragedy.

Still, it doesn't seem reasonable to complain that Montaigne is too sane, too reasonable. At its best his level-headed clarity can produce beautiful moments of comprehension, like his explanation of why Homer gives his gods human failings – so that he can also give them virtues that are constructed from our imperfections. Montaigne doesn't shy away from certain ranges of human weakness, but they are usually flaws we can take a wry satisfaction in admitting, like our foolishness in pursuit of sexual thrills. In Montaigne people led far afield by their desires look silly; they don't find that their lives are irreparably ruined.

You cannot imagine Coleridge writing in such an unanxious way about sex; or imagine him writing about it at all. I suppose it is an important moment in the history of self-disclosure when Montaigne tells us that his penis doesn't perform as well as it used to, but it is not a great surprise. More interesting and more revealing of Montaigne the man is his thought-experiment on whether it is harder to think of something else entirely at the moment of sexual climax or at the moment just before the kill in a hunt. He decides that the latter is more difficult for a couple of quite plausible reasons.

Coleridge's self-revelations are more scattered and less continuous, but you can't imagine Montaigne finding himself in the spot Coleridge does right after offering wonderfully detailed and inspiring advice to a young poet. At the bottom of his marginal comment he signs himself 'A map of the road to Paradise drawn in Purgatory on the Confines of Hell by STC July 30 1819'. This is Coleridge who believes that poetry is the highest literary calling, and has just said so above; Coleridge the poet who believes that he has permanently lost the gift. At this moment he has broken through the calm surface of the page as Montaigne never does.

One of Montaigne's best discoveries was to grasp the truth and power of contradictory structure, which is consistently built into the essays at different scales. 'On thumbs' is followed by 'Cowardice the mother of cruelty'. 'On cruelty' begins with a long discussion of Virtue, hard and easy varieties. At first it seems just perverse, and then you notice that the two themes are practically contraries, and that you've been set up, rather subtly, to oppose cruelty without Montaigne needing to give you advice that you'd probably resent.

He says he doesn't like following the accepted view, and we could find lots of examples of quiet contrariness, but this profession sounds odd coming from someone who bolsters every opinion by citing classical authorities until sometimes the text is virtually a patchwork of quotation. There is a real contradiction here. Montaigne is often read as if he were an instance of wisdom literature whom you go to for popular versions of philosophical truths. At one point he says he only wants to be more wise, not more learned. This is not Montaigne the adventurer but the purveyor of well worn if solid truths, the man who decorated the beams of his library with the 50 wisest sayings he could remember from his reading.

Wisdom literature, continued

Soon after Kafka had been diagnosed with tuberculosis his writing changed direction, becoming pithier, and so brief there could be no question of narrative continuity. So is this the turning toward wisdom literature it is sometimes thought to be? Yes, if you mean aphorisms that sit uncomfortably in the world, lonely fragments. No, if you mean philosophical tips that want to help you with life's problems.

Of course Montaigne has his disconcerting moments which do not encourage the view that reason can solve your problems or reconcile you to not solving them. One of these practically defines our situation in the world as not-knowing. One day Montaigne has the rare, probably unique, chance to meet one of the Indians from the New World. He wants to ask so many questions; there are so many forms of sameness and difference to explore, and time is short. The conversation has to be conducted through an interpreter. As luck would have it, this European go-between is stupid and does not understand the questions Montaigne is trying to ask, so sitting a few inches away from a visitor from another world who could tell him many things, Montaigne is betrayed by the failings of his local assistant and the meeting is largely wasted.

He seems unusually modern at a moment like this, doing his own fieldwork like a twentieth-century anthropologist, and venturing into territories where there are no authorities or hallowed texts. The frustrations of this particular enquiry confirm, paradoxically, its novelty and its boldness. Launched on this sea, one doesn't expect or even desire safe havens. Montaigne's preferred perspective on historical material is quietly subversive and undermining of the pomp and dignity of standard histories. He wants to know what Brutus said in private conversation rather than public oration, what he did in the workroom or the bedroom rather than the Forum. And although his marginalia, such as they are, cannot vie with Coleridge's – he saves his energy for other things – they mark a crucial historical stage. Montaigne has already been noting in the backs of his books when he read them, and then at a certain point he begins writing summaries of what the book has meant to him, why it is important, what its failings are. These comments are further defences against his weak memory, reminding him of his reading long after. But they also assert the primacy of the reader's experience, and you can almost imagine that Montaigne is sometimes more interested in his own response than in the dry old text that provoked it. Certainly by the time you get to us, it's his comment rather than what he comments on that we care about. It's a stage, as his writing is altogether, in the dethronement of authority, now jostled by the irreverent outsider with an opinion of his own.

There's a powerful recent expression of this inversion of significances, a careful scholarly study of Montaigne's copy of Lucretius, only identified for the first time in 1989. It's not the case that Montaigne has permanently upstaged Lucretius, as Joyce has Le Fanu, whose novel *The House by the Churchyard* must now be read almost exclusively by people following up clues in *Finnegans Wake*. But Montaigne now seems a more vivid subject to most readers than those great writers of antiquity on whom he leans, turning them into a patchwork that in the end has a stronger collective identity than any of them individually.

A very English hoarder

A figure of the next century, Robert Burton, bears a fascinating relation to Montaigne. Both of them claim that they began to write to combat melancholy, both produce something like a giant patchwork sewn together out of fragments of their reading, and both make readers feel that every imaginable topic will find its way into the book eventually. A first and highly determinative difference between them is that Burton has decided to combat his melancholy by an exhaustive investigation of . . . melancholy, a plan of such perversity it is hard to take seriously. Can anyone believe that this method will work? In fact Burton cautions actual sufferers against reading large portions of his book at all.

He presents himself in surrogate form as Democritus, an ancient recluse-philosopher regarded as insane by contemporaries. Burton says he has read much to little purpose, penned up in his study, a prisoner of learning. So he may have mainly himself to blame that features of the life of Democritus have got themselves attached to him, including the picture of escaping his confinement to laugh at bargemen swearing at one another at the bridge-foot, Oxford, like the Greek recluse collecting rustic slang in the harbour of Abdera. Perhaps worst of all, Burton has occasionally been given a fitting end to his labours in the service of sadness: the eighteenth century believed he had hanged himself in his rooms at Christ Church. Montaigne presents himself as normatively human, just more honest than most of us in confessing petty weakness. Burton makes himself seem a crazed eccentric, and is believed.

One thousand pages on the subject of melancholy sounds an absurd project. It didn't start this way though; improbably the book proved popular, and Burton added compulsively to the later editions while at the same time leaving unchanged what he knew was faulty in the earlier form. Apparently the new parts aren't always particularly apposite or well joined up to the rest. It is a work bewitching in detail and out of control overall, like *Finnegans Wake*, another accretive product of which there is much too much for normal purposes. I don't know yet and am afraid to find out what it feels like to become so happily lost in the labyrinth of such books that there can't be too much or even enough of them.

How to read Burton

There are at least two main ways of reading Burton, as poetry and as prose, slowly and dreamily or like Sherlock Holmes compulsively, following up every clue. Maybe anyone who sticks with this impossible book will fall into both of these modes, at different times. One of the first things you notice is a certain kind of endless sentence like a dream monologue or the so-called stream of consciousness. Except that these don't flow smoothly forever, and one suspects that the main reason for this is that they don't really know where they are finally headed, so they may come to a dead end there's no obvious way out of, or at least to an awkward spot they need to jump over. A real enthusiast might even like these hitches in Burton's stride best of all, sometimes papered over by sticking in 'I say', which doesn't signal a pause for breath but a decision to press on even faster over a rough spot.

His lists

Lists are one of the trademark features of Burton's sentences – I don't call it prose, it's too unquiet and disrupted – but these lists are not one kind of thing. They are floods that sweep away any firm grip the reader may have had, or eruptions or explosions, an overheated bursting forth. If he is genuinely popular with melancholics (and Dr Johnson is a famous example who said this book was the only one that ever made him rise two hours earlier than he wanted to), maybe this frantic energy or almost demented liveliness is the cause.

Burton's lists can also be simply exhausting, twenty words when two would do, but a reader of this book is lost if he lets himself notice small flaws. Just as it feels wrong to call Burton's prose *prose* or his lists *lists*, it seems almost stupid to decide you are going to talk about him as a scholar. He has so clearly spent his life with books that you wonder if there's ever been time for anything else. Perhaps there are other semi-Burtons or almost-Burtons in his century; maybe he is a more generic phenomenon than we imagine. Certainly there is a particular world of thought which he inhabits: the same authorities recur, including some like Cicero just about current now, and lots of obscure medical writers, and then most interesting of all, his near contemporaries, mostly Continental and thoroughly outmoded by now. I say this, but I was very pleased to find one of them, Pontano, recently reprinted in the I Tatti Renaissance Library. These writers wrote mostly in Latin, as Burton claims he would like to have done, not comfortably accepting that his historical moment was rapidly leaving Latin behind.

One of my teachers was given to sharing scholarly secrets. One day he told us the bibliography was the first thing he looked at whenever he picked up a new book. Burton's bibliography weighs down his book in a way all its own. Not that he gives orderly references or provides a list of his sources. Normally he calls them by abbreviated names that are almost nicknames, and sometimes they are just 'mine author says'. So one of the ways to read Burton is to try to look up the names and find out who his authors are and what else they may have done besides giving Burton a dodgy idea about the effect of a prolonged rainy spell on a fragile psyche. In an obvious sense this is a perverse approach: authorities are usually the merest conveniences to

Burton. He reaches for a musty scrap of information that will provide a springboard for a diatribe about how British towns are sleepy and poorly drained compared to Continental ones. An essential part of the joke is that Burton never travelled anywhere – he has a wonderful way of putting this: he calls himself a map-traveller – and concocts his pungent views of foreign places out of a combination of reading and his own fancy, so that they are both colourful and unreliable. But then no one reads Burton for up-to-date knowledge.

My old teacher (who was young at the time) should have been interested, if he had thought about it, in the peculiar work of scholarship that Burton's book is. *An Anatomy of Melancholy*, a bewitching set of words to me long before I ever opened this book, which proclaimed that a psychic condition could have a body which you could dismember, making a long and tedious discussion grisly like an autopsy. Burton gets round to saying many things about his subject, and one of them that recurs is that surprising fact evoked for me by the title on its own before I had opened the book, that sufferers from this affliction find something almost hypnotically alluring about the idea of discussing it. So, that word *melancholy* in the title is strong enough to overshadow the contrasting suggestions of system in *anatomy* almost completely.

The allure of the index

Haunters of tedious scholarly forms like indexes and bibliographies will find them enchantingly combined in many editions of Burton's *Anatomy*. That is to say that the index of authors includes details of their occupations, their dates and titles of their books. I suppose all this impacting of information on top of itself is a response to the incredible density of reference in Burton's text. It isn't at all unusual to have twenty authors glancingly referred to on one page, and for others to be drawn on without being named. How can anyone keep track of all this divergent detail? Should he or she try? Before long the idea of an annotated edition of Burton occurs, but one quickly decides it is unthinkable. The book is already an elaborate exercise in annotation, which takes voluminous and disorderly reading and tries to digest it into some kind of connected order around a particular topic; it's like a series of notes, each of which could be expanded, perhaps infinitely expanded, creating a sense of not-yet-exhausted plenitude that can be alternately exhilarating and suffocating.

If one set about annotating Burton's long marginal comment on his reading, already a mosaic of tens of thousands of glittering fragments, where would one stop? And how long would it be before one forgot the way back to the original stimulus and went off sideways on a track of one's own? There's a pleasantly amateur edition of the *Anatomy* put together in 1927 by a pair of editors who are clearly not regular academics. In its index it indulges in some Burtonian flights, commenting garrulously on a few of Burton's obscure but recurring authors. One who particularly caught their attention was the *Hungry Spaniard*, which is no more than Burton's whimsical nickname for a Portuguese navigator, Federigo de Queiros.

Of course, as some readers will know, it has proved possible to produce a scholarly edition of Burton's book after all, but only recently and just barely. It fills six volumes and several thousand pages and involved two distinct teams of editors, one for the text, the other for annotations. Three text volumes print a daunting listing of variants collected from numerous early editions, variants the vast bulk of which are of no literary interest to speak of, and could only be charted using the latest computer technology. Three volumes of commentary, longer than the text but not much longer, really flinch at the whole idea, not that they aren't an impressive achievement but they are far from complete, and distressingly un-Burtonian in spirit. They point out places where the source does not discuss the topic Burton credits it with, they translate the Latin that peppers the book, though keying both versions to line numbers in the commentary always takes time, and by then you've lost the thread. Altogether, it's as if dealing with someone as wild as Burton has brought out double-strength sobriety in the annotators.

Chasing Burton's sources

It is true that Burton's sources, which often sound like phantoms, actually exist, and you can not only look them up but hold them in your hands. Seventeen-hundred books survive from his library, and more are being discovered all the time by sleuths who report on them in *The Book Collector*. Maybe these pursuits are just ways of not reading Burton, who himself often treats his learning less momentously, deploying it like bric-a-brac, setting out a series of place names at such odd angles to each other he creates a little tract of utmost inconsistency. His lists are often lightened by variegation in detail or a shift of gears in the middle when he begins to dawdle over elements in a series that had begun as simple naming. Sometimes it's impatience, sometimes inattention, and all the deviations from the grammatical format of the series increase the immediacy that is one of Burton's trademarks.

These little lapses from regularity are just failures to follow his own rules, lapses which individualize moments that threatened to line up too neatly with other moments. Occasionally Burton's impatience breaks out more crudely – 'Read Galen himself', he insists, or throws a long list of further reading at you, to get you off his back. His temper isn't reliable, which doesn't feel, as it does in Sterne, like a calculated ploy. When he addresses the reader Burton often sounds truly fed up with the task he has set himself. But of course this easily turns into playacting: he has discovered a trick he can repeat.

Latin mixed with English

The most glaring inconsistency in Burton's pages has barely been mentioned, a mixture of languages like the jumble of leftovers in a coarse peasant dish. Like his educated contemporaries, or most of them, Burton was deeply at home in Latin, and his English is consequently larded with Latin phrases, snippets and longer quotations, woven in so seamlessly that they can't comfortably be separated out. In fact at many points it ruins the experience of reading to get held up by them. A Latin-less reader must either skip them, mouth them over without much understanding or find an edition that prints translations right under the Latin. The scholarly edition makes no concessions, and so won't do as a reading text for non-Latin readers. The all-English version of 1927, so scorned by the scholarly 'not an edition at all, but a curiosity', probably makes things too easy, because all trace of the Latin has disappeared.

The macaronic variegation of texture caused by the two languages bumping against each other is an important part of Burton's bearish, cross-grained intention. The 1927 edition also leaves out his short-hand references to his sources like 'fracast. cap. 2, sig. 1', which pepper the pages like tiny signs of the author's indigestion. Both the Latin and the scholarly shorthand are ways this scrambled text is broken further apart, a process of fragmentation that gets worse as the years pass and Burton's style of learning resembles our own less and less.

But as he admits, his writing is already the dregs of learning, a ruin of books, what's left behind after a lifetime of reading promiscuously, without purpose, until too much time has gone by to start thinking systematically. Some of the most poignant pages, on idleness and on solitariness, evoke a vast landscape of waste with suppressed passion that suggests these subjects come too close to home for comfort.

'The Anatomy' as poetry

Burton's only other surviving work is a satirical play which is said to anticipate Ben Jonson's *The Alchemist*, but Burton's play, unlike Jonson's, is in Latin. If there's a buried dramatist in Burton he is only peeping out in sudden flashes of vivid particularity, often of briefest extent, like shooting stars. Tertullian's cloak, Zeno's heart, Anacreon's grass-hopper, Epictetus' lantern – such are Burton's ways of concretizing the discussion by linking a famous person to an everyday object and thereby making it seem that an important meaning is sealed in the freak encounter between the special and the ordinary. They aren't by any means parallel instances, except linguistically or poetically, but this trick is a small instance of what still keeps a few readers devouring Burton avidly: he turns scholarship into poetry.

When he is striving most doggedly to be systematic he is liable to create the most inextricable tangles, as in the digression on the types of devils that cause melancholy. At first he says confidently that most experts agree that there are nine kinds of demon, and then he enumerates them: 1) false gods of the Gentiles; 2) liars and equiv-ocators; 3) vessels of anger, inventors of all mischief; 4) malicious revenging devils; 5) cozeners, such as belong to magicians and witches; 6) aerial devils, that corrupt the air and cause plagues; 7) a destroyer,

Captain of the Furies; 8) that accusing or calumniating devil Diabolos [printed in Greek characters]; and 9) those tempters in several kinds.

The neat numbering helps us keep the welter straight, but we soon wonder if it doesn't make pervasive disorder in the content more glaring. At first the categories are large groups, separated according to attitudes, techniques or location, that is to say arranged along completely discordant axes, one after the other. And then in the seventh kind, it's a single individual, likewise the eighth, and back to multiple groups for the wrap-up in a ninth kind. Burton doesn't bat an eye; in fact he is busy muddying the waters further with extra details at each step, non-matching ones of course, which send us off on little detours.

As soon as the list is complete, without a break comes this:

> *Psellus* makes 6 kindes, yet none above the Moone: *Wierus*, in his *Pseudo-monarchia Daemonis*, out of an old booke, makes many more divisions and subordinations, with their severall

A page of *The Anatomy of Melancholy* without paragraph divisions and with a constant peppering of citations and translations in the margin. On the left the tail-end of a confusing chart of the book's overall design.

names, numbers, offices, &c. but *Gazaeus* cited by *Lipsius* will
have all places full of Angels, spirits, and Divels, above and
beneath the Moone, aetheriall and aeriall, which *Austin* cites
out of *Varro lib. 7. de Civit: Dei cap. 6. The celestiall Divells
above, & aeriall beneath*, or as some will, Gods above, *Semidei*,
or halfe Gods beneath, *Lares, Heroes, Genii*, which climb
higher, if they lived well, as the *Stoicks* held; but grovell on
the ground as they were baser in their lives, neerer to the earth:
and are *Manes, Lemures, Lamioe, &c.* They will have no place
void but all full of Spirits, Divels, or some other inhabitants;
Plenum coelum, aer, aqua, terra, & omnia sub terra, saith
Gazaeus; though *Anthony Rusca* in his Booke *de Inferno, lib.
5. cap. 7.* wold confine them to the middle region, yet they
will have them every where, Not so much as an haire breadth
empty in heaven, earth, or waters, above or under the earth.
The aire is not so full of flies in summer, as it is at all times
of invisible Divels: this *Paracelsus* stiffely maintaines, and
that they have every one their several *Chaos*; others will have
infinite worldes, and each world his peculiar spirits, Gods,
Angells and Divells to govern, and punish it. (1.181–2)

Wonderful moments like the air full of flies in summer have to be
salvaged from the flood that threatens to obliterate all distinctness.
You almost feel that you need to point out Burton's most wonderful
phrases to their author; he has rushed on already and forgotten them
– grovelling on the ground, *invisible* devils like barely visible flies,
the word 'stiffly' so unexpected and so out of keeping with the
summer evening to which it effectively puts a stop.

Then after a few lines of verse, a swarm of more authorities who
get confused with even more crowds of demons, the two masses
momentarily overlaid like a double exposure, until putting the devils
inside a parenthesis sorts them. Modern readers already have trouble
with the lack of paragraph divisions in sixteenth- and seventeenth-
century texts as they were originally printed. Perhaps the lack of
visible distinctness dates back to times when writing surfaces were
precious like vellum, making scribes reluctant to give up half-lines
to allow new paragraphs. There are other ways of marking divisions

that don't leave empty space of course, and besides, running without visible breaks forces on us a different idea of the unity or singleness of the text. Modern texts are by comparison short-winded, insubstantial, pseudo-aphoristic. If it weren't so implausible on the face of it, we might say that they aspire to the condition of poetry.

Burton has his own quirks or problems of continuity. The passage above comes from 'A Digression of the Nature of Spirits, bad Angels, or Devils, and how they Cause Melancholy', which interrupts the setting out of the causes of melancholy. Does it break in because it is a subject close to Burton's heart? In any case the division which follows, on witches and magicians, seems to have been inspired by the digression, which has thus diverted the discussion from its course in a more prolonged way, and apparently without the author's noticing. Further on, Burton announces that he wants to introduce a digression on imagination that he is sure some of his readers won't like. He apologizes for the delay but goes ahead anyway. The trouble is that digressions in Burton are hard if not impossible to pick out; no part is more digressive than any other, and any single sentence, almost any extended phrase feels as if it is straying from its starting point or the assumptions on which the previous sentence was based.

At times nothing is more wonderful than a book which doesn't know what might come next, which therefore catches the reader out continually with surprises on different scales, a startling word (like 'stiffly'), a sudden picture (like the summer flies) or a completely new way of arranging the same material (like new rankings of devils). At other times it is intolerable: I cannot imagine wanting to read Burton if you were deeply sad or seriously preoccupied in whatever way. Then Montaigne would be a better choice.

Montaigne vs Burton

Montaigne and Burton occasionally tell the same stories, like the one of the famous commander: 'that great Captain Zisca [who] would have a drum made of his skin when he was dead, because he thought the very noise of it would put his enemies to flight.' Burton's version is more vivid and impinging to start with, and contains a wonderful sting in its tail: 'I doubt not but that these following lines [all thousand pages of them!], when they shall be recited, or hereafter read, will drive away melancholy (though I be gone) as much as Zisca's drum could terrify his foes.'

Much more lively than Montaigne's treatment of the same material and self-reflexive in a thrilling way of its own, if you ever manage to find it, lost in the enormous thicket of an unreadable (in a superficial but crucial sense), untranslatable book. Or not even book, for the way it arrives at its length is probably more heedless of the reader's needs and circumstances than almost any verbal construct known. So is it any wonder that Montaigne can be translated into dozens of diverse languages, that he is universally recognized as signalling a new stage in human consciousness, someone who changes our sense of ourselves, while Burton recedes steeply from our view, a very special but unreachable variety of seventeenth-century hoarder?

5

Ruined Narratives

BUT MAYBE A LINE can be traced from Burton via Sterne to Joyce, a line secret and undisclosed, which is and isn't there. Sterne's greatest work, *Tristram Shandy*, is continually boasting of its kinship with Rabelais and Cervantes and never mentions Burton, but borrows from him in unacknowledged chunks, parodies his collaging of authorities, out-digresses him and any other writer, and matches him in unlikely obsessions (noses, fortifications and the education of infants, among others). It is the slipperiest of works, least or most like a novel of all novels, the first anti-novel or the most typical novel of them all (Shklovsky), a self-absorbed literary prank or an impossibly rich and vivid representation of consciousness that anticipates and exceeds Joyce's experiments toward the end of *Ulysses*.

Whatever possessed Sterne to cast what he was saying as a novel, if it left him liable to commit the maximum number of breaches of narrative decorum? He keeps inventing problems of novelistic presentation and then apparently forgetting they are there, except that he keeps reminding us that he has left Uncle Toby starting a sentence, or Walter stretched prostrate on his bed or Trim holding the knocker on the Widow Wadman's door half raised and about to strike. Parts of the story are continually getting into the wrong order, and then Sterne tells us that the inn in which Le Fever died isn't even built yet (so some other place for Toby to stay will have to be found), but however reasonable it sounds this is an impossible statement. If the inn isn't there, the man hasn't died. Except of course that this conundrum *can* happen, not in reality, but in the head.

Most of Sterne's jokes arise from misalignments between the realm of thoughts and that of physical objects, or between one person's thoughts and another's. You don't need to set many of these trains going at once to achieve an effect of unencompassable complexity. A reader can view this as an elaborate hoax or as a multivalent rendering of the wealth of our experience on a par with one of Mozart's operatic ensembles. Sterne's materials are wonderfully humble, two men dozing by the fire until disturbed by an uproar in rooms overhead, stirred into action by hazy reports and sending various people off on errands that we already know are unneeded or will go wrong, delivering results too late to be useful. This whole scene downstairs by the fire is the way Sterne has chosen to narrate the birth of his hero. It would be so easy to break through the veil and find out what is really going on upstairs, except that various preoccupations prevent this, and the big event the novel has been waiting for happens without even the reader realizing before it is all over.

Everything in the wrong order

From one angle it is a preposterous joke that everything takes place here in such scrambled and fragmentary form, so that Toby's funeral is narrated before his great adventure of replaying battles in miniature in his garden. This is not a flashback contrived by a novelist to explain something; it pops into Tristram's head and it spills out, a kind of helpless effusion, one of the accidents of mental life. As each deviation from regular progress is announced, we may view it as an amusing prank – certainly the Preface finally appearing in volume three reads this way – but with a little distance, or maybe, having built up sufficient stock of such surprises, we begin to see it as an expression of the way reality works. And finally we come to feel that the whole effect is a symphonic version of the ungraspable flux of our consciousness, which moves with a life of its own, essentially out of our control.

Walter Shandy serves as a constant warning of what happens to those who imagine that they can give mental life rules to obey. The simplest attempts to impose order on the world, like giving names to children, fail most ludicrously. Walter has a particular horror of the name Tristram, for its suggestions of sadness and inertia among other reasons. He has chosen the name Trismegistus for his son, tells the serving girl who misremembers it as Tris-me-something, and she tells the curate who mis-corrects it to Tristram, and so the mistake is made, prompting a long debate about baptism and how it can be undone or negated, including detours into baptism of unborn embryos by injection and pre-baptism of sperm en masse.

Logically this debate should follow the misnaming of the child, but actually (that is, in the novel) it precedes it, as part of Sterne's impossible project of making a fabric consisting entirely of disruption, of interrupted sequence and of missing parts. A chapter is left out – by inadvertence? – and then its contents are recounted. Another chapter is omitted because it is so high-flown that it will make the rest of the book look pedestrian by comparison. At a crucial moment in the affair of Widow Wadman two consecutive chapter headings have blank pages under them, because the material is too embarrassing or intimate for us to see, or so we guess. This wasn't the reason after all, and when Sterne is ready, these inoffensive chapters are inserted out of normal order. 'Normal order' is a necessary notion here, but only so that it can be violated. The most prosaic, unthrilling goals are held out before us and then moved further off as we get near. We are told we are about to meet the midwife, but then we don't, and again we don't, and so this idiotic meeting begins to seem important. In the end we have to add it to the large list of destinations announced but never reached.

Straightening out 'Tristram Shandy'

In more sober moments it probably passes through our heads that for all its surface complexity, there isn't really so much there in *Tristram Shandy*, meaning that we could make extremely short work of re-counting what happens in the novel. Many readers must have felt an itch to straighten it out and put everything presented by the novelist in such intricately disrupted sequence 'back' into proper chronological order, the way we imagine it must have started out. This was done years ago very expertly by Theodore Baird, a professor at Amherst College (and one of the most interesting teachers I ever had).

His purpose was to show that the book is anything but scatty and slapdash, and has been carefully constructed to say something serious about our subjective experience of time. Baird's reordering of the material gives the military campaigns a prominence and weight they don't have in the novel. Tristram's story becomes a tail attached to a larger body of more momentous stuff. Maybe the straightening gives you more respect for Sterne, as it was intended to do, by exhibiting him as a serious historical researcher. But this isn't what he's best at or memorable for; it's just the underpinning of the book, like Joyce's dovetailing of all the movements in Dublin for his 'Wandering Rocks' episode. Maybe Baird's essay is an early instance of genetic criticism: 'How I wrote *Tristram Shandy*.'

The life of the book lies in its disruptions, like the constant reminders that we are in a book, which do not lessen but increase the intensity of our experience, because that is our primary reality, that we are readers, so the most violent occurrences are punctures of the narrative surface, like the sudden glimpse of Tristram on 9 March 1759 writing what we're reading and remembering that only a week ago Jenny did something a lot like what just happened in the novel. We've never heard of Jenny. She must be his girlfriend, mistress, wife – these words don't flit through our head; we just accept that Tristram goes together with Jenny. A little further on, Sterne teases us with all these possibilities in turn but won't choose, provoking a female reader 'Fy, Mr Shandy!' In the amazing film based on *Tristram Shandy* made in 2005, Steve Coogan the actor who plays Tristram has a wife named Jenny who visits the set for the film. Confusingly, the actress who plays Mrs Shandy is called Jenny too. 'Jenny also, not Jenny two', Coogan says.

The film doesn't observe the scrambled order of the novel; the opening scene of the book, in which Mrs Shandy throws Walter off stride at the moment Tristram is being conceived, is thrust further into the film, which is scrambled too, but differently. The film is called *A Cock and Bull Story*, which is the punchline of the book, sprung dramatically on the last page. But the book isn't finished, only a fragment of what Sterne promises in black and white to write on various occasions. There's a map of the Yorkshire neighbourhood of Shandy Hall 'now with the engraver', which will be included at the end of volume twenty. Elsewhere he says he has 40 volumes still to write, and another time he plans to write two volumes every year (as he did at the beginning) for as long as he lives. He sounds sincere, but he mentions his health, and Sterne's illness slowed down his intended production and finally intervened to end it all with that abrupt putdown.

That is the kind of sentimental story that Sterne in certain moods would have enjoyed telling, but there are signs toward the end that he is running out of conviction; the fooling is often more throwaway. Life and fiction converge too neatly: Sterne did try Continental travel as a cure, just as Tristram does without much warning in the book. This shift produces wonderful moments, like walking home to dinner across the marketplace at Auxerre with his father and Toby, entering Lyon with a smashed carriage and moping in a borrowed pavilion somewhere near Toulouse, all three foreign encounters occurring simultaneously though they are years or days apart, a convergence which is possible because consciousness is more fluid than the external reality it sits nestled in. But the Continental interlude is a sign of withdrawal, and Sterne is being led away from *Tristram Shandy* to another kind of fiction, milder, more resigned.

We've seen the deaths of most of the main characters, including Tristram's own, though they are also all still gathered there, alive, on the last page of the book. Mrs Shandy's disappearance slips past us at the end of a scientific discussion: 'She left the world without knowing whether it turned or stood still.' Tristram's is imagined in the Continental interlude when he has illness on his mind: his preferred scene for his deathbed is a room in an inn, like Le Fever's, which will crop up again further down the page. I'm not sure if life imitated art and Sterne got Tristram's wish; I think not, but I could look it up, as Tristram periodically tells the reader to do.

The lull around Tristram's birth is the supreme example of a space in which everything happens and nothing does, a space squeezed impossibly full of incident, or stretched out with almost nothing in it, broken apart into jarring fragments but full of hectic life. It contains the tiredest of literary devices, the interpolated text or story, familiar in every long fiction since Cervantes or for that matter Homer and the Hebrew Bible. We've lost track of when and where the first interruption took place and of what the ur-situation is that we should periodically be reporting back to. But we're still surprised to be witnessing the interruption of an interruption of an interruption . . .

The volume of Stevinus that Toby has sent for, having misunderstood a reference in the discussion, which is now being set aside, from which a few interpolated pages fall out – what are these? Could Trim read them and we will try to figure out? This sounds like a sermon, far from a joke. Sterne was a clergyman who wanted to publish his sermons and finally did on the back of the present book's popularity. Could this actually be one of those, placed here as a kind of taster like those Amazon gives you, 'Look Inside!' Of course the present audience doesn't sit still for long: Slop is a Catholic and the sermon is offensively anti-Catholic, reducing Trim to tears when it reaches the prisons of the Inquisition. He also notices that the tower in a biblical allegory is over-guarded. 'You wouldn't need seven Watchmen; two would do.' In fact the sermon is so disrupted you couldn't possibly give a connected account of what it is saying, so Sterne the self-promoter has shot himself in the foot. Or the comic has got the better of the promoter and couldn't resist the chance for sabotage.

Presumably the entire sermon is there, and could be read consecutively if you persisted in the task, but reading just what's in front of you produces a deeply unsatisfying result like eyes which won't focus. It's a problem that arises from Sterne's excessive allegiance to the sermon, which is seriously disrupted, but not seriously enough. If we could take a more theoretical view, we would see that this was a necessary station on the whole spectrum of possible disruptions, the least fun of all, but a space that needs filling.

Visual jokes

Most of Sterne's jokes take much less time to tell; the visual ones are over in an instant. The black pages and the marbled pages (two of each) that make such a strong effect before you've even begun, stronger than their impact in their proper place, aren't supplied with the expected explanatory text, as if they're speaking a different language that doesn't convert to English. Martin Rowson's graphic novel of the book is extremely faithful to the text, but I liked it even better the

Tristram's pre-history – the perilous journey of the homunculus as interpreted in Martin Rowson's cartoon version of *Tristram Shandy*.

second time, looking without reading, when it becomes a much faster, more phantasmagoric version of the book. *Tristram Shandy* sometimes acts as if it would like to be a wordless enigma, in those marvellous squiggles that are meant to represent the progress of the narrative in the first four books, reputed to be extremely accurate in their own

——Lord have mercy upon me,—said my father to himself——* * * * * * * * * * * *
* * * * * * * * * * * * * * * * *
* * * * * * * * * * * * * * * * *
5 * * * * * * * * *.

CHAP. XL.

I Am now beginning to get fairly into my work; and by the help of a vegitable diet, with a few of the cold seeds, I make no doubt but I shall be able to go on with my uncle *Toby*'s story, and my own, in a tolerable straight line. Now,

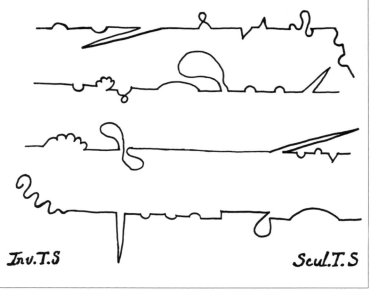

The narrative structures of the first five books of Tristram Shandy graphically depicted, with a detailed key provided for the fifth book only.

These were the four lines I moved in through my first, second, third, and fourth volumes.——In the fifth volume I have been very good,——the precise line I have described in it being this:

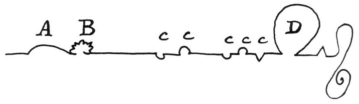

By which it appears, that except at the curve, marked A. where I took a trip to *Navarre*,—and the indented curve B. which is the short airing when I was there with the Lady *Baussiere* and her page,—I have not taken the least frisk of a digression, till *John de la Casse*'s devils led me the round you see marked D.—for as for *c c c c* they are nothing but parentheses, and the common *ins* and *outs* incident to the lives of the greatest ministers of state; and when compared with what men have done,—or with my own transgressions at the letters A B D—they vanish into nothing.

In this last volume I have done better still—for from the end of *Le Fever*'s episode, to the beginning of my uncle *Toby*'s campaigns,—I have scarce stepped a yard out of my way.

If I mend at this rate, it is not impossible——by the good leave of his grace of *Benevento*'s devils——but I may arrive hereafter at the excellency of going on even thus;

which is a line drawn as straight as I could draw it, by a writ-

way, and printed upside down or backward in the Russian edition
Shklovsky used, or so I have read, and most economically in the rip-
pling diagonal line Trim makes with his stick, an argument for celibacy
if you can believe it, that you need to read from bottom to top if you
want to take it seriously as physical performance.

Sterne and pornography

Of all the book's visual elements the slyest and at the same time least
conspicuous are the series of asterisks standing in for obscene words
or risqué scenes, first the words, then the scenes, and in further prospect whole sections of narrative that will be left to the reader's own
dirty imagination to fill in. I wonder if other readers feel as awkward
as I do about Sterne's leering lewdness. Of course we can dress it up
as a valid philosophical investigation, albeit carried out at the reader's
expense. Saying 'nose' when he means 'penis' gives a writer an unexpected freedom to produce some fairly explicit pornography, freedom
Sterne isn't that serious about exploiting, but the very idea of a clergyman finding out this secret makes us sit up. The answer that 'I never
said that, it's you who had the indecent thought' is always available,
but it doesn't take a very alert reader to see that there's no other way
to fill in Sterne's blanks than with whatever names for the male and
female parts one prefers.

A more interesting experiment with embarrassment arises from
the need to explain Toby's famous wound in the groin. The question
of what exactly happened to him and where exactly it occurred cannot
be settled unless it can be deflected, so that it's no longer a matter of
intimate places on the body, but of a certain location in the complex
fortifications of Namur. The sequence begins with Toby flat on his
back, spending four years recovering from his mysterious wound. Part
of the cure is explaining to visitors exactly how the wound occurred,
and as Toby interprets the task this requires a lot of technical language
– ravelins, counterscarps, redoubts and the like. He ties himself in
knots trying to explain, until one day he thinks that all he needs is
a good map of Namur and he can dispense with the specialized ter-
minology. It turns out that this is only the first step in a multi-stage
progress from words to things, like an un-discovery of language and

regression to an earlier world of objects. The map raises as many questions as it answers, and soon Toby is studying the theory of projectiles with the help of a huge number of books on the subject that have arrived one by one in a narrative full of detail about how one led on to another, which was sent for, arrived, mentioned still others, and so on.

This whole process is treated as a kind of laboratory demonstration of key mental operations. Locke is brought in to provide the theory of knowledge that Toby's recovery illustrates, with the hilariously vivid embellishment of a stick of red sealing wax dropped from a chambermaid's pocket as an image of the impressionable human brain. Ever since, Sterne has proved surprisingly vulnerable to one-stop theories of his intellectual sources. Critics have argued that Locke's *Essay Concerning Human Understanding* (or Bayle's *Dictionary*) is the key to all the book's oddities, and in this reading *Tristram Shandy* becomes a kind of illustrated Locke for readers who can't cope with real philosophical treatises. This is just an extreme case of the syndrome all the writers in these chapters suffer from, a deflection from the writer to his sources, even a substitution of the one for the other.

The journey from words to things

Books on military architecture eventually pile up in Toby's sickroom until he needs a larger table to consult them properly and spread out their folded-up illustrations. It takes Trim, the manservant, to point out that the space isn't big enough, but if they were to move . . . Toby has been left a modest manor house in Yorkshire with a kitchen garden and just beyond it a bowling green that would be perfect for building a bigger but still comfortably reduced model of the fortifications of Namur. Toby can project and Trim can execute all the fosses and counterfosses, the covered galleries and defended gates, and the spot where Toby got his wound will take its place in a well-rounded landscape.

The journey from words to things will then be complete, after a few days in which Toby hardly eats or sleeps, and a coachride, the final stage of anticipation before a magical fulfilment. It is an escape from language and a conversion of adult life into a board game which can be mistaken for reality because it is as big as life, or nearly.

Toby's experience of war has been interrupted, but can now continue in extremely accurate but peaceful form. After all, the war hasn't ended and is reported daily in *The Gazette*, which Toby and Trim use to enact each new development. Bad weather doesn't stop them, except when sea squalls hold up the mail boat with the newspapers. Finally the Treaty of Utrecht calls a temporary halt to their play, and Toby brings out serious military reasons why the fighting should have carried on.

Sterne has incorporated in his so-called novel a thorough put-down of literary form as at all adequate to represent experience. He does this over and over again and seems happy to let the result fall apart into misshapen fragments. Somewhere Joyce says – maybe early in the composition of *Ulysses* – that he could easily have written a whole shelf of Victorian novels if he had wanted to, but the ease ruled out such a course, and so *Ulysses* falls apart in the later episodes into incompatible techniques, at least one new one per chapter. The idea of a series of separate stylistic experiments is pretty hostile to narrative continuity or to characters' lives as the fundamental material of fiction.

The trouble with 'Finnegans Wake'

In Joyce's next work this impulse has gone a lot further, and the difficulty of *Finnegans Wake* is in a class of its own, even after 75 years and a host of imitators. At the simplest level, this book is largely made up of words which are not exactly words but semi-recognizable distortions of known ones. Already on the first page a sprinkling of foreign words and expressions, similarly nudged away from their familiar forms without losing touch altogether. Over 60 languages turn up in this text in bigger and smaller quantities, and so native-speaker investigators have gone through the book looking for Polish, Hebrew, Malay pidgin, Croatian and lots of others, not an easy task where words are almost always hiding in other words. One of the author's most baffling techniques is to transliterate a whole line in a foreign language into nonsensical English, which then sticks out as particularly resistant to comprehension. For random examples, see a battlefield telegram in German on page 9, line 5: 'Leaper Orthor. Fear siecken! Fieldgaze thy tiny frow', a transliteration of *Lieber Arthur, wir siegen. Wie geht's deiner kleinen Frau?* (or *Dear Arthur, we conquer. How's your little wife?*); a Danish greeting on page 9, line 5; conventional French phrases on page 16, lines 4–5; and the same bad-tempered lines in Ibsen's Norwegian repeated on pages 364, line 28 and 530, line 23 but transliterated differently each time.

It isn't hard to make Joyce sound perverse; he was, and some wonderful instances are waiting their turn to speak. But you don't need to read far to pick up hints of a profound understanding of how language works. He isn't content to write in English exactly as he finds it in 1923, intent as he is on driving it back to become its old self, or more itself than usual. Samuel Beckett wrote something around this time about Joyce's ideas about language influenced by conversations with Joyce. He says that Joyce wants to de-sophisticate English, the European language that has been pushed furthest toward abstraction, and that he views words as living beings that go through Vico's cycle of germination, maturation and putrefaction, before starting all over again. The fourth term in Vico's series is missing, and the idea of individual words each obeying the biggest rhythms of human history seems unlikely. Still, Beckett's remark remains revelatory about the way words behave in *Finnegans Wake*. The word, the phrase and the sentence seem unstable, parts of it decaying or expanding at different rates or in different ways. The wild permutations taking place before our eyes appear to be based on the belief that pulverizing language until it doesn't yield much everyday sense will release primitive energy locked inside it and ordinarily unable to get out. Words have to lose their conventional clarity in order to recover their lost physicality. For the reader of *Finnegans Wake* these are hazy intuitions hard to get hold of, of something hiding deep in language but not voiceable in that medium after all.

Language as the book's protagonist

Beckett says that one of the things uniting the two of them was a distrust of any kind of transcendence, but the reader of *Finnegans Wake* must wonder if Joyce isn't deifying or at least mystifying language in this book. His profound unbelief in the normal motivating forces of fiction seems to drive him to look for the kind of individuality in words that most novelists find in their characters. So *Finnegans Wake* is bursting with a certain kind of drama, but of a microscopic variety that arises from turning a compulsively searching gaze onto individual words. There's a story in practically every word, if only there were time to attend to every one.

It isn't nearly as simple or as uniform as that, and yet one despairs of capturing the highly improbable scale on which things happen in this book. It is the most wonderful and most maddening case of the world in a grain of sand, and in one grain after another, stretching ahead into the distance. I wonder if many of the friends, colleagues and admirers of Joyce brought together in 1929 in *Our Exagmination round his Factification for Incamination of Work in Progress* had any idea how much of this book there would finally be, or of what that would feel like.

So the reader's difficulty has something to do with exactly how this book is long. More like Burton's *Anatomy* than most, it seems to be made of a huge number of pieces that don't join up in a way we can immediately discover or fit under an overarching form. The life of the individual line is almost unbearably vivid, but we cannot see the wood for the trees, so we hope no one is going to ask us for directions or to say where we think we are. Anthony Burgess claimed there are more jokes per page than in any other book, and more chances to laugh out loud. It is true that the number of jokes is incredible and this is the main thing that keeps one going, but why do there need to be so many? They're finally quite disruptive, like a walk through a wood full of traps and snares.

Another sign that something is amiss in the overall form of *Finnegans Wake* is the unexpected character of Joyce's commentary on his own book, on the infrequent occasions he feels a need to make any. There's usually something resembling plot summary, and it is staggering how grateful the little reader is to find out that a particular bit of action takes place in an inn where everyone is asleep, or that another section is based on a children's street game common in Joyce's youth.

Joyce's treacherous notebooks

How have the most basic features of the situation become so obscured that no one can find them anymore, like the stair in the hoarder's house buried under such layers of debris that it looks like a cliff-face? Maybe in some sense the underlying narrative isn't there anymore, or isn't fully intact after suffering a process of expansion and revision that can now be traced minutely through a frighteningly complete set of notebooks, drafts, earlier part-publication, and finally proofs, multiple sets of them, with scribbled revisions on each. It seems to have become a fact through constant repetition that there are 20,000 pages of this kind of source material connected with this book, though few can have much idea what this figure means. If, as I have restricted myself to doing, you stick with the latest version, you'll mainly experience *Finnegans Wake* as a tumultuous dream or murk so dense with crazily varied references crowding in on each other, interfering with if not obliterating one another, that trying to keep a tight grip on them all at once seems a task both hopeless and wrongheaded. Paradoxically, in a book where annotation is a major industry, it spoils the fun even more than usual to look things up, just because there is so much to look up.

But who can resist completely? We have it from Joyce himself that the first ten lines of *Finnegans Wake* incorporate references to Commodus, a Roman emperor, the Italian theorist Vico, the 1st Earl of Howth (Sir Amory Tristram), Tristan and Isolde, the Napoleonic wars, Dublin, Georgia, USA, St Patrick and peat-burning peasants, gypsies and non-gypsies, Jacob and Esau, Parnell and Isaac Butt, *Vanity Fair*, Swift's Stella and Vanessa, and ideas about the surface of the sea, peninsulas and rainbows, among other subjects that flit in and out of view in so slippery a fashion, no one, maybe not even Joyce, can register them all in the time allowed. It is perhaps a sort of ideal that one will look up references in a couple of the wonderful resources for doing this which have sprung up in the last few decades, and then one will fold it all back into the text and do another, integrated reading. An unattainable ideal! Suppose that Joyce had fully explicated the whole book, not just a few random pages: the commentary would dwarf the parent many times over. In any sense you try to think of, the idea of a comprehensive commentary on *Finnegans Wake* is unworkable, yet it is certainly underway and getting closer to realization all the time. Just last night I added two explications of a single word and a two-word phrase to my favourite website of this kind, *fweet*.

The important thing about *Finnegans Wake* is the metamorphic life of the linguistic surface where words are more like things than in any other book, where being lost in the trees can be rapturous, where the sense of a plenitude one can never exhaust makes it seem more like an entire universe than just another book.

And yet one cannot stop hankering for the ordinary kind of progression and overarching coherence that just isn't there. Of course there are parts of the book which are more like conventional narrative, perhaps above all the final monologue in which a female figure, not too clearly defined of course, reflects on her whole life from near the end of it when she finds she's ready to let go and drift out into the sea from which all life emerged. It's very beautiful in its way, but it's also a reprise of the end of *Ulysses* carried out at a later stage of life. Although the overriding attitude is that all life is helplessly cyclical, there's still an acceptance here of time and progression that marks this out from most of the book.

There's an earlier ending oddly similar to the final monologue, the washerwomen's conversation that concludes the first book, similarly elegiac and reminiscent in tone. Joyce feels less need to pack things in at this point and lets himself dwell on nightfall: two women on opposite banks are less and less able to hear one another and seem about to subside into simpler existence as stone and tree. At the end of the whole book the doctrine of eternal return requires that death and dawn be conflated, unlikely as that feels to normal time perception.

In the rest of the book opposites are regularly merged with each other in the same word. The amazing density resulting from Joyce's habit of loading existing text with further suggestion, by making the words already there carry other words through a process like punning, eventually makes the reader uncertain about the identity of most of them. The result is a reader suggestible, susceptible and hypnotized by all the shifts of meaning he has seen, hallucinating presences that aren't actually there. Joyce's puns then work something like Sterne's asterisks. Sexual entanglements are never far away from the very basic human situations Joyce deals with, and Joyce loves puncturing the solemnity he's built up with suggestive hints of male and female body parts and functions.

Coming back to the book after an interval one can be appalled at how little one is able to make out and also by how little past experience seems to help. Yet this feeling of being lost spurs us to new sorts of mental activity and turns our idea of what reading is upside down. If you're mostly in a dark forest, you can blunder into occasional clearings. Perhaps these are just passages that have escaped the reviser and been through fewer stages of development. Or perhaps as one gets more familiar with the text the number or proportion of clearings will increase. Unfortunately, I don't think this book works like that: my grip on parts I think I know seems subject to rapid decay. Perhaps I will get along best with only the vaguest idea of the sequence of parts, which anyway appear to repeat themselves – catalogues of HCE's failings and bills of complaint brought by the uncreative brother against the other one. We're better off, more fully engaged when not sure of our place in the whole, and yet . . . there is so much of it. Beckett has no trouble throwing out the whole idea of progression, though; maybe we need to emulate him.

Finding the plot

If there isn't much of a plot, maybe there's something like an overarching metaphor that gives the whole thing unity. Joyce's own version of this is to say that *Ulysses* treated a single day and that *Finnegan* takes place in a corresponding night, not the night of 16 June 1904 or any other particular day, because nights aren't specific or time bound in that way. He also says he wants to put language to sleep and show it reshaped by the unconscious impulses of the dreamer. Seizing on this, some readers have tried to interpret the book as the extended dream of a single sleeper, HCE in bed in his pub at Chapelizod on the outskirts of Dublin.

The idea that this immense, encyclopaedic work could take place in a single consciousness, even Joyce's, is far-fetched. The book has its eye on a kind of synthesis far beyond the capacity of an individual or set of characters to embody or contain. It isn't written entirely in the language of sleep or any other single dialect. At times it veers into the groggy consciousness of someone waking up, but elsewhere it strives for grand cultural conspectuses through associational conflations that hide their complexity in order to take the reader by surprise and overcome him all at once as lyric poetry habitually does. *Finnegans Wake* is more like a 600-page lyric poem than a novel, and more like an enormous historical rhapsody than a single story or even an interlocking set of stories.

It still baffles me that it is as long as it is, but perhaps like *The Faerie Queene* it insists that you should become lost in it, because the vision really is grand in spite of the micro-scale of the pieces of the mosaic. Not that there is an extensive picture you're meant to decipher, but that the book's accumulated reference is finally miraculous.

Joyce and the Koran

Joyce was very taken with the idea that the author of the Koran was illiterate yet had produced a text each of whose words had 70 meanings. For him this double ideal had tremendous force, and in his own way he sought to achieve both parts of it. His work would increasingly approximate a preliterate text by incorporating so much popular language in the form of cliché and cant phrase, proverb and traditional saying, song and speechmaking, curse and diatribe that it seemed to come from an utterer vaster than any single writer. At the same time, by techniques that only a highly educated intellectual could apply it would conceal the fruits of extensive research into ancient cultures, remote languages, the main world religions (or at least the lives of their founders, more directly accessible than later transmutation into exclusivist doctrine), terrestrial geography, food, drink and costume. Thus the illusion of something like 70 meanings per word would be produced by doubling, tripling, quadrupling the loads that sentences carried, until there was more there than any single reader could ever apprehend. The feeling of too much was achieved at least in part by a painstaking incremental process, at times by going over and over the same patches adding more each time, at times by sprinkling new ranges of meaning over large areas by adding, say, 200 river names to a chapter whose main focus was a girl he wanted to turn into a water goddess.

Here are a couple of exhibits to show how far Joyce thought he could go, and to suggest the outer limits of certain kinds of meaning in the book. The first is one of those theatrical scenes the book is full of, 'the truly catholic assemblage gathered together in that king's treat house of satin alustrelike above floats and footlights' (32.26), recognizable as the Gaiety Theatre in Dublin to anyone who remembers the Protestant condemnation of this place (in a local paper) as 'the House of Satan in King Street'. The second paints another picture of HCE caught in a compromising position on a public thoroughfare:

> Ah, dearo! Dearo, dear! And her illian! And his willyum! When they were all there now, matinmarked for lookin on. At the carryfour with awlus plawshus, their happyass cloudious! And then and too the trivials! And their bivouac! And his monomyth! Ah ho! Say no more about it! I'm sorry! I saw. I'm sorry! I'm sorry to say I saw! (581.20–25)

Here you would recognize the donkey with the name of the Roman general Aulus Plautius if you had been to dinner with the Joyces in a Paris restaurant sometime in the 1920s when their Irish friend Phyllis Moss told the story of this donkey from her childhood. 'Monomyth' conflates HCE's erection with the Vendôme column (monolith) in the square outside the restaurant, where the character's disgrace is now conveniently located. Mrs Moss didn't think Joyce had been listening, and didn't know what he was talking about when he told her later he'd put her in his book.

This donkey is only retrievable because Phyllis Moss wrote a memoir in which she tells the story. Surely Joyce wasn't counting on this form of gloss on his obscurity. There must be thousands more such references, picked up here and there and then stored by the writer somewhere in its pages over the 6,000-plus days he worked on the book. Maybe a really important text (like Homer, Shakespeare or this one) needs cruxes, which usually arise after centuries have garbled the words in their passing, but which it turns out can also be built in from the start (though there isn't really a true starting point with this text), the last refinement or badge of antiquity supplied by the canny author himself.

Irishness

Both of these obscurities are Irish in different ways, and Irishness certainly preoccupied Joyce. Being Irish was clearly a handicap, as he knew too well and expressed poignantly on many occasions. It was also a distinction and allowed the erection of a ramifying and self-contained system of references that outsiders would have to learn, however incompletely, if they were to read him.

Dubliners have sometimes gloated over how many details in Joyce belong exclusively to them, because no-one else will recognize them. Perhaps Joyce relied on his own reading of Shakespeare among others for a sense of how much obsolete, remote and recondite meaning can be restored by the determined excavations of later readers. He's reputed to have said he wanted to keep the professors busy for a hundred years. But it's hard to believe he wanted to be read primarily by inhabitants of Dublin and the universities. Maybe all the local obscurities are just traps for the unwary.

And yet, you miss some very good jokes if you don't know the languages Joyce knew or haven't read some of the not-very-worth-while books he read or at least cannibalized to beef up the factuality or factedness of the book. Is it possible that Joyce could have projected forward to the French translator of *Finnegans Wake* who identified himself so thoroughly with his author that he read all the books Joyce is known to have read, haunted all the places he is known to have gone and learned the six (?) languages Joyce is thought to have known? These feats of sympathy haven't stopped Philippe Lavergne from believing that mathematics, his own area of professional study, holds the key to *Finnegans Wake*. Another reader who knows the book extremely well, its Polish translator Krzysztof Bartnicki, thinks the whole book turns on a single source, the Egyptian *Book of the Dead*. But if anything is obvious about this labyrinthine work it's that it doesn't have a single key or source or path through. If you can't have a labyrinth without a solution, then this isn't a true labyrinth.

By the time he finished *Finnegans Wake* Joyce hadn't set foot in Ireland for 27 years, the whole period in which he wrote his greatest books, *Ulysses* and *Finnegans Wake*, both profoundly located in Ireland, but an ideal Ireland uncontaminated by contact with the depressing reality, maybe increasingly a compendium or god forbid, an abstract. One of the most interesting improvements made in the new restored *Finnegans Wake* of 2010 is the addition of two Dublin churches which had been dropped out of the list of 29 on page 601.21ff by a printer's mistake. Of course 29 has special significance for Joyce because of the lunar cycle and his 29 rainbow girls who represent the colours of the spectrum, but had anyone noticed that 27 names were not the full set that we'd been promised? For Joyce had played an additional strangening game with the names that made them hard to recognize even for the most hardened Dubliner. He had substituted street names for saints' names in every case, using addresses rather than persons to identify the buildings and then turning the street names into imaginary early Christian personal names, mainly female. Maybe this is a more ancient Dublin than the existing city, but it's also unnervingly dislocated.

Lists, again

A list is one of the most primitive kinds of verbal order and occurs profusely in the most ancient, and especially in oral, compositions. In writers like Rabelais, Burton and Joyce the list may sometimes signal an archaic urge and a disintegrative tendency in the book's thinking at the same time. Lists start as rigid orders – the list of 29 non-existent patron saints keeps neatly within boundaries – but a list can always turn into a frame that allows, almost invites, decorative detail to be hung on every one of its members. Or even more disrupted, onto an arbitrary selection of them. In *Finnegans Wake* the list to end all lists is announced as running to 1,001 items, a number which just means 'a great many' in its best-known occurrence, the *Arabian Nights Entertainments* (to which there are at least 48 references in *Finnegan*), or hugeness plus one. This list, of gifts ALP gives to a confused assemblage of recipients, 'stinkers and heelers, laggards and primelads,' including (or entirely consisting of?) her 1,001 'furzeborn sons and dribblederry daughters', runs for three pages or so (pages 209–12). The list is doubled: each item is a pair, a gift and a recipient – 'an x for y, a z for a, a b for c,' until somewhere in the middle it switches to 'for d an e, for f a g'. That's the template, but from the beginning it is always threatening to disintegrate into the peculiar thingness of each elaborated item, as in the following random sample:

Wildairs' breechettes for Magpeg Woppington; for Sue Dot a big eye; for Sam Dash a false step; snakes in clover, picked and scotched, and a vaticanned vipercatcher's visa for Patsy Presbys; a reiz every morning for Standfast Dick and a drop every minute for Stumblestone Davy; scruboak beads for beatified Biddy; two appletweed stools for Eva Mobbely; for Saara Philpot a Jordan vale tearorne; a pretty box of Pettyfib's Powder for Eileen Aruna to whiten her teeth and outflash Helen Arhone; a whipping top for Eddy Lawless; for Kitty Coleraine of Butterman's Lane a penny wise for her foolish pitcher; a putty shovel for Terry the Puckaun; a potamus mask for Promoter Dunne; a niester egg with a twicedated shell and a dynamight right for Pavl the Curate . . .
(210.25–36)

This melee reminds the reader of the midden heap we explore near the beginning of the book, a rubbish dump of history left behind on a battlefield and now containing a museum of those fargone days. The disjected nature of the list is a sign of its authenticity, its badge of something like antiquity, leftovers of language teeming with suggestion.

Lists are origin as well as final form in *Finnegans Wake*. The notebooks, now so avidly studied, appear to consist of lists of random phrases collected by Joyce from his reading, and in some interpretations, simply stuffed in verbatim at different points in the text. In fact the closer you look the more you see the transformative effect of Joyce's tampering with his readymade phrases. And the context is often wildly different from that in his 'source'. One of the funniest passages I know comes in the description of the miserable hovels of medieval Dubliners in the style of a nineteenth-century government report. Now we learn that Joyce went to Seebohm Rowntree's study of poverty in York published in 1901 for authentic detail. Drastic slippage in the context creates some startling effects:

This missy, my taughters, and these man my son, from my fief of the Villa of the Ostmannorum to Thorstan's, *recte* Thomars Sraid, and from Huggin Pleaze to William Inglis his house, that man de Loundres, in all their barony of Saltus, bonders and foeburghers, helots and zelots, strutting oges and swaggering smacks, the darsy jeamses, the drury joneses, redmaids and bleucotts, in homage all and felony, all who have received tickets, fair home overcrowded, tidy but very little furniture, respectable, whole family attends daily mass and is dead sick of bread and butter, sometime in the militia, mentally strained from reading work on German physics, shares closet with eight other dwellings, more than respectable, getting comfortable parish relief, wageearner freshly shaven from prison, highly respectable, planning new departure in Mountgomery cyclefinishing, eldest son will not serve but peruses Big-man-up-in-the-sky scraps, anoopanadoon lacking backway, quasi respectable, pays ragman in bones for faded windowcurtains, staircase continually lit up with guests, particularly respectable, house lost in dirt and blocked with refuse, getting on like Roe's distillery on fire, slovenly wife active with a jug . . . (543.15–34)

I suppose we have to admit that this is an extremely literary form of joke and that *Finnegan* is the oddest of learned works usually hiding as well as deranging its sources. It is a book made of books in a more literal way than almost any other, but propelled also by this powerful destructive urge to dig down in language to its preliterate origins, a book that will dismember itself or swallow its own organs and spit them out disorganized: a more universal, less provincial kind of stuff.

HCE, ECH, CHE etc.

One of Joyce's strangest ideas about structure is to break his characters down into their most featureless components and bury these in the soil of the book like seeds that might sprout at some later time. Being creatures of a book, these characters are made most basically out of letters, three each, as it happens, like the Trinity or a triangle. HCE for male, ALP for female. Maybe he began as Humphrey Chimpden Ear-wicker, but these words are soon just a memory, hardly seen except in many avatars. The letters rarely make persons, but entities like Howth Castle and Environs or Here Comes Everybody or Hush! Caution! Echoland! or hod, cement and edifices or How Copenhagen ended. As time goes on, the letters appear more often reversed or scrambled, as in Earthside hoist with care or Eglandine's choicest herbage. Apparently there are over 500 permutations on the pattern in the book; the list on *fweet* is that long and it probably hasn't caught them all.

Beckett makes the inspired suggestion that this is the character refusing to disappear from the page but lingering like an afterimage on the retina. But after 600 pages it feels more like the dissolution than the persistence of the character, reduced to something less and vaguer than a name, rarely deserving capital letters any more, barely an interruption of the surface of the ground, probably a figment.

The looming or hovering presence of all those HCEs is the surest sign of the author's maniacal control yet it feels like a helpless consistency, as if it just happened, as if planning by a conscious agent couldn't extend so far down into the separate molecules of a giant verbal artefact. *Finnegans Wake*, one of the most meticulously orga-nized texts in existence, has lent itself to surprising theorizing about the impossibility of authorial intention surviving in a published text. Features of the book's plan, like the looping back of the last words to the first ones, giving it the momentary appearance of a Moebius strip, are used to show that this is a book fundamentally unlike all previous books, built as a textual ruin that accepts and incorporates its own decay as part of its deepest, most elemental being.

'Finnegans Wake' as a decaying artefact

What is the evidence that Joyce wanted his book not just to look unstable, an aesthetic effect, but actually to degrade over time both through the intrusion into it of foreign material and the disap-pearance of (small) pieces of its substance? There's an old story that Beckett was taking dictation from Joyce when someone knocked at the door, and Beckett typed Joyce's 'Come in' into the text. Beckett wanted to correct this, but Joyce liked the idea of leaving it in. You could say that Mrs Moss's donkey has about as much business in *Finnegans Wake* as this 'Come in', and that Joyce welcomed all kinds of intrusion in his deliberately interrupted text, which is always disconcerting us by losing the thread and starting over. It should be noted that this 'Come in' has proved impossible to locate in the text as it stands, but maybe the anecdote remains true nonetheless. Much more than this one phrase remains lost somewhere in *Finnegans Wake*.

The argument over whether we should welcome the slow destruction of this text over time, or try to stop it, narrows itself to the question of whether it is possible to correct errors in *Finnegans Wake* and hence to produce an improved edition more like the version Joyce intended. Obstacles are enormous: the book is full of deliberate misspellings and of grammar that loses its way with terrible hitches in the middle of many sentences. It was written in a curiously circular way, not from beginning to end but in fragments whose eventual location wasn't known at the start. Before long Joyce was revising and expanding a large number of these over the same period. Selected portions were published in little magazines, which usually meant they were revised in a different way on printed proofs. So there's uneven, inconsistent evidence for different parts of the book. At one point Joyce's eyes were so bad he had to write entirely in capital letters using a stick of charcoal. When these sections were printed they were turned into uniform lower case, and all capital letters he might have intended were lost, and perhaps never systematically restored.

So the text starts ruined in various ways, perhaps uniquely ruined, and some observers despair of making it better. There are others who positively relish the author's inability to control the text and the inevitable, if partly inadvertent, contribution of printers and publishers to how the text looks and what it says. One of the most persuasive advocates of this view has even gone so far as to argue in favour of a mistake in the first American edition which substituted 'pronosophical' for 'pornosophical' somewhere in the book. He claims that the mistake actually contains or implies the original meaning as well as a whole new range of suggestion around 'prone' and 'proneness', a concept or posture of great significance to Joyce as he demonstrates with examples from *Ulysses*. In the same piece this writer contends that by incorporating one word of Ki-swahili in *Finnegans Wake* Joyce intended that every word and every part of every word (he's the same man who talks about 'the so-called "words" of the book') in his text should be read graphically and phonically in relation to the entire Ki-swahili dictionary, so that resemblances to Swahili words that Joyce wouldn't have recognized because he didn't know them now become part of the book's resonance.

These attacks on the idea that a book belongs to its author are only carrying out on a supra-literary plane intuitions integral to the techniques of Joyce's book. Such critics want to claim that *Finnegans Wake*, considered as a physical artefact, is itself subject to the rules of distortion and disintegration that Joyce has applied to the English language and his invented characters inside it. In furthering this project, they welcome the errors the book already contains and project further actual and imaginary intrusions. In this projected afterlife the book has to undergo trials like those of its characters; maybe there is a cockeyed sort of justice in that.

6

Art and Destruction

What doesn't kill me, makes me stronger
Nietzsche

LES DEMOISELLES D'AVIGNON must come nearer to an act of pure destruction than almost anything else in the entire history of art, with its cleverly jagged pieces of sky jammed in between its dismembered bodies, coated for large stretches in deceptively bland pink. If it looks incomplete, hastily thrown together, the violence of a moment, that is another deception, for its lengthy and torturous gestation has been carefully recorded. Picasso is deliberately working himself free of all kinds of things, some of which remain trapped here in helpless residues, references to various historical stages, all of them virtually prehistorical and defiantly 'primitive', at least viewed from inside the protected realm of European painting of the just-finished nineteenth century. African, Iberian, Egyptian – these alien mentalities stare out of the faces of all five women, who wear what look like masks but go deeper: these are stone or wooden heads.

In spite of everything this isn't an African carving but a painting on canvas with a classical subject that fills the entire frame, five female nudes and fruit, a dream of bliss it might have been. Nothing as violent appears again in Picasso's work for a long time, but the contradiction persists in his and Braque's pictures between idyllic subject matter and an unsettling way of approaching it. The subjects include fruit, bottles of rum, musical instruments, seated musicians, female nudes (Picasso), rooftops and landscapes (Braque), all of which get harder and harder to recognize, culminating in the best period of so-called analytic Cubism from 1909 to 1911.

Unrecognizable at last

It almost seems that we've been waiting for objects in these paintings to become truly unrecognizable. Clear outlines have disappeared, along with distinct textures and specific colour. Everything is earthy brown or metallic grey, the overall effect a kind of grisaille that is no respecter of the character of particular substances. Who can help looking for traces of 'Fan, Saltbox and Melon' as advised by the title of this Picasso canvas of 1909? Like the reader of *Finnegans Wake* encouraged by brief glimpses of narrative progression or recognizable characters, the student of Cubism keeps trying to uncover a relation to ordinary reality. There have been various attempts to supply a logic for the destructions in these paintings that leave only splintered ruins of things and spaces behind. Braque told an interviewer that a single painting included multiple views of the same object, like plan, elevation and section for representing buildings in architectural drawing. The Picasso version of this is more frantic or disordered: different aspects of the object are collided not separated, as if different moments of vision could happen simultaneously.

The paintings usually feel less comfortable, less rational and less coherent than what seem like retrospective justifications of a process more anarchic, that experiences the disintegration of everyday reality as an explosive release of energy. Now the prosaic titles seem catalogues of what has disappeared, though still, paradoxically, a form of specifying. The list of unrecognizable things in the title just marks out how far we've got from recognition, and have almost an opposite function from naming what is there. Joyce's chapter titles (which he put in and then took out of *Ulysses*) would probably have worked that way too, but they are undeniably a form of interpretation and therefore taboo.

Objects appear to multiply by refraction or another kind of optical illusion, or to migrate round the picture space, a space which often wages war with the orientation of the frame. In Braque's work later in this period specific details, which might help us identify a particular musical instrument or type of armchair, detach themselves to become unrelated fragments. Perversely, the most distinct elements are set free from performing any stabilizing task: the best clues are all in the wrong places, or at least are the least connected parts. Perversely, this description too makes confusion and irresolution in these paintings sound like a failing or a problem. But uncertainty and irresolution are what they are most centrally about. It is thrilling to see ordinary objects made so convincingly problematic, to have an unacknowledged and barely guessed complexity in the makeup of the physical world brought out with a force impossible to ignore.

There are two main ways of regarding these early Cubist pictures – a name which never becomes entirely comfortable, however much one tells oneself that by now it's just a name, pure convention, and not an attempt at describing – as a whole new kind of perception or way of registering how the world shows itself to the mind, or as a series of experiments with the picture space, resulting in paintings *about* representation. There's probably a time for everyone when this second perspective seems the more exciting one, a higher form of interpretation.

At least since Rubens and maybe beyond it has been possible to view many Western paintings in these two ways, switching back and forth between looking at forms and looking at brushstrokes practically without thinking. The second attitude has a shorter history, and Cubism plays a key part in it.

Sometime in 1912 an important shift occurs in what both Braque's and Picasso's canvases look like. Roughly speaking, they flatten out, become less confused and more like collages, as if they consist of thin flakes or sheets of material overlaid in a more orderly way. At a certain point elements that look paper-thin turn up as actual pieces of paper stuck to the canvas, even bits of newspaper printed with part of some lurid story.

Words had made an earlier appearance in Cubist pictures. They gained entry because they were part of the subject, which was a table-top with drink, glasses, pipe – and a newspaper. So the name of the paper, or part of it, is there like the rest of reality, but different, clearer and more insistent, always something of an intruder, the most intelligible element but also the most disruptive, in a different register from everything else, rightside up and frontal like nothing else, as if language is so powerful it can force paint into forms it doesn't really want to be in, emissary of an order that makes painting into a formal game.

Art made of junk

At the end of the First World War Kurt Schwitters says that everything has broken down and new works have to be made from the
fragments. In 1918 he produces his first collages, which look as if
they're made of scraps found in the street and rescued into the painting, trampled pieces of paper, used tickets, torn patches of cloth,
lengths of wood and bits of machinery, the flotsam of urban existence
washed up in gutters or in the pockets of drifters through the streets.
Unlike the early Cubist pictures these collections of leftovers don't
send you searching for the narrative that lies behind them, as if they
were the ruin of a particular event. Occasionally they might resemble
a machine being taken to pieces or flying apart, or a wall from which
the wallpaper has been imperfectly stripped, showing other layers
underneath, or a more public version of this same situation, the
palimpsest of posters and notices built up on an abandoned shopfront
or the side of an unused building.

Schwitters's collages appear in the midst of a particular historical
catastrophe, and give voice to the pain of their time and place, yet
Schwitters must have seen the shredded words and objects in Braque's
paintings of five or six years earlier, where broken-off pieces of familiar things acquire enigmatic power. Schwitters's words begin as the
debris of day-to-day commerce and are raised to almost sacramental
status. By accident or design part of a bank's printed name (*Commerz
und privat Bank*) on a letterhead got broken off and became a powerful nonsense syllable – *Merz* – with suggestions of sorrow (*Schmerz*)
that Schwitters hung onto and attached to all his works from that
moment onward, a meaning that could never shake off a residue of
meaninglessness, an untranslated survivor from an unfamiliar language.

Narrative fragments burst out of the picture surface and then bury
themselves in it again, like the toy motorcycle with its crouched rider
in *As You Like It* of 1943–4. He's been painted over as if to camouflage
him and he burrows into a crease in the fabric like something hiding
in an armpit. The range of debris in this picture – actually a deep relief
– is unusually diverse, one meaning of the title, that there's too much
here to give it a descriptive name. The reference to Shakespeare that
jumps out at us seems to lead nowhere. Schwitters's English titles are

sometimes arch, sometimes idiomatic like this one; Schwitters was a poet who Herbert Read for one took very seriously, comparing his use of language to Joyce's in *Finnegans Wake*, but that may have been an opportunistic stab at connecting the alien with an English audience.

The attempt to forge a backward link between Schwitters and the British Pop of Richard Hamilton similarly misfires. For Hamilton popular culture is shiny and up-to-the-minute; he incorporates it almost bodily via superreal graphics in a spirit mainly celebratory and only marginally satirical. Schwitters buries or obscures the popular material, which doesn't feel up-to-date anymore, though still trivial. Trivial the way that most of what archaeologists find is trivial, evidence of common not special activity and in its way all the more revealing for that. Trivial the way cooking debris in the *Iliad* is trivial, leftover from a sacrifice on the beach.

In this perspective the collages made entirely of paper and fabric are often the most moving, because these materials show wear and tear more vividly and also age more quickly than most, granting these works more of a history than contemporaries made of more durable stuff. There's a collage of 1940 called *Pink Green and White* in which the colours have faded so completely you can't even be sure which scraps were the pink and green ones. A wrinkled stretch of tissue paper was probably *Pink*, chosen for its frailty and distressed further in the rough way it has been pasted down.

Ephemera are trivial and even foolish – expired tickets, empty wrappers, thin strips of stuff like the striped edges of air mail envelopes, labels lacking both container and contents. Schwitters imparts disturbing life to all the debris in a piece like *Very Complicated* of 1947, with its title either dazed or deadpan. Here different sorts of paper are ageing differently: newsprint has yellowed dramatically, but wrapping was brown to start with and others have been attacked with scissors until identities are lost. The scattered assemblage gives an accelerated idea of passage, of civilization ruining or becoming unrecognizable.

This is such a tiny space in which to detect these great developments that we are bound to wonder if we're not exaggerating. Schwitters was after all a light-hearted not a gloomy character, and the same pile of shattered fragments that signalled the breakup of the old order in the collages of 1918–20 must mean something different

Kurt Schwitters, *Very Complicated*, 1947, where the scattered assemblage of scraps hints at civilization coming unstuck.

in the visually indistinguishable work of the 1940s. It is still expressing a quintessentially urban sensibility, but it emerges from the years of isolation in rural Cumbria.

Schwitters's own comments are not much help, with their focus on questions of technical mastery. Other observers will find other messages in Schwitters's late work, even in some of the collages, ones like *Windswept* and *Pine Trees*, both of which treat weather and the natural world, if you believe their titles, and suggest coordinated upward movement, which is enough to lend them an optimistic air. All of which casts serious doubt on the attempt to read vast cultural statements into Schwitters's collages. And yet . . . even the trees (formed so unexpectedly of the inner surfaces of corrugated cardboard) and clouds (made from a cheap paper doily) fall apart at certain moments into scenes of destruction. All the fragments form both a buoyant creative game and a world which can't even hold itself together.

Schwitters as an architect

From early in his career Schwitters showed an interest in realizing the space of the collage in three dimensions and much bigger, at first on the scale of the room, and finally as a twisting tower of space stretching through a couple of storeys that constitutes a kind of building. He did this in his family's house in Hannover, colonizing progressively larger amounts of the living space which remained visitable but not truly habitable. This experiment was known initially as the Cathedral of Erotic Misery and then as the *Merzbau*. The justification for the earlier name was the series of shrines, mock-sacred spaces which filled little offshoots and crannies in the larger assemblage. These sometimes secreted grotesque relics, like a phial of a famous person's urine or a discarded piece of Max Ernst's underwear.

Such human interest feels at odds with the overall aesthetic of the later *Bau*, austerely modernist in its pure whiteness and nondescript materials. The excitement of the *Merzbau* lay elsewhere, in its impossible and illogical assemblage. It looked just like architecture throughout, being composed almost entirely of boards, beams and posts which formed straight lines but were combined in a disarray so precarious it was a wonder it didn't all collapse. Large elements defied gravity and seemed to be plummeting toward the floor, a sensation increased by the pointed shapes they ended in. Schwitters's construction is anti-architecture that deliberately upturns all the comfortable certainties of buildings. It could never be built, yet here it is, or was, until destroyed in an Allied bombing raid in 1943.

Buildings made from holes

Maybe there's a bitter aptness in that attack on Schwitters's denial of architecture, an actual destruction of his conceptual destruction of the whole idea of building. For different reasons Gordon Matta-Clark's partial destructions are also short-lived. Unlike Schwitters operating in the seeming safety of his own living space, Matta-Clark tackles buildings derelict or already slated for demolition and tampers with them in a short breathing space before the real destroyers move in. He had studied architecture at Cornell in the '60s but then moved sideways into the art scene in lower Manhattan without giving much sign of wanting to practise architecture, favouring forms closer to street art or performance instead.

Maybe his final projects combine all three of these activities. These start in the suburbs with different ways of taking houses apart, first by slicing a facade free of its building (*Bingo*, 1974), then cutting through the whole depth of a wooden frame house from top to bottom (*Splitting*, 1974), and doing this twice with less than a foot between the incisions. The result was an opening which left identical ruined pieces on either side. Views from inside through the crack present something like a strange eclipse. All four corners of the building under the eaves have been removed to create four cubic voids about four feet on one side. In the videos that Matta-Clark made you can see more of what he is driving at. The views he chooses are consistently disorienting. Stairs, doors, walls and floors lose their point and gain a kind of independence from reality from within which they defy you to make sense of them.

The two halves of *Splitting* soon began to sag away from each other and the neat slit became a gaping wound that Matta-Clark was quick to accentuate. The finished work lasted three months before its site was cleared for urban renewal. In his report on the project Matta-Clark puts quotes around 'renewal'. After this his ambitions or at least the size of the architectural cadavers he worked on grew. He had been busy for two months on a derelict pier shed along the Hudson River before being detected, creating solar effects by cutting out a huge circle with a piece missing in this building's end wall. As soon as the work was discovered, the City of New York sued Matta-Clark. The suit was later dropped, but perhaps didn't entirely displease him.

Consider his project for Peter Eisenman's Institute for Architecture and Urban Studies, perhaps an ironic title but almost bound to provoke Matta-Clark. He was invited to show work there, and had been looking at the projects (as they are called) in the South Bronx, public housing in a sad state of early ruin, where windows are regularly broken by stones or shot out with airguns. Matta-Clark took some monotonous close-ups of these broken panes and mounted them in the gallery. Then he went down and shot out all the windows of the exhibition space. Eisenman didn't appreciate the logic of this, and Matta-Clark's photos were removed. It is his least architectural project and probably the shortest-lived. I wonder how much he thought about the aesthetic effect of broken windows letting in light onto pictures of broken windows, a convergence few people ever got to test.

For me this is the most dubious of all his works, mainly because it is so physically bleak, without the rich textures or impinging thereness of the others. But you cannot really give the rationale of any of his best work, which is always deeply unreasonable. To find such clear thinking devoted to the un-realizing of construction, to see a building falling away from itself, how can we explain our fascination with that? Matta-Clark is always creating or hastening ruin, but not like eighteenth-century dabblers by playing with miniatures. It's the palpable sense of danger that thrills us, the knowledge that a wrong cut could make a floor collapse or a building fall, sending someone plunging through space or crushing him flat. A sense of danger long past in reality, but vivid before us in the gaping hole this architect manqué has made in architecture.

Why is it no more upsetting than it is that none of Matta-Clark's works survive? That they have all been bulldozed, as we can watch the Paris project, which is probably the greatest of all, undergoing in a murky homemade video whose crudity is its own analogue of ruin. Photos of architecture can tell you things that the buildings themselves cannot, but no one thinks they're an adequate experience of buildings. Yet with Matta-Clark we are all stuck scanning photos of the work, idealized single views of what were spatial experiences to start with. Still, each of these images is a kind of multiple in which spaces lead to other spaces. In careful dissections of buildings like these you can see many different places at once. If it is only a conceptual view, it is conceptual like a cutaway drawing that shows all parts of a machine at once, as never happens in reality. Matta-Clark has turned this x-ray vision onto architecture, yet it is still a stationary glimpse, frozen at one moment in a process, though all the rough edges help us imagine other stages than the one we can actually see.

Conical Intersect takes its place in the bigger destruction of Les Halles, a whole area of central Paris still mourned by anyone who remembers it, which felt like the bowels of the city where the gruesome acts that underlie and sustain human life including culture were embarrassingly displayed, and jostled you as you passed in the form of steaming carcases of animals being carried past and then torn to pieces to get them ready for consumption in more decorous forms elsewhere.

Matta-Clark was allowed to do his more refined architectural butchery on a worn-out seventeenth-century townhouse at the edge of the condemned district, cheek by jowl with a new cultural landmark, a museum disguised as a gasworks or gigantic piece of machinery that looked hardly anything like architecture. So Matta-Clark was producing his subversive anti-art right next to a big display space for art, a daring piece of un-architecture that carried the name of an important French politician at the end of his career.

It's a bizarre fact that by now *Conical Intersect* has mislaid its interesting location beside the Centre Pompidou and could perfectly well be displayed inside it without mentioning its own helpless involvement in the destruction of Paris. There is a way to remember the connection though – by watching the video which records the whole sequence, starting with the intact dwelling in a neighbourhood of similar buildings. The film shows the first tentative probes of the wall from inside, the slowly widening wound which for a long time has no recognizable shape, punctuated by views outward that catch glimpses of cars in the street below going past this small hole. Before long the building is coughing up rough bits of itself as lumps are thrown out through the hole. Rooms inside gradually disappear as the cut progresses. It's very messy along the way, attacking the building repeatedly, producing waste that must be ejected via the hole.

From time to time we look out at the ruins of the district and a big stretch of cleared ground between us and the other ruins, a sight indistinguishable from that of a bombed city, but not the same, because self-inflicted. The hole begins to make sense, neater but still rough-edged. Now it extends over a couple of storeys and partial membranes are revealed between the main geometric forms.

Some of the complex structure of Matta-Clark's design is only revealed when a digger attacks the whole building from behind in order to bring it down completely. Now we can see remnants of a kitchen in the hollow cone Matta-Clark has made, an old stair laid bare looking really venerable, and lots of views through into Matta-Clark's spaces we hadn't gotten till now. After the digger breaks into Matta-Clark's zone it tears away at his big circular hole and reveals a structure like a fish's rib cage, a skeleton discovered inside the building which survives briefly after the main facade has gone.

After watching this destruction we find it harder than ever to believe the commonly repeated story of the work's genesis, that it was inspired by Anthony McCall's film *Line Describing a Cone*, which materializes an empty space, practically bodiless, without any of the unsettling visceral thereness of Matta-Clark's. I'm not sure the 'construction' of *Conical Intersect* should form part of the story, but I want to say that its destruction *is* an essential element of the work. Rather than this illogical claim, perhaps we could just recommend that you should see the still photos of this project in its completeness before you watch the video. In fact this is how most viewers will encounter the work anyway, without any special staging or theorizing.

One of Matta-Clark's last projects, *Office Baroque*, in Antwerp, attracted the attention of the city authorities who held up progress for a time, even though like the *Merzbau* this project dealt entirely with interior spaces. It does look alarming however in the way it eviscerates the building, creating voids that shoot off in several directions and give the feeling of complex falling movement. It's a ruin where things are happening, in a prevision of a structure actively disintegrating. Like the most extreme Baroque interiors it makes architecture feel ephemeral, molten, something that changes from moment to moment.

It was the last surviving work of its un-architect and the subject, after his early death, of an attempt to preserve it, which failed in spite of the promised donation of lots of artworks by friends and admirers to fund its salvage. There's something quixotic and paradoxical about the whole notion, but not long before he died Matta-Clark had married a curator and perhaps would not have found the idea absurd of

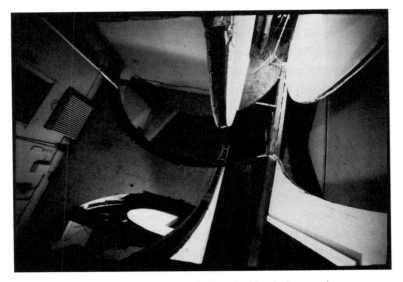

Gordon Matta-Clark, *Caribbean Orange*, 1978, silver dye-bleach photograph.
The deconstructed, soon-to-be-demolished building was adjacent to a
contemporary art museum in Chicago.

one of his large works turned into a monument with opening times,
tickets and guards.

Matta-Clark's descendants in earlier times

Searching for Matta-Clark's spiritual kin among regular architects
leads in surprising directions. Sir John Soane, an English architect
practising a century and a half earlier, looks like a neo-Classicist when
seen from certain angles or in certain projects, but when most himself
reveals one of the most subversive and Romantic architectural imag-
inations of all. At the back of his own house in Lincoln's Inn Fields
the building appears to come apart into a rickety skeletal framework,
a ghostly remnant of its original self, a structure half destroyed by time
with the unintended benefit of multiplied architectural possibility.
Walls that have mainly disappeared let us see through into whole
other worlds, overhead and underfoot, irradiated and weightless,
gloomy and heavily burdened, a tower, a cellar and a middle ground
in-between, all present at once. This complex space is visceral yet
conceptual, crammed full of rich sensation but only visitable along

little walkways, a feast for the eye and the spatial sense but otherwise oddly inhospitable.

Like Matta-Clark's voids carved out of the dead flesh of condemned buildings, Soane's mysterious and bewildering space achieves its phantasmagoric sensations by destroying the conventional integrity of the structure. In a sense, no explanation is needed, and yet we would like to know what possessed a man with such a powerful interest in worldly success to create something so disruptive.

As it happens, Soane left a strange manuscript that reads like a dream-narrative which has found a way to let loose his deepest fantasies and fears about architecture, the self and death, as all three of them are crystallized in this building of modest physical dimensions. This text is called 'Crude Hints towards an History of my House in L.I.F' and dated 1812 but was first published in 1999 as an appendix to an exhibition catalogue, where it fills fourteen oddly spaced pages and looks like a work that is still evolving.

In one sense 'Crude Hints' is a hoax, of a kind that Soane had already perpetrated at least once before. It treats a building, which is just going up and therefore has no history, as if it were venerable, incorporating elements dating back to Roman times and even beyond.

The so-called Dome at the back of Sir John Soane's London house, whose questioning of the certainties of architecture eerily resembles Matta-Clark's punctures of 150 years later.

Soane's earlier experiment in building ruins, attached to his villa at Ealing, west London. A view of them at an imaginary earlier stage.

Earlier Soane had built a fake ruin in the grounds of Pitzhanger Manor, his house in Ealing. To amuse his friends he had written an antiquary's account of these ruins, speculating about their origins and producing an imaginary reconstruction of the antique building, an impressive temple the lowest levels of which still lay buried in the ground, like ancient Rome beneath the streets of the modern city.

The little ruin at Ealing, which has since been built over though the rest of Soane's villa survives, differed from most other mock-ruins in being attached to the modern house, as if the whole might be a reworking of something much more ancient. So the ruin might embody more or less serious intentions to establish a continuum between the living and the dead. Soane returned to the ruins at Ealing 30 years after his little hoax about them, long after selling the house, to hypothecate the missing temple in greater earnest. It seems to have been an idea that meant more to him than he could rationally explain.

'Crude Hints' dates from ten years after the imaginary manuscript at Ealing. Soane conceives it as his house is going up, right after the demolition of the previous occupant of the site. So the plot is a building site, not pristine, but a space from which debris is being cleared while the new structure is sketched out on the ground. Still, it is a strange conceit to view a building under construction as if it were a ruin, a place incomplete and mysterious because, so long abandoned, many signs of what it was have disappeared.

I wonder if Soane knew the paintings of that favourite subject of sixteenth-century Flemish artists like Bruegel and Valckenborch, the Tower of Babel, which show a building site as if it were a ruin. This tower is an unfinishable project that has already been going on a long time, a whole city of separate acts that make just one big useless lump, a vision grandiose and pessimistic at once. It's a subject which also attracted Kafka, via Bruegel's paintings I would not be surprised to find, who imagines all those lives losing track of the plot completely, getting distracted onto peripheral arrangements, until finally eaten up by fantasies of destruction, not building, and the wish that a huge supernatural fist would appear and smash their futile routines.

'Crude Hints' pursues the idea of the incomplete house as a set of clues to the intentions of the builder and the lives of the inhabitants. We've come along centuries later, and we can't decide whether the complex – undoubtedly larger originally than what we see now – was a classical temple, a magician's palace or a convent of nuns. Each of these options is enthusiastically pursued, arguing from bits of construction and fragments of statues found in the ruins. The fragments are pieces from Soane's collection, now roped in to take part in fanciful

The building site as a ruin: Marten van Valckenborch's *The Building of the Tower of Babel*, c. 1600, oil on panel.

narratives, no longer inert but vigorously animating the surrounding masonry, giving it human point. Every part of the house as it will finally materialize makes an appearance in this story: the basements of Soane's house were formerly the above-ground graveyard of the monastery; the top-lit stair was formerly a windowless prison cell *à la* Piranesi for driving recalcitrant nuns mad; the cast of Apollo Belvedere is the magician turned to stone.

The whole exercise is a spoof and simultaneously the most profound expression of Soane's architectural intentions in existence. He is making a burrow that will be a temple, a scholar's hideout, a convent and a necropolis all at once. Its equipment, consisting of precious fragments of practically every civilization and every epoch known to us, is meant to work like the shaman's kit-bag to summon up spirits, to help us travel to all places and all times within the confines of a single terrace house, which turns almost imperceptibly into three as you move from back to front.

The most surprising and unorthodox inclusion happens in the lowest depths, an underworld or sepulchral region as real as Soane can make it. This section raises most uneasily the question of how real all of this is meant to be. Soane tries to have it more than one way at once. He is creating an Academy of Architecture where poor students who can't afford the Grand Tour can have the physical experience of Greece and Rome, through the actual and fictitious but always fragmentary remains he has brought back. But he is also creating mock-ups of successful persistence through generations that backfire when he remembers that his sons are not going to play the game of succession and continuance, leaving his elaborate piecing together of a universal and personal history nothing but a wreck, of fragments forlorn without the saving haze of fantasy. So the meditation, which began so jauntily, ends with the despairing thought of a pen dropping from a palsied hand. Or is that, too, just the conventional close of a Gothic tale? This is the thought about architecture Soane is most anxious to avoid having, that it is finally as futile as more ephemeral-seeming activities, because if it survives long enough all those who understood it will have disappeared and it will be a ruin without anyone realizing it. Foreseeing his buildings as uninterpretable ruins is finally no fun at all.

Even more lethal attacks

Soane's architecture in moments when it is barely there, eaten away by intimations of ruin like the so-called Dome at the back of his house, is among the most gripping of all. But can we really count art which has been so effectively attacked it hovers on the verge of non-existence or is no longer there as just another version of ruin? For these are destructions carried out by enemies who would probably be happiest if it didn't exist at all. Though the route by which the mangled text or damaged sculpture gets to us is more torturous, maybe the reader's or viewer's experience has more in common with the pleasures brought by Matta-Clark or Soane than one initially supposes.

The oldest Norse poetry has been largely destroyed and we cannot even reconstruct the process by which this happened, except in the sketchiest way. The surviving remnants are of several different kinds, the oldest a hodgepodge of poems and poetic fragments collected together for safe keeping in the thirteenth century in Iceland and copied out in semi-logical sequence into a compendium which at a later date lost a sizeable piece of itself – just how large we cannot tell – leaving a gap behind which has become known as the Great Lacuna. That absence can stand in for many others, poems never written down or lost destroyed forgotten in the centuries between the arrival of Christianity in Iceland in 999–1000, when it was adopted as the national faith by something resembling legislative decision, and the antiquarian salvage of poetic remnants three centuries later.

For the principal destructive force was indeed Christianity, which discredited if it didn't entirely stamp out the old Norse gods, giants, elves, ogres and valkyries. There's the strange story, like something from myth, of the pagan priest entrusted with the decision on whether the Icelanders should convert to Christianity. After a lonely night of pondering he decides that they should. He throws his own idols into a waterfall, but preserves the right for pagans to perform the old sacrifices as long as they do it in secret. Old religions don't just vanish from neglect; they're actively suppressed, but in Iceland provision is made for a long twilight in which the old ways can continue if they stay hidden.

Poetic fragments are not the only remains of Norse myth. There is also a highly organized prose compilation, apparently the work of a thirteenth-century Icelandic writer and politician called Snorri Sturluson. This is a variegated collection, evidently produced over many years and finally including patches of extended narrative as well as treatise-like elements and whole sections which are glorified lists. This text is now known as *Edda*, or *Prose Edda* to distinguish it from the *Poetic Edda*, a name given retrospectively to the poetic remains after the matching name for the prose had sunk in. 'Edda' is a linguistic curiosity, a rare word which means great grandmother in one of the old poems. Our 'edda' is probably a different word entirely, a linguistic ruin whose history and meaning remain obscure. So we cannot take it as just a quaint way of saying 'something very old'.

Snorri's lists

At its most methodical the *Prose Edda* is indigestible, listing various names for Odin or kennings for gold without explaining what they have to do with each other. In fact we come to doubt that all those names are talking about the same being or substance. The compiler has forgotten something vital about why you have so many names for the same thing in the first place. You really need to come across the strange names for Odin first in their ancient habitats, where the god-hero is hiding behind his father or remembering his duties to the slain. You can't make a single composite being out of all those names, nor do you feel the expected thrill on simply toting up all the ways of mentioning gold. Each name turns out to be an encapsulated story, so at any point in the narrative you are never far from all the other things that have ever happened to this interconnected throng. All those names are signs that this is a whole ramifying world, and there is no short route to coming to feel at home in it.

Perhaps ideally you would be able to linger over each item in Snorri's catalogue of Norse kennings when he reaches gold:

How shall gold be referred to? By calling it Aegir's fire and Glasir's foliage, Sif's hair, Fulla's snood, Freyia's weeping, mouth-count and voice and words of giants, dripping from

Draupnir and rain or shower from Draupnir or from Freyia's eyes, otter-payment, Aesir's forced payment, seed of Fyri plains, Holgi's mound-roof, fire of all kinds of waters and of the arm, stones and rocks or gleam of the arm.

In this form the lore is simply a ruined heap, a set of things that once meant powerfully and still could, but are now stacked up to form a confusing dazzle. The principles or whims by which the list is ordered are distracting or misleading. Snorri certainly knows better, but it seems as if he wants to wear out our attention.

Abruptly, unreasonably he follows this with a flood of explications of all the kennings for gods, heroes, places and substances one by one, hundreds of them, that sometimes lead into unrelated stories and continue for pages before he pulls himself back to the next kenning. The lore is wonderful in itself but maddening in its density and confusion. Precious nuggets are lost in the heap, like this: Gold is called Aegir's fire because one time Aegir invited the gods to visit him and when they were all seated he 'had glowing gold brought into the middle of the hall which illuminated and lit up the hall like fire, and this was used as light at his feast, just as in Val-hall there had been swords instead of fire'.

Gold is scattered everywhere in the Norse tales, most grandly and ominously in hoards buried underground and guarded by dragons. Buried because that is where it came from in the first place, or because it is deathly and always brings death along not far behind. At the end of *Beowulf*, the eighth-century Anglo-Saxon epic whose close relation to Norse material seems obvious to me but is not universally accepted, the dying hero sends young Wiglaf back into the dragon's burrow, which is also an old burial mound, to survey the treasure, which strikes him initially as ruined: rusting, broken and spoiled. But then the glitter of gold wins out and the sense of waste and uselessness passes.

Yet the connection between gold and death remains: the hoard's rescuer is dying and his thoughts turn to architecture. Emerging from the mound fatally wounded, Beowulf perches on the ramparts and admires their construction. Now he gives instructions for his burial mound on a promontory overlooking the sea. This will be a monument known by his name which will guide seamen; it will no doubt contain treasure and attract fortune hunters in its turn, and the cycle will begin all over again.

Ruins as seeds from which epic poems spring

The filiation of ruin and poem runs even more strongly in the other direction: no epic without a ruin to set it in motion is apparently still a respectable theory as it was for Schliemann. The ruins of Troy provoked the *Iliad*, as the ruins of Ur did *Gilgamesh* and burial mounds of previous cultures presumably did *Beowulf*, and now one can follow the trail backward in the other direction. Apparently the poem ends with an archaeological site you can visit. Already in the oldest Norse fragments the gods are finding gold playing pieces in the grass, ruins of former feasting and carousing. Nostalgia has already crept into the purest layer of remains.

Even worse, the whole search for Norseness in its pure form may prove hopeless. I'm told that *Völuspá*, weirdest and most alien of the poems, is shot through with Christian ideas, though I still can't see them except at the very end where the gloom suddenly lifts and life is beautiful. In *Beowulf* Christian intrusions are easier to spot, but no more feasible to remove.

Norse myth was extinguished by Christianity and then revived by nineteenth-century agnostics like Morris and Wagner in flight from Christianity. You could find a version of your own pre-Christian roots there, but then what did you do with it? Import the savagery back into the nineteenth century? Nietzsche was one of the great theorists of such switchbacks, though Viking tales had no charms for him and his own behaviour fails the test of the new morality.

A more circumscribed search for roots is the attempt to cleanse English of later overlay and return it to its Anglo-Saxon self, a struggle waged by the Dorset vicar and dialect poet William Barnes among others. He produces strange coinages that are like kennings in their straying from recognizable sense, like *wortlore* for *botany* or *sunprint* for *photograph*. They are artificially created ruins of language based on the wishful supposition that English hasn't progressed from its provincial origins at the edge of the civilized world, willing that lots of cultural pollution (or you could say exchange) had not happened.

Gerard Manley Hopkins's response to Barnes's coinages is fascinating. He loves the new words, like *pitches of suchness* for *degrees of comparison*, but thinks the campaign quixotic. His own poems are the nearest thing to English with the whole Latin overlay entirely swept away, and the man who wrote them was making himself into a fanatical Roman Catholic at the same time, perhaps as conflicted a character as Snorri, who thinks up ingenious justifications for the old heathen poetry he loves.

Almost no one is completely immune to fantasies about roots, leading you on to find the ruins which are *your* ruins, signs of your connectedness to ancient layers. I've formed a special fondness for one of the Norse poems, 'Völundarkvida', which tells the grisly tale of the smith who talks with birds and kills the children of his oppressor and buries the pieces under his anvil. This tale is purer, truer and more primitive in its violence than most, but its key feature for me is that it may have been written near here, somewhere on the Yorkshire coast. I try to forget that this is a mostly exploded theory of its origin, in spite of some linguistic resemblances to *Beowulf*, and distract myself by cherishing all the Norse placenames nearby, like Redcar, so mysteriously but nonsensically clear that it has always puzzled me, now explained as meaning 'reedy marsh'.

Placenames as ruins

Placenames are among the most bewitching and concentrated of ruins, the more battered beyond recognition the better. Wonderful to find Welsh coasts littered with Norse names like Fishguard and Swansea, whose seeming Englishness is a delusion arising from a later effort to make sense of them. All etymologies are folk ones, I sometimes think, or at least have an imaginative component, but so what? The basic principle feels right, that every placename is a secret hoard containing unexpected layers and contributions from places – mental locations that is – far afield.

They are the most venerable remnants, usually the only ones, of vanished cultures in the place I come from. Every American knows that all the strangest and most interesting names in the u.s. were left behind by Indian tribes as they were chased westward across a huge continent. Here is probably a much more detailed routemap than the traces of the Norsemen on British coasts.

Norse words lie buried all around us in great profusion, of which we are unaware and bound to remain so, because they are so common and so easily mistaken for Anglo-Saxon. Most English speakers know that English is one of the world's least pure, most hybridized languages, but practically no one realizes Norse borrowings have affected it more deeply than the better-known influx from Norman French.

Anger, awe, awkward, axle, bag, bark, bask, billow, bleak, boulder, bread, bug, bulk, clip, crawl, crook, cur, dirt, drag, dream, dregs, drip, droop, egg, fellow, flat, fog, freckle, gap, gape, gawk, gift, glitter, gosling, guest, gust, haggle, heathen, irk, keel, kindle, knife, knot, lad, leather, loft, mistake, muck, muggy, oaf, odd, outlaw, plow, raft, ransack, rive, root, rotten, rugged, scant, scarf, scrape, scrap, skid, skin, shirt, skull, sky, slaver, sleuth, snare, snub, stagger, stammer, thrift, tidings, ugly, until, weak, whirl, window, wrong.

These are English words derived from Norse, taken from lists that run into thousands and include common pronouns, basic verbs and many more names for everyday objects. Can this really be an influence more powerful than the French? Probably not, because it only intensifies what we think of as the Anglo-Saxon element of the language – gruff, monosyllabic, inescapably physical, language made of solid, earthy material and used by speakers who have their eyes on the earth not the heavens.

That's the myth anyway. And besides, the list smoothes over a lot of complexity: these words aren't all Norse in the same way or to the same degree, because words are more like fragments of ruined, dodgily transmitted poetry than pieces of vanished buildings dug out of the ground. They haven't stayed put, and figuring out where they came from often requires a complicated narrative built on intelligent guesses.

Noticing all the Norseness in English makes the language and its connection to place feel realer and richer, built on even more gnarled ruins of the past than we had thought. It pushes our origins further toward the peripheries, as does the key role of Iceland in preserving the Norse sagas. Only in this outlying place are these cultural relics treasured and collected. The stories don't start there or take place there; in Iceland there is nothing much you could call a court, and certainly none of those heaps of gold gear lying about. But the poems are in some way made at home in Iceland, where the parchment is like as not sealskin and the ivory is whalebone.

Back to that grisly ruined story

Not just a phantom Yorkshire link draws me to the story of the smith who buries his victims under his anvil, but also its rude depiction scratched into whalebone on the Franks casket, most of which has made it back to Britain and the British Museum after improbable journeys. Its main runic inscription refers to the material's journeying before it fell into human hands: 'The fish beat up the seas onto the mountainous cliff; the king of terror became sad when he swam onto the shingle: whale's bone,' which tells you what the object you're holding is made of, in a riddling, circuitous way.

This casket isn't the best argument for cultural isolation as strength or a badge of authenticity. It combines classical, Biblical and Northern stories, or history, religion and myth, blithely, greedily, as if determined to encapsulate all culture on one modest domestic object. Of course it was the purest accident of passage that the casket ever became either modest or domestic. It ended its life out in the world as a woman's workbasket in a French farmhouse, but in the early eighth century in northern England when it was made, it wouldn't have been an everyday object but an unheard of marvel in a rare material, to which impressive learning had been applied.

What can the promiscuous medley of stories on the casket have felt like to the deviser? Has one range of stories won out, leaving others as outmoded ruins? But the Northern story, though crowded into the smallest space, seems to hold its own, the most enigmatic of them all. Like the old Northern interlace which fills the richest pages of the Lindisfarne Gospels it doesn't act like the last gasp of a superseded culture. But it remains a mystery how such survivals are possible, and it is hard to believe that the illuminators saw themselves as subversives, any more than the Indian carvers of the facades of Jesuit churches in Mexico. One can still wonder if they knew what their hands were drawing or carving, in any conscious way.

Franks casket of whalebone, early 8th century, mixed Christian and pagan stories surrounded by an Anglo-Saxon riddle written in runes.

Four or five centuries after Lindisfarne, Snorri arrived at an intricate explanation for where the old Norse material came from that is either a sophisticated version of how myths arise or simply a riddling narrative device that turns a story inside out as a means of detaching ourselves from literature to return to life. It goes like this: an immigrant race with wizard powers have been recounting the stories of the old Norse gods for the local Swedish king. When they reach the end there's a crash and he finds that the hall and the castle in which these stories were being recounted have disappeared. So he goes home. The tellers reconvene and decide to award all the names of gods in the stories to people in the neighbourhood (themselves?) so that people centuries hence will believe that the two are the same, and that someone called Thor is the god Thor. A final twist is then added, like a clinching afterthought: Thor is part of the story of Troy, where his feats will be found attributed to Hec-tor. The Turks also tell stories of Ulysses giving him the name Loki.

Which story has the most authority, the classical or the Northern? Which is a type of which? European royal families are all descended from the heroes of Troy. Even more improbably, so are the figures of Norse myth, and we authenticate gods by tracing them back to human warriors, bigger than us but decidedly mortal. Snorri's (or someone's) attempt to historicize the old story-material has ended in riddles. As far as we can understand this confusing passage, Snorri seems to turn the stories into anthropological exhibits, diminishing them in order to save them.

Later iconoclasm and the passion for destruction

Some of the most violent instances of ideological destruction of cultural material take place within the boundaries of a cult, not when a foreign cult storms in and takes over an indigenous one. From our distance Byzantine iconoclasm of the eighth and ninth centuries might seem a limited affair, confined to arguments over how the interiors of churches are to be decorated, while English iconoclasm of the seventeenth century is an overspill from social revolution and thus part of one of the largest shifts in human consciousness from medieval and magical ways of thinking to increasingly rationalized modern modes. So the Byzantine case can continue to be seen as an episode in the history of art, while the denuded English interiors get their poignancy from their unwitting participation in the story of scientific progress.

In both cases ruin shows itself as emptiness and absence. Old things haven't mouldered – they've simply been removed. How do we recognize blankness as ruin if we never get to see what formerly filled the space? Intuitively (because the remnants don't feel complete)? Or by laborious reconstruction via written texts, which describe the old state, usually while pursuing other courses entirely – recounting an important visit or recording a repair – and less often than these, by using those rarer texts which itemize what's taken away.

Then one looks again at the spaces and notices broken-off heads or arms and blocked up openings. Aside from the general impression of bareness, perceiving ruin in English churches becomes a kind of historical study. On top of which these are usually ruins currently in use, many of which underwent re-medievalization in the nineteenth and early twentieth centuries. By an odd twist of human intention we get most in our present search from restitutions carried out in a different Puritan spirit by architects following the abstemious rules of spab or something like them.

The later history of Byzantine churches has often ruined them much further, because they were eventually taken over by an alien cult in most of the old empire. This is Islam, which has been aggressively iconoclastic through much of its history, or aniconic as some experts prefer to call it. Churches in Constantinople were regularly converted to mosques, often in such a rough and ready way that much survived under plaster and whitewash, so the most magnificent survivors could be de-simplified again in the early twentieth century and opened as museums. Greater numbers continue to function as mosques, realigned to face Mecca. These are among the world's most affecting ruins, whose old identities are clumsily and unintentionally treasured under their current use.

Iconoclasm in Byzantium originally proceeded in see-saw fashion, periods of destruction followed by restitution and then another return of the smashers. Passions ran extremely high in the first period of state-sponsored iconoclasm. The city had been seriously threatened by a Muslim siege in AD 717 and these misfortunes were blamed on the barbarous images inspired, it was alleged, by demon-worshipping Gentiles. Perhaps it seemed that the pagan gods had somehow insinuated themselves into Christian spaces. Milton found a roundabout way of introducing heathen gods from the Hebrew Bible into *Paradise Lost*. He did it by assigning them places as devils in Hell, and then went on to create a lot of sensuous excitement in their vicinity. They needed to be destroyed, but their downfall made it possible to relish them as you bid them goodbye.

The eighth-century iconoclasts were driven by a more literal-minded fury. It was thought particularly insulting to represent the living God with dead matter. Extreme opinion held that the only legitimate images were those made of the same material they wanted to represent, so Christ was truly depicted only in bread and wine. There are stories of painters forced to trample and spit on their own paintings if they wanted to live. I haven't found any painter-martyrs, but these are not hostilities safely confined to the history of art.

The iconoclasts were so successful in getting rid of icons that the only earlier ones to survive – just fourteen of them – escaped by being holed up in the remote monastery of St Catherine in the Sinai desert. The iconoclasts have in their turn been obliterated by history;

A Byzantine
church ruined
and salvaged
as a mosque:
Kalendarhane
Camii, Istanbul.

their arguments survive almost entirely in accounts by their successors. These throw up wonderful puzzles of literalness: images lower down the walls are more likely to have been destroyed, not because they are easier to reach, as we lazily suppose, but because they are more often objects of adoration by ignorant believers who offer them candles and incense, though images can neither see nor smell. A certain family is ridiculed for choosing an icon as godfather to an infant, though it must have been the saint and not the picture they expected help from.

Where does the urge come from, to clear out and destroy elaborate furniture which instantly becomes worthless junk? Eighth-century Constantinople had two models nearby, an exuberant and powerful Muslim court in Syria, and the Hebrew Bible with its prohibitions of divine images and its stories of the destruction of idols. Muslim influence is never admitted, but the Hebrew examples are often dragged in, yet the distaste that powers iconoclasm runs deeper than any mandate from whatever authority – a monkish hatred of worldliness, which would extend its anathema much further than rulers, who are only using iconoclasm, ever feel the need to do.

Violence in English churches

Like Byzantine, English iconoclasm comes in waves: Tudor destructions followed by reassertions of the image and the old ritual complexities under Archbishop Laud, followed by further cleansing and then by another Restoration. The earlier phase, which included the Dissolution of the Monasteries, has left more dramatic ruins, not just whole abbeys, convents and priories, but chancels falling into ruin because parishes couldn't afford to take them over after the Dissolution. The later phases produced nothing so dramatic but have left a stronger mark on the country's imagination. Religious painting practically disappeared in England for a couple hundred years and after that it was too late. A revival by the Pre-Raphaelites (so cumbrously named) produces genre paintings on Christian subjects enhanced by ethnologically accurate detail, a laborious way of returning religion to its roots.

The seventeenth-century iconoclasts aimed to re-primitivize Christianity using the same source as the Byzantines, the Hebrew Bible, but in a different way. The most notorious iconoclast of the period, William Dowsing, visited 100 churches in Cambridgeshire and 150 in Suffolk, smashing stained glass, mutilating sculptures, ripping up brass inscriptions, destroying altar rails and steps, and pulling down crosses, crucifixes and wooden angels. He wasn't a mindless vandal though; he had a public appointment and carried out the destruction in an orderly manner. Dowsing had lived in Suffolk all his life, a solid yeoman farmer and a learned man in his own way. He had a sizeable library, mostly religious controversy but including the Greek historian of Rome, Polybius. Dowsing was an especially avid collector of Parliamentary sermons, which he annotated meticulously with biblical references. In the end he bound 146 of these into six volumes and then sat down to read through them all over again.

Dowsing kept a journal, which records each of his visits and the action taken. These are mostly a bare tally, 'We brake down 40 superstitious pictures, destroyed 68 cherubim, removed 2 Orates, took down the altar rails and gave them to the poor, gave order for the steps to be taken down.' The orate is the Latin request to pray for the dead, considered superstitious by Puritans; the steps set off the chancel as special, like screens and rails, also always removed. Intense concern is focused on the altar, which the Puritans want turned into a table and detached from the eastern wall. Facing the east and inclining the body toward the altar are positions and movements the reformers want to make impossible. It feels as if we have entered a maze of detail and that to appreciate Dowsing's work we need to become involved in a set of minor liturgical disputes.

The bulk of Dowsing's campaign lasted only four months from Christmas week of 1643 to April of the following year, 1644. He began with the chapels of Cambridge colleges. The longest entry in the journal finds him among the doctors at Pembroke College. He begins by breaking and pulling down 80 superstitious pictures, but the legality of his action is immediately challenged by one of the Fellows. An account of a lengthy disputation follows, in which Dowsing confidently rebuffs one sally after another, armed to the teeth as he is with biblical pronouncements about idols. It's his own version of the contest we are reading, to be sure, but it feels as if Dowsing's reading of the Bible has been more focused and intense than theirs, so that if you take Scripture as the final authority, he will win the argument, and he does.

Only once is there a clear expression of class feeling when Dowsing in exasperation or triumph tells the dons that his child could preach as well as they, meaning has as good a command of Scripture, perhaps. Starting at Cambridge and wading fearlessly in, Dowsing is asserting a kind of social authority that religious conviction has given a new class of self-taught citizen. He has been called a bureaucratic Puritan, but is something more, a quiet revolutionary of an alarmingly methodical sort.

There's now a careful edition of Dowsing's *Journal* which would permit a Tour of the Ruins, checking the current state of each church against Dowsing's tally and trying to picture the missing images and appliances in their original richness. The editors have supplied detail about later alterations that have sometimes destroyed features which escaped Dowsing. At least one set of wall paintings whitewashed by Tudor reformers and rediscovered in 1874 has since vanished; brass memorials overlooked by Dowsing have occasionally been stolen since.

There have been attempts to calculate how much stained glass was destroyed in the English Reformation, both branches, a melancholy exercise. The big west window of Winchester cathedral is composed of thousands of fragments left over from a seventeenth-century window-smashing spree. Apparently visitors sometimes mistake it for a recent piece of abstract art, abstract art which is regarded by some writers as an even more lethal attack on the image than any that preceded it.

Sometimes it is easy to think that bleak later cults regularly come in to cancel earlier richness, more or less brutally, as the Spaniards did the Mayan, as Protestant fundamentalism does all over Latin America again today. Christianity began, in Rome at least, as a know-nothing movement of dumb conviction: that is how it looked to refined urbanites. So we find ourselves holding out against one rough beast after another slouching toward Bethlehem to be born.

Early Soviet Russia produced a whole sub-genre of iconoclastic art. Posters and disruptive graphics are the most familiar, but the most satisfying fulfilment of these impulses occurs in film. First you have the straightforward iconoclastic act, like tearing down the colossal statue of an enthroned tsar, which occurs as an impromptu festival attended by a large crowd, but short-lived. On film the pleasure in destruction is both speeded up and prolonged, and the statue is taken down and then jumps comically back onto its pedestal, only to be pulled to pieces all over again, so that the flimsiness of the exploded ideas can be seen again from new angles. Maybe the process, deconstruction followed by mocking reassembly and further less momentous decompositions, running reality first in one direction and then its contrary, forward then backwards, gave ideas to Constructivist designers, to reproduce in their own productions both the moment of energetic splitting and that of falling back into unforeseen disarrangement. Melnikov and Rodchenko's work often looks as if it has been

Lower panes of the great west window of Winchester Cathedral assembled in the 1660s from the debris of Puritan iconoclasm and now sometimes mistaken for abstract art.

broken or even smashed, but has gotten a burst of energy from the trauma and come out stronger than ever.

Graffiti in the history of art

Modern graffiti did not begin with the paintings on New York subway trains but that is where they first attracted serious attention and reached a wider audience. A better reason for starting there is that this is where the illegal activity of dispossessed teenagers connects with some of the key themes and methods of modernist art. From the mid-nineteenth century if not before, the modern city has been seen as a place of exhilarating but alienating speed and movement, of ceaseless self-devouring change. Various forms have been devised to capture these daunting inhuman forces set loose by the monstrous explosion of cities since the Industrial Revolution, including, above all, film, where the medium itself moves and studies movement, as in Vertov's *Man with a Movie Camera*, which follows the camera as it rides around the city on cars, trams and trains.

Graffiti begins in downtrodden neighbourhoods like the South Bronx or North Philadelphia where it finds a ruined landscape and degrades it further, adding an extra layer of ruin. At least that is how it looks to the uninstructed viewer, tired surfaces embellished with senseless scribbling that often cancels itself with overwriting at a competing slant so the combined effect is an interlace it would take an expert to untangle. Not that careful decipherment seems the right way to tackle this written-out aggression. Graffiti at Pompeii are interesting; graffiti that obscure a timetable at a local station are a nuisance.

You're right to think the letters aren't trying to tell you anything, but that doesn't mean they have nothing to say. This is the most primitive form of graffiti, the name of the scribbler which will only be known to a few of those passing, but that apparently is who the message is meant for, and the rest of us just have to put up with this teenage code taking up public space. Of course that is part of the message too; this is a crude political statement and that's what we don't like. But like art or primitive life-forms, graffiti evolve and begin to get more interesting. Even in the earliest there is already a certain play of imagination, if only we could see it. For the names are all pseudonyms, and with fiction, art rushes in: Tracy168, Phaze2, Stay High149, and five further aliases of Dondi: Naco, 2Hot, 2Many, White761, Asia. The numbers generally tell you where the graffiti writer lives, approximately. Painters go on being called 'writers' even when they've evolved into more conscious artists, keeping a link to the origins of the art in pure lettering, leading on to deconstructing individual letters and inventing new forms for them.

So the sides of subway cars are where this happens most flamboyantly. It is a site which appeals because of the danger of the yards, and is possible because the trains are still when parked at night, the time when vandalism can go undetected. But most of all because this is how graffiti can escape the ghetto neighbourhood and roam freely in the city from one end to the other. At some time in the early 1970s writers begin covering whole cars in single unified compositions that often ignore the windows, painting right over them.

At least one writer has been inspired by the WPA murals of the 1930s which decorate the interiors of post offices, train stations and government buildings. This is the legendary Lee, now Lee Quinones, who exhibits successfully in galleries. Legendary is what writers about graffiti call the most prominent artists, perhaps in rueful recognition that graffiti compositions, however magnificent, never last. So Lee got the idea of transferring the murals onto a huge moving canvas that travelled round the city ceaselessly, and he sloped his designs to make them seem to be rushing past even faster. It was work which borrowed the heroic monumentality of the trains and their elusiveness as well, work which vanished as quickly as it had appeared.

Graffiti evolved from tight black scribbling on despised surfaces into gigantic rainbow-hued paintings moving freely through space, but they never left behind their roots in the painter's nickname which still formed the main material on the hundred-foot canvas, the letters now bloated or twisted beyond recognition. Wilful obscurity had been part of graffiti from the beginning, and as they got more pleasing to look at, it seemed to increase. Graffiti had begun as something like the code of a gang, a private language, but as it became more successful or more noticeable this innocence became hard to preserve. Writers and photographers produced books about graffiti as an important urban phenomenon, forming relationships with the kids in the process, who had already been trying to record their work with primitive paper cameras and began to cooperate with professionals to get better images.

New York subway car with graffiti, 1989.

Successive mayors of New York decided that graffiti represented a serious threat to social order, and even claimed that if graffiti could be controlled then crime would drop and peace return to the city. After some false starts, the kids were successfully kept away from the trains and the most monumental and exciting graffiti all disappeared. Now like the work of Matta-Clark they can be seen only in books.

The books show graffiti in their natural habitat, and in the case of the trains, one habitat after another. It's a vision of urban decay both exhilarating and frightening. So if not ruins themselves, graffiti are drawing attention to the fact that we live in a ruin, and therefore the politicians may not be entirely wrong to see them as enemies of this particular social order and of the complacency rulers depend on.

The photographs show that graffiti are making much more powerful comment on the condition of the city than their creators can possibly be conscious of. Many 'writers' are articulate and self-aware, but they don't theorize themselves or their work, and erecting big intellectual superstructures on them seems a travesty. These works are so authentically rooted in particular places, and so illustrative themselves of the world they grew up in, they rebuff explication as if by some powerful magnetism.

Maybe the code of the graffitists is the best explanation of what they are about. Graffitists cannot buy their materials; they must steal them, not only because they couldn't afford the amount of paint they need, but because the activity is outside legality and ordinary ownership from start to finish. The location must be highly visible, forbidden and if possible dangerous to reach. A recent graffiti film takes 'Tonight the Streets are Ours' as its theme song, and the surge of the music sweeps us up in not just infringement on property but complete capsizing of daytime possession. Is it immature machismo or deep utopian longing and a vision of a world remade?

There's a tradition or at least a precedent for regarding damage as a kind of form or anti-form that can express certain kinds of truth. Film-makers like Stan Brakhage welcome flaws in filmstock as humanizing or particularizing the material, and at other times attack the film surface, scratching, gouging, eating away at its bland integrity to produce a ruined result which represents a form of experience. Graffiti are supremely vulnerable, look tattered before they are old, get written on (though this is taboo for other graffitists except in certain circumstances), get rained on, and can't control their edges. They read continuously with the peeling wall beyond, are islands in a sea of filth or of soulless order, and hang onto a precarious existence in the face of general hostility. They give a speeded-up sense of how fast a city ruins and changes.

After graffiti go up, a strange inversion takes place. Now the writer must police the work and make sure it isn't attacked. Sometimes the subculture of graffitists sounds like a tightknit community; alternatively it is vicious war in which artists get beaten up, knifed, shot, warned off patches they thought were theirs. And then there's arrest and jail; those who keep at it for long often end up in prison. The worst stories of violence I've heard come from a white graffitist who, bored by life in a middle-class suburb, fled to the ghetto; he couldn't be stopped, but someone certainly tried. The rare white graffitists seem possessed and driven beside the more common Hispanics and blacks: they don't have automatic entry to the subculture, but then maybe no one does – there are interesting descriptions of lengthy apprenticeships.

Maybe in my fascination with how completely the painter fits with, belongs in or owns the places he works, I'm simply caught up in an outsider fantasy of the denizen united with the *terroir*. Sometimes territory is chosen not given: one of the most ingenious choices is to claim a bus route and keep up lots of sites along it, from one end to the other, that need regular checking and maintenance. Now we are entering the world of turf wars, and maybe watching *The Wire* on power relations in the ghetto is what we need to do next.

In fact it's possible that the best training for understanding graffiti would be to sample the enormous genre of graffiti films, beginning with *Wild Style* (directed by Charlie Ahearn) and *Style Wars* (directed by Henry Chalfant) of 1983, and ending with *Infamy* (Doug Pray) of 2005 and *Exit through the Gift Shop* (Banksy) of 2010. At times these are like those wildlife films that try to catch shy creatures behaving naturally. Some of the most interesting graffitists, like Dondi, are practically mute, but nevertheless you get a strong sense of thoughtful people intensely engaged by the places they are in, not mindless vandals but contrary folk who've forced the world, which ordinarily leaves no place for them, to sit up and take notice.

The line between graffiti and street art: one of these artists includes a website and e-mail address in his composition. The website is still active in 2015.

But nothing stands still, and at some point in the 1990s more conventionally trained artists become interested in the idea of the transient, stumbled-upon urban location as a more authentic venue for their work than the gallery, so they move outdoors and onto the battered and neglected surfaces of the inner city.

Street Art, sometimes known as Post-Graffiti, has been called the quintessential art movement of the twenty-first century. It can be tricky to distinguish clearly from graffiti, but roughly speaking it appears when images replace glorified lettering and graduates of art schools take over from the denizens of urban ghettos – take over in the sense of occupying the same kind of illegal urban sites and filling them with images that comment on the squalor and decay that surround them. Graffiti are often inspired by the imagery of cartoons, comic books and advertising. Street art draws on the same sources though it's more likely to treat them with conscious irony. Irony isn't a main ingredient in most graffiti, but maybe Lee, who's been called the Picasso of subway art, is an exception. The more layered results in street art are often fascinating, but its arrival resembles what happened when well-heeled buyers drove out the artists from Manhattan lofts and London docklands.

Street art's practitioners can hop on planes and turn up in Berlin, Tokyo, Nairobi or the West Bank, making their own *engagé* comments on the inequalities they find. It doesn't seem fair to fault them for not being ghetto kids, and yet . . . graffiti as a global phenomenon cut loose from place seems even more crazy than an architecture in which the main buildings in Beijing are designed by architects who've barely visited China.

A graveyard, the ultimate ruin

Tony Harrison's poem 'V' begins in a graveyard, a common site for archaeologists, an archetypal place of ruin where there's more beneath than above the surface. This one is a particular derelict cemetery in Leeds, the poet's home town, which lies on a short cut to a nearby football ground. So the only signs of current life are left by drunken louts who drop their Harp cans and scrawl one-word curses like 'Cunt', 'Nigger' and 'Paki' on the tombstones.

Harrison is the right poet to confront them, who wrote a satyr play like a kind of graffiti scrawled on the dignity of high tragedy and who dredges up a childish vandalism of his own that helps him collapse the lout and himself into one, standing on shaky ground eaten out by coal mining underneath the graves, older vegetable ruins even than the corpses – corpses which are the ruins that underlie all others for anyone who is getting older and more visibly a ruin himself. Being rooted in a place, which I feel it is essential for true graffiti to be, strikes more restless people as too much like standing on your own grave.

Death in the 'Iliad'

There are an extraordinary number of corpses in the *Iliad*, or at least of separate deaths. Death is always individualized, but only up to a point, because once underway it is over in a flash, and the victim's shield clatters on him like the lid of a coffin that marks a clear end. Enemies always recognize each other, sometimes insult each other by name, but even when there's not time for that and the kills are just lists, they are lists of *names* of the dead. One of the most surprising moments in the whole poem comes when the poet says out of the blue, 'I'm not a god, I don't know the names of all the dead' as if the battle he tells is only the tip of an iceberg, which is not how it feels at all. The deaths in this poem of slaughter can be counted, and they add up to 140-odd, far less than we would have predicted.

Death is never far off, and is famously presented with an unflinching directness. The spear enters the victim's body at a particular place, just above the nipple or where the neck joins the shoulder, and there's often a dramatic unpacking, the intestines spill out or the brain, but it takes no time at all and we move on. These carefully confined bits of gore are like diagrams or Russian Futurist paintings that come into focus at a few key nodes and leave the rest of the canvas blank.

There are extraordinarily few wounds in the whole poem; I think you could count them on the fingers of one hand. Death is grim but not a lingering evil. Corpses don't hang about, don't pile up, don't rot. Homer saves the whole idea of the body as the most heartrending sort of ruin until near the end of the poem, after announcing in the first lines that dogs and birds have had lots of flesh to chew on since this war began.

The idea that this poem had a distinct author and that he wrote it down will violate the preferred theories of many current readers. There are plenty of signs of the oral rather than literate culture that we prefer to imagine it springing from, first of all ready-made phrases that help the poet produce lines of the right length at the required speed without having to think much, and then more sizeable repetitions of whole speeches that a messenger is now relaying in a new setting. The first time we meet this it probably seems naïve but before long we're relishing the reappearance of the already known like the return of a musical theme.

So maybe we are able to think of the poem as a grand cultural relic miraculously surviving into a alien world, composed by a wholly different method from anything later Greeks are used to, by nameless non-individual singers who nonetheless manage to preserve a vast, intricately organized edifice without really comprehending what they are passing on. There have been critics like Wilamowitz who think our present *Iliad* is the ruin of a great poem, spoiled by the tampering of lesser writers who came after. But the commonest view for much of the last century is that the poem has the delicious innocence of an illiterate product in touch with the Mycenaean times it treats, though it is widely accepted that there was a cataclysmic cultural break between Mycenae and any of the possible dates for the poem. Writing was lost for four centuries, and material impoverishment bred nostalgia for the lost heroic age.

Maybe there's a better case for thinking that the poem issues from an early stage of written culture, and the relics of oral culture we find in it are ruins of an earlier mode frozen there like insects in amber or chance burials in a peat bog.

Whatever its roots in a preliterate past, the poem's later history is literate through and through in ways both trivial and profound: its division into books happens to match the number of letters in the Greek alphabet, so each book can be identified with its own letter. One of these books is practically turned over to the peripheral and paradoxical subject of the earthen ramparts the Greeks have built to wall off their ships from Trojan attack. This construction mirrors the walls of Troy and prompts the poem's strange foreshadowing of their eventual ruination. Everything human is eventually reduced to indistinguishable rubble: even the proud signs left by the winners will eventually rot and leave barely a trace, besides one last reminder, the poem we are reading, inspired as we now know by those sad remains.

The most perverse waste in the conflict is the inaction of the greatest hero, Achilles, who has been festering in his tent or hut through most of the poem, holding up the action and thereby allowing space for all the indecisive happenings which constitute the poem to occur in. Of course we've known all along how the poem will end, or rather how the war will. We know much less than we think about how Homer will conduct the working out.

Christopher Logue notices that fighting doesn't really begin until Book 5. The early parts of *War Music*, his magical rendition of the *Iliad* material, make it utterly strange and foreign in spite of language of great directness, language so violent it presages or pre-empts the battle and raises the fear that there will be no more stops to pull out when wilder events come along. Logue's *Iliad* has no ordinariness, no lulls, and recalls the French sculptor who said that the poem made him imagine all human figures a foot taller.

Maybe Logue participates in the inverse romanticism of an illiterate Homer after all, who brings to his jaded audience, like *The Wire* in our day, the freshness of a brutal, preliterate world where death is everywhere but barely exists because it hasn't fully entered consciousness. Modern audiences are horrified but intrigued by the ubiquitous cruelty of these worlds, which sticks out particularly in the harsh treatment of suppliants. There is the terrible case of Achilles meeting a young man again whom he had sold into slavery after catching him in an orchard. Heroes don't feel pity, and re-meeting him, Achilles spears this clinger to his knees without any of the regret we want him to feel.

Pity is fatal to the idea of heroism abroad in this poem, and it begins to creep in toward the end. Now nearly everyone is experiencing or foreseeing ruin of one kind or another. Achilles thinks the blow-flies will start infesting Patroclus' corpse; Priam has a hallucination of being ripped to pieces by his own dogs; Andromache fantasizes her son thrown off the ramparts by a Greek and dashed to pieces.

A similar process overtakes both Hector and Achilles, whose fates, one achieved, the other still to come, double one another. Cornered outside the walls of the city, Hector becomes almost a kind of Hamlet in imagining various possible courses of action. Imagination is paralysis, and it overtakes Achilles too. He becomes more interesting, and the most beautiful moment in the poem now appears, but this deepening is fatal for the single-minded hero. The Trojan king visits the Greek camp to reclaim Hector's body and kneels and kisses Achilles' hands before he says a word. It is an indescribably horrible act, yet it allows Achilles to relinquish his anger, at least temporarily, thinking of his own father he won't see again. At this point, with killer and victim both united and divided by tears, the heroic certainties of the rest of the poem break down, and after this there can never be another poem like this one.

In *The Wire* the drug culture of the black ghettos of Baltimore is just a primitive bubble or preserve in a wider world, but with its archaic hierarchies, its alarming physicality and the abruptness of its deaths, it serves many of the purposes for us that the stark society of the battlefield supplies later readers of the *Iliad*. Apparently many English speakers watch *The Wire* with subtitles, their way of saying that this language isn't entirely recognizable as English. Is it an archaic, earlier stage of English whose strangeness is partly pre-literate, at times of great rhetorical power, at others of fearsome brevity?

Among Homer's archaisms are certain ruin-words, mainly adjectives, that no one can claim securely to understand, which, it has been proposed, he didn't understand either, but saved into his verses out of respect for their supposed antiquity. One of them – amumon – had usually been translated 'blameless' by analogy with a similar known word, until Anne Amory Parry insisted that the word couldn't apply to Aegisthus, Clytemnestra's accomplice in murder, so it is probably better understood as 'handsome'. Even so it remains a patch of obscurity, like a knot in wood that there's no way to straighten into intelligible, smooth running grain.

Archaisms like Spenser's are easy to recognize as conscious expressions of the ruin-mentality treasuring quaintness that isn't quite intelligible, like a spot of mental mist. Archaism in Shakespeare isn't usually like that, but an accident of the later history of the language, which has left this one stranded while welcoming other equally eccentric coinages into familiarity. So I wonder if we couldn't posit something like that in Homer, and admit that we can't always tell how deliberate the peculiarities (as seen by us) in his language are.

The famous misplaced epithets that are such a disconcerting feature of the poem have often been read as moments when the poet is overmastered by the verse form. These are epithets applied when they don't fit the context or even violently contradict it, like calling Achilles 'swift footed' when he's immobilized by grief, or Hector 'killer of many' when he's a helpless battered corpse. Those are crude examples: the effect can be more muted or more complicated, so that we can hardly unravel all the implications of reminding us of some talent or propensity in the character that doesn't seem operative at this particular moment. The misplaced epithet can be a way of calling up other places and times, specific ones, or more generally widening our field of view.

Toward the end of the poem its main characters are much given to foreseeing their own ends, more often than not ends which aren't going to happen in just the way the character supposes. I. A. Richards speaks of 'poetic enjoyment of the foreknowledge of death' as a main feature of the reader's experience. Rather early in the long history of Wagner's *Ring* cycle the composer, fed up with hostile responses from opera critics, imagined building a special theatre and filling it with a sympathetic crowd of devotees who would enjoy one performance of this proto-*Ring*, *Siegfried's Death / Siegfrieds Tod*, after which he would take down the theatre and burn the only copy of the score. This kind of ruin-enthusiasm is more an Achillean than a Homeric impulse: when the hero has his mind fixed on the decay of his friend's corpse, the poem is also remembering that the other soldiers must eat: here in Achilles' compound, rotting and replenishment go forward at the same time right next to each other.

That might be called a synoptic vision of how a battlefield works, but Homer seems to feel strong reluctance to paint vast landscapes of war; when he finally gets round to writing about the war itself Christopher Logue creates a filmic panorama steeped in the pervasive stench of carnage, something which, Logue makes us realize, Homer himself has studiously avoided. Even David Jones writing about the trench warfare of 1914–17, whose perspective is the most individual and inward imaginable, sets his own gnarled thoughts in a wider ruined landscape. So far the ruin keeps its distance from the men: trees are the principal casualties, their big corpses split open by explosives, exposing leprous flesh.

Jones is narrating the 'Great War' from so far underneath that no one knows where they're going, why they're stopping or what it's all for. Their immediate goal is to stay as dry as they can. Their larger goal is the Big Ship, a mythical item that will appear some day and take everyone home. We're down among the nameless, but here they are the ones who have names. The men who would appear in the *Iliad* or *Flandriad* of this war, if there could be one, make fleeting appearances, and aren't known by their names but by their braid and eerie self-assurance.

It's probably true that when Homer says he doesn't know the names of all the fighters he is making a similar social distinction, but the comparison seems misguided, as does the description of Homeric fighters as an aristocratic society. If they're aristocrats, that's virtually all there is, so the word becomes practically useless in try-ing to describe the poem. Speaking of inclusions and exclusions, it is much more remarkable that the Trojans – the enemy – get as much space as they do. By a strange twist, since fighters are paid special attention when they die, and since the Trojans lose more men, the losing side attracts more sympathy. Rachel Bespaloff makes the most fervent case for Hector as the real hero of the poem. I can't help read-ing it this way: suffering and the prospect of suffering humanize the Trojans, and at the end there's even heroism in defeat, acknowledged by Achilles looking at Priam, who has done something Achilles could not.

There's a tradition of portraits of losers which might at times over-lap with but doesn't coincide with tragedy as a genre, which includes the Pergamene sculpture of *The Dying Gaul* curled ingeniously into the circle of his horn which lies on his shield, very satisfying but a fantastical coincidence. The last moments of life before he becomes a corpse, cold as marble, are magically suggested by the carver's skill, which casts a spell on both of us. This figure in warm yellow marble

A corpse as the ultimate ruin: *The Dying Gaul* from Pergamon, Roman marble copy of 3rd-century Hellenistic bronze, originally part of a larger victory monument.

is only a copy: the original was bronze and much larger, but only a part of a complicated victory monument crowing over the defeated, or giving them their due.

Seamus Heaney's 'The Grauballe Man' resuscitates one of the bog burials found in the 1950s in Denmark, corpses ruined and preserved by water and the tannin of the bog which is supplied by rotting vegetation. These are usually victims of harsh punishment, adulterers, false accusers, outcasts who by an odd twist in the rules of decay have outlived their tormenters in ruined but shockingly recognizable form, unintentional sculptures that Heaney all these years after likens to *The Dying Gaul* at one end and the latest reprisals in Northern Ireland at the other, in a long continuum of slaughter.

Apparently the *Iliad* has been translated many more times into English than into any other language. How to explain this – is it the triumphal spirit of Empire claiming kinship with the colonizers of the distant past? It depends what kind of poem you think it is, a strong anti-war piece as Simone Weil found it in 1940, that spoke sharply to her situation in occupied Europe, or a sort of ruin-poem, a relentless catalogue of waste. Not everyone who sits down to translate the *Iliad* is thinking the same thing, but maybe a sense of the sadness that is part of victory as well as defeat that runs so strongly through the poem has often been a part of its fascination.

Apparently the *Iliad* is unusual among epics in being centred on a war fought over a city. The fall of Troy never happens in the poem; for that we must consult Book 2 of the *Aeneid* with its spectacular scenes of nocturnal destruction lit by flames and the moon. A huge city burning became a favourite subject for exquisite paintings on copper in the sixteenth century, and inspired wonderful patches of rhetoric that get lost in Shakespeare's *Hamlet*.

Berlin, 1945

The Second World War produced plenty of ruined cities, Berlin and Tokyo among the most emblematic, powerfully conveyed in grey photos showing places barely recognizable as cities, more like archaeological digs stretching improbably far into a desert somewhere, so thoroughly pulverized that nothing stands out.

Detroit was saved by that war from crippling unemployment in the auto industry, and got back on its feet for a last fling of chrome and fins and unconscious fantasy. With hindsight, it is possible to see signs of the impending ruin stretching back as far as the end of the war, but no one saw it coming in the Fifties.

From early in its history the whole mechanism of car manufacture has spread devastation wherever it turns. The assembly line on which the industry is founded is a powerful destroyer of the souls of workers, memorably catalogued by Studs Terkel in the 1970s. Planned obsolescence, possibly the brainchild of Alfred P. Sloan of General Motors, treats last year's model as junk and fills the world with virtually indestructible rubbish as recorded in *God's Own Junkyard*. Early in the period auto executives began to treat the city of Detroit as junk, abandoning it to construct new towns at its edge which avoid its complexities and use the car and its needs as the main principle of planning. Since you've already destroyed the streetcar network to encourage car use, these suburbs need to be connected to the centre with freeways,

The centre of Berlin reduced to rubble in 1945.

Ruined automotive plant, Detroit, from Julien Temple's *Requiem for Detroit?* (2010).

for which you need to plough wide corridors through neighbourhoods along the way.

So perhaps it should have surprised no one that when U.S. auto manufacturing proved incapable of adapting to the world of scarce oil which no longer wanted its deliberately oversized, deliberately inefficient products, Detroit became the most complete urban ruin in the developed world. But it did surprise and still surprises almost everyone. The opening scenes of Julien Temple's riveting film *Requiem for Detroit?* show derelict cars which were once gorgeous, with their portholes, scoops and mock torpedoes in chrome now dulled not glittering, with all their elaborate devices now vandalized. Then come the ruined hulks of factories and theatres with sagging roofs and decaying decoration.

Our method of negotiating the deserted districts is of course the despised automobile, in its most egregiously outmoded forms. Our guides are the urban explorers, small farmers, activist-authors, rehabbed criminals, street artists, recyclers and sociologists who have sprung up to inhabit the post-urban landscape. Is Detroit a freak or the city of the future, some of them wonder?

Judging from a sample of the baroque excesses of the current stage of capitalist decay, huge enterprises like Wal-Mart that send customers wandering down the aisles of aircraft hangars, a much cheaper alternative to city streets, or others like Amazon who pen up their employees in secretive warehouses like forced labour camps, or a financial sector so oblivious to reality that 2,700 investment bankers in London are each paid in excess of £1 million in 2013, judging by signs like these, multiplied many times, social ruin on a daunting scale is only hidden from us because we are conveniently shielded from the truth.

7

Dreams of Recovery

RUSKIN OFTEN TURNS BUILDINGS that are complete in reality into ruined fragments in his drawings. He isn't doing this simply in order to break off a feasibly small chunk for the kind of attention he intends to pay. Ruskin's fragments are often lopsided in their proportions and uneven in their level of finish, wayward in technique and defiantly incomplete. Wayward, but not really careless: even an element that seems whimsical to start with, like the inconsistent colouring in a famous rendering of an upper corner of the facade of S. Michele at Lucca, actually helps convey the blinding glare of the afternoon sun. And the cockeyed straggle of the drawing showing through gives a faithful impression of the disorderly vitality of the medieval design.

In its haste (more apparent than real) and insouciance (not incompatible with a highly intellectual approach) this drawing gets you much closer than a more balanced rendering could to the spirit of the building, or to the Ruskinian ideal of the hand of the carver making itself felt continuously across the surface, lending the whole building a quivering intelligence like a creature's.

A drawing like the study of two incomplete niches on a flamboyant Gothic church at Caen makes the point instantly why for Ruskin nothing but the true medieval surface, dirty and overgrown though it may be, is the only thing that will do. Irregularity is piled on irregularity – the sensitive variance of the sculptor's hand, which can't be made to obey mindlessly like a machine, is overlaid by vagaries of weather shaping the stone further. By frost breaking off the most fragile bits of carving, by rain finding weak seams in stone that erode

Ruskin called this drawing 'Part of the façade of the Destroyed Church of San Michele in Foro at Lucca sketched in colour', 1846, and he collected pieces of green serpentine which had fallen out of its mosaic.

Ruskin, detail of niches at St Sauveur, Caen, 1848, pencil and wash, where radically inconsistent treatment increases the sense of movement and of ruin.

faster and, most fugitive of all, by light and shadow, which the work caters for but can't control. Drawings like this are powerful teachers of how to find an infinite complexity of form and sensation in the smallest stretches of old masonry, and they mount the strongest arguments against improving decaying buildings by renewing parts of them as they wear out. For someone infected by the spirit of Ruskin's drawings, the best buildings are often the most ruined or at least the ones whose principles of construction let them accept decay gracefully.

Against restoration

Inspired by Ruskin, a group of anti-restorers appeared at the end of the nineteenth century, whose ideal was repairs that didn't show, that left ancient walls leaning and floors uneven, stabilized by new support that hid itself inside the walls. If visible elements needed to be replaced, they weren't faked but renewed plainly in a different material without pseudo-medieval detail, as in the famous case of wooden tracery in Gothic openings of a church in Lincolnshire.

So it was a more strenuous allegiance to Gothic detailing that eventually drove some English architects away from imitation of recognizable historical styles and toward more generic inspiration from vernacular buildings. A parallel development in theatrical performance and stage design aimed to strip away the expensive and distracting sets of Late Victorian productions and return to what was imagined to be the bare Elizabethan stage. The stated purpose of the Elizabethan Stage Society, founded by William Poel in 1894, was to produce Shakespeare's plays in the closest approach to the physical circumstances of the playwright's own time, that is, practically without props, in simplified costumes and intimate settings where the text would again have pride of place.

Along with this return to an original purity of performance arose the project to reconstruct the physical theatre of Shakespeare's time in its original location at Bankside in Southwark. In some ways this dream couldn't have been further from the Ruskinian inspiration of the Arts and Crafts. The idea of a Shakespearean theatre was almost entirely conjectural; no physical traces were known to survive. Only in 1989, when plans to rebuild Shakespeare's Globe were far advanced, did minimal remains of the old Globe and a fuller floor plan of the Rose appear as if on cue on commercial building sites nearby.

But when the project began there were only sketchy drawings and prints of the overall form of these buildings from Shakespeare's time, and a single sketch of the stage itself by a Dutch visitor, discovered by a German researcher in 1888. Besides this, there existed brief verbal allusions and far from full descriptions in the journals of foreigners (mostly) reporting on plays they'd seen, and building accounts for another early theatre that had no direct connection with Shakespeare.

Then – so slender is the record – the plays themselves, and especially the stage directions they contain, were meticulously combed for clues as to what the old spaces of performance were like.

Lack of evidence could not be allowed to put the brakes on this compulsion forever, a compulsion which has overtaken so many, and not just native English speakers. The great German Shakespeare translator Ludwig Tieck commissioned the greatest theatre architect of the day, Gottfried Semper, to produce a design. Sir Edwin Lutyens did a half-size mock-up for the 'Shakespeare's England' Exhibition of 1912 in which fragments of the plays were performed, complete with boisterous groundlings and girls selling oranges.

Shakespeare with all the trimmings

This sounds like a prank, but there is more to this movement than that, stemming perhaps from the feeling that Shakespeare's genius is a mystery we cannot penetrate – perhaps a physical crutch could help us become Elizabethans so Shakespeare's work would no longer be so utterly beyond us. The number of replicas or reconstructions of the Globe worldwide seems to stand somewhere between fifteen and twenty at any moment, most of them in the USA, followed by Germany and Japan. Britain has one of the latest but certainly the most serious entry so far, the brainchild of one man, Sam Wanamaker, an American actor of heroic persistence, who was fascinated by a model of the Globe he'd seen at the Chicago Fair in 1934, went to live in Southwark in the 1950s and devoted himself to the project of a new Globe from 1970 onward. He assembled a team of experts of all kinds to advise him, including theatre historians, literary critics, architectural theorists, authorities on London, on early maps, on Elizabethan dress, diet, art, furniture, music and of course architects, builders and designers.

The whole process lasted 27 years and the result is a building that Wanamaker, the real projector, did not live to see in use, a building of the 1990s built almost entirely by Tudor methods, without steel or concrete in its main body and without nails: the frame of English oak is held together by wooden pegs. It has the first thatched roof allowed in London since the Great Fire of 1666, made possible by a chemical spray for treating thatch that appeared in the 1980s. One of Wanamaker's advisors read about the new method in the *Financial Times*, which reported that insurers had accepted it.

Such are the twists and turns that chasing after authenticity sometimes throws up. It can be a hard taskmaster: the pit where the groundlings stand has a floor of concrete, not beaten earth covered in rushes, and the groundlings began by sitting on it, which is apparently not authentic behaviour, so the ground was lightly sprinkled with water before performances to keep them standing.

A performance at the reconstructed Globe, Bankside, London.

Once the building is up and functioning the idea of authenticity isn't finished with, but shifts to performance, and actors begin to think they're researchers into what Shakespeare is really about, which has been hidden or obscured until the Globe reveals it. Now the possibilities of what the new theatre can uncover seem practically limitless. Not all performances go all the way, but those following Original Practices lay special burdens on performers. Elaborate costumes made by Elizabethan methods, all buttons no zips, can take hours to put on, and constrain the body so that many familiar movements are impossible; you have to learn to walk and sit all over again. At a certain point Elizabethan cosmetics became a focus of interest: male actors taking female parts in the interest of authenticity are feminized by white face paint, but the main original ingredient, lead, has to be changed to chalk, to which oil must be added to produce the lead sheen, occasionally finished off with a dusting of crushed pearl, to achieve the ethereal shimmer seventeenth-century romantics required.

And so, increment by tiny increment and by the most circuitous route we are back at an overelaborated result. Decorative clutter has replaced purity and Shakespeare's text has been buried again under layers of distracting detail. In spite of the hazards and pitfalls though, in spite of the quixotic pursuit of the unattainable goal, there's something deeply touching about trying to put ourselves back into Shakespeare's time via such extravagantly literal devices.

The relation of such reconstructions to their present-day settings are always problematic: apparently Sam Wanamaker wanted the Globe to play a part in regenerating Southwark, formerly vibrant, currently (in 1970) depressed. Maybe it has happened somewhat as he wished. Another commentator insists that every visitor to the reconstructed Elizabethan space should first see the shrunken ruin of the Rose. Sixteenth-century people were noticeably smaller than us, and I've read that everything at the Globe has been scaled up by a tenth. Some experts think Wanamaker's calculations for the diameter of the building are much further off than that: it is 35 per cent bigger than the original. But after all the piecing together of fragmentary and finally inconclusive evidence, we must come out with something buildable and also habitable, by people as big as we are now.

Inventing American history

A visitor to the rebuilt colonial town of Williamsburg, Virginia, notices at once how spacious it is, with so much room between the scattered buildings it sometimes doesn't seem like a town at all. Is this the spaciousness of a settlement dispersing itself in a big continent, or is it just a sign that records and remains are sparse? Like the Globe, it is primarily the work of scholars in the first place; there was very little to start with, and especially the most important buildings, like the Governor's Palace, are reimagined from scratch.

In some way it's a much more momentous enterprise than any parallel in England like the Globe. Colonial Williamsburg adds a whole century to a nation's physical history, a century tinged here with an aristocratic, even monarchical flavour. The gardens are among the most satisfying but also the most entirely hypothetical elements. No English eighteenth-century garden is so complete. Looking down on the Palace garden and the streets that unfold beyond is like looking at a model of the whole eighteenth century. How satisfying it must have been to call an entire civilization back into existence.

Behind the Palace eighteenth-century vegetables are happily growing right before our eyes, while in the lean-to nearby cooks in eighteenth-century costume are preparing historically accurate meals. But in Williamsburg work isn't work but play, just as in Marie Antoinette's faux-rural hamlet at Versailles. The spaces between the buildings are left by the missing shops, now quarantined in a special district adjacent, called Merchant Square, which charms me with its tastefulness and then goes too far: 'Gentlemen's Clothing' a discreet sign says.

Williamsburg is the brainchild of the local rector and his friend John D. Rockefeller Jr, one of the richest men in America, made rich by oil and now in flight from the social consequences of that enterprise. There are no cars in Williamsburg, one of its most soothing features. By a strange twist, all the historical sites of the region – Jamestown, Yorktown and Williamsburg, all named after kings and dukes – are linked by a beautiful road, Colonial Parkway, where the route follows serpentine bends scaled up from a Picturesque garden, and overpasses are built of mellow old brick.

Colonial Williamsburg with reconstructed buildings and generous paving for visitors.

One of the most extreme quirks of the Globe is the occasional performance delivered in OP (original pronunciation), a rustic kind of speech much easier to understand than you would expect. At lunch in Virginia a man behind me is speaking in an accent I once knew very well, and I realize that he sounds exactly like my grandmother, who died in 1952. Now I feel I'm getting closer to what this journey is all about, the enthusiasm for ruins and for elaborate mock-ups are not really so far from each other, for that which is visibly collapsing and for extreme and quixotic forms of putting it back together.

When work began at Williamsburg in the 1920s, the colonial town was largely a hypothesis or figment lying almost two centuries distant, which meant none of the workers were reconstructing the town from physical memory. For many observers the project must have seemed dilettantish, without even the mild patriotic urgency of contemporary memorials in Washington to actors at Williamsburg like Jefferson. In 1945 everyone in Warsaw remembered what the city was like before its deliberate destruction the previous year. A German plan dating back at least to 1940 had proposed the obliteration of the Polish capital and its replacement with a much smaller German city. In the end it was bombers, not urban planners, who flattened the city much more quickly and probably more thoroughly than the planners had envisaged.

Undoing bombing

Soviet armies are reputed to have stopped short of Warsaw and watched the destruction, perhaps because Stalin wanted right-wing defenders of Poland eliminated before he took the city. So the buildings and inhabitants of Warsaw were caught between these various forces, with results you can read about in contemporary journals, and see in some astonishing aerial footage of the destroyed city in which barely a recognizable building remains. Maybe our eyes are too ready to read the destruction as more perfect and complete than it was, for there is also footage of workmen bashing away at nineteenth-century commercial buildings which could have been salvaged. Maybe a clean slate suited the new government of Poland better than the reminders of bourgeois institutions.

The impulse to rebuild the shattered Old Town of Warsaw didn't come from the government, who resisted such plans at first as not fitting with a new socialist Poland. Popular allegiance to the old core of the city proved impossible to repress because it was more than nostalgic and antiquarian. The German enemy had tried to obliterate the idea of Poland altogether, by attacking, displacing and degrading its people, and also by destroying physical evidence of their existence, particularly in cultural forms and above all in architecture.

So detailed reconstruction would be the only satisfying answer to the assault on Poland's identity. So much is riding on this effort and there is so little to go on. The old town is only a fragment of the whole but it will have to carry the burden for all the rest. The passion of the Polish restorers was extraordinary and their expertise was later drawn on across the Soviet bloc. Nonetheless severe restrictions on what they could achieve remained. So little of the actual fabric survived that the reconstructors were forced to depend on paintings by Bernardo Bellotto, Canaletto's nephew, one of the last eighteenth-century Venetian providers of 'picturesque views'. Bellotto's pictures are remarkably detailed given their modest size, but show buildings from one side only and give no clue about interior divisions or decorations. So we're left with facades.

Heavy dependence on Bellotto rather than later photographs predisposes the reconstructors to favour eighteenth-century structures

Market Place in the rebuilt Old Town of Warsaw. The reconstruction depended heavily on Bellotto's paintings and pre-war architecture students' drawings.

stripped of later accretions. Such historical cleansing is more accidental, more a solution thrust upon the devisers than the radical cleansing of the Acropolis in Athens in the early days of Greek independence, but the effect is the same, a certain bleakness and lack of sensuous complexity. The result sometimes looks more like a model of itself than the real thing. In Athens, other choices were possible; in Warsaw they were not.

The reconstructed Warsaw has been called a Disney fabrication by Fredric Jameson. Maybe we could concede that it feels decidedly false but can still count it a heroic and moving failure, not an instance of culture hijacked by entertainment, however much it appears now just the equipment of tourism.

Pictures taken right after the bombing of Dresden and Hamburg are the nearest thing to the images of Warsaw destroyed. W. G. Sebald writes about the strange German response to these horrors in some perplexity; he regards it as a response that is no response, which does not acknowledge what has happened. Finally Sebald has ventured so near the horror that he has to describe it himself. He does this with surprising force, but even this much is enough to show that it is an impossible task. Nonetheless, the glimpse that Sebald gives of the physical destruction of a very few of the thousands of victims in the firestorms of these cities is enough to cast many human concerns into the shade. Standing under this cloud, and in the perspective of all this meaningless pain, the reconstruction of a few buildings in Warsaw does look, momentarily, almost ridiculous. The rest of the rebuilt city was largely an exercise in the obliteration of memory, even more monotonous than those that Sebald finds in West Germany, decked out with a few false memories, street names honouring obscure communist martyrs, since removed.

It is bound to seem frivolous to compare ancient ruin-fields in Turkey, Sicily or Cambodia to devastated European cities at the end of the Second World War. Archaeologists wondering what can be done with a vast rubble of scrambled fragments no one alive has ever seen in any other state aren't under urgent necessity of helping people live among the debris. At Ephesus Austrian archaeologists could afford to spend nine years (1970–78) reassembling one building, or more precisely, one facade. True, it is a very special facade, a rare survivor of the most extreme late Roman building type. This is a ceremonial form inspired by theatre backdrops, which resembles the extravagant fictional architecture painted on the walls of rooms in Roman villas surviving at Pompeii above all. The wall dissolves in a filigree of spindly columns and delicate pediments that weave in and out like a whole city squeezed into the space of a single dwelling. A library occupied this building in Ephesus, built by an official to commemorate his father, and incorporating his tomb. So it's a multi-layered repository which blurs together historical piety and self-advertisement, as philanthropy has sometimes been known to do.

The Library of Celsus (the father's name) had been unearthed as long ago as 1902. Photographs show it as a collection of disconnected fragments only assembled into courses in one corner and not rising more than a couple of feet above ground level. Looking at these images, it is impossible to guess how you'd get anything resembling a building out of this mess. Besides, pride of place is given to something that has nothing to do with the Library, an impressive frieze of lifesize figures taking part in a procession. This artefact seemed important and detachable and was sent back to Vienna to be installed in the new Ephesus-museum. Later it was established that the so-called Parthian reliefs didn't belong to the Library in its original form, but had been

Library of Celsus, Ephesus, excavated in the early 20th century, and finally
reconstructed in the 1970s.

borrowed from another building to help in turning the library facade
into a grandiose fountain, following the destruction of the building's
interior in fires caused by an earthquake.

So the less distinguished rubble is left behind in Ephesus. But it
turns out that by carefully picking through the remaining pieces you
can find enough of them to do a decent reconstruction of the whole
facade, though why this project didn't get underway until the 1970s
remains a mystery. Even a non-expert can see a fair amount of fresh
stone in the result, especially in the inner layer of this layered composition, where it shows less. But the richness of the surviving carving
carries the viewer away, and the ingenuity of the overall design, which
took a lot of patient detective work to discover, makes this one of the
highlights of Roman architecture. Not long ago there was nothing to
be seen, and then it sprang out of the ground fully formed, as in the
old wartime trope of 'rising from the ruins'.

Anastylosis in the jungle

It is hard not to be swept up in the enthusiasm for whole buildings rather than miles of rubble, the illusion of buildings it has to be, for they remain paper-thin and less complete the closer you look. Why, other than luck, is it possible to reassemble some and not others? The library at Ephesus is richly carved and florid in overall geometry, which means that many of its separate pieces are distinctive and therefore easier to place correctly in the puzzle. When French archaeologists set off on a huge campaign of reconstruction at Angkor in Cambodia in 1931, they began with the smallest, most richly carved set of shrines, which always seemed to me an odd choice, but in fact it was eminently practical.

The miniature complex at Banteay Srei in Cambodia in an outlying location was one of the last to be 'discovered' and therefore hadn't been as extensively cleared, rearranged and trampled over as the better known precincts at Angkor. When reconstruction at Angkor began, Cambodia was still a French colony, and it carried on under French direction even after independence in 1953, until interrupted by fifteen years of civil war from 1970 onward, was resumed in the '80s and continues now as 'the largest outdoor university of archaeological conservation in the world.' Already in the French time most of the major complexes had been taken apart and rebuilt in the biggest campaign of anastylosis ever.

Why did it happen here? The Angkor site is probably the biggest archaeological site of comparable richness in the world. In the early years it was remote and hard to get to, buried in jungle and virtually uninhabited. Perhaps in those days, 1907–53, the sparse local population was easily discounted by the colonizers. Anyway, the French had a free hand in deciding what to do with the monuments, which had made a powerful impression on the first Europeans to come upon them. But apparently the archaeologists were initially haunted by the spectre of Eugène Viollet-le-Duc, the nineteenth-century restorer who had reconstructed French castles, cathedrals and fortified medieval towns, inventing and supplying missing features in pursuit of perfected versions of each type.

Lack of funds might have had just as strong an effect, limiting archaeologists' work at Angkor to clearing the jungle and propping up masonry on the point of collapse with wooden or concrete posts or strapping leaning walls with iron bands. A visit by a Dutch archaeologist in 1929 changed all that. The Dutch found Borobudur, the biggest ancient site in the Dutch East Indies, in a collapsed state, and between 1907 and 1911 they had taken it apart and put it back together so it stood up straight, more or less as originally constructed.

French architect Henri Marchal, the head curator at Angkor, paid a visit to Java, where he learned the Dutch technique, called anastylosis, and returned to put it to work at Angkor. Over the next fifteen years many of the most important buildings on the vast site received this treatment and were converted from disorderly ruins into intelligible models as close as possible to their original forms.

Anastylosis is a beguiling term which sounds both scientific and magical. It is appropriately Greek in origin, for it began on the Athenian Acropolis in the early days of independence when the ideas of Klenze won out over those of Schinkel, who wanted to plant a new royal palace on the hill, and then to use the world's most famous ruins as ornaments in its gardens. Klenze preferred to return the site to its classical state as far as possible, which entailed clearing away all the barbarities of succeeding ages, Byzantine and Ottoman above all.

When taking down Ottoman fortifications, the archaeologists found pieces of a building they recognized as the little temple of Athena Nike, which everyone assumed had been lost in a seventeenth-century explosion similar to that which blew a hole in the side of the Parthenon. Eventually enough pieces were found to guess at the overall form as well as the details of this building and to reconstruct it. This re-erection is generally regarded as the first anastylosis, which in this case consisted of extracting a ruin from inside another ruin, collecting and identifying all its pieces by laying them out on the ground in disassembled form, working out how they fit together and then reassembling them.

It sounds logical and unproblematic. But in the case of the Nike temple no one since the seventeenth century has ever seen it standing. Luckily a base is found that probably fits this building, so spacings of columns are known, but not their heights. Luckily too, not much is missing, though the fabric needs to be patched with significant amounts of new stone, and the whole project becomes more questionable as this eking out of gaps grows larger.

At Angkor anastylosis usually means taking apart a semi-collapsed building, keeping careful track of the pieces and then putting it back together. The taking apart of the Nike temple has already happened before the arrival of archaeologists, and no one has kept track of the pieces, which were used as filler inside a later building and therefore hidden from view. Something wonderful in these diminutive buildings, which burst out of more stolid larger ones, like the exquisite barque shrines buried in enormous pylons at Karnak in Egypt. They're jewel-like in more than one way, in their fineness and in their isolation from context as well. They become portable, like objects in museums, and are plopped down at Karnak in a little compound of their own, in sight of the main temple but not properly connected to it.

Old photographs of Banteay Srei reveal that the neat sequence of taking apart and putting together doesn't adequately describe what actually happened. It wasn't just a matter of levelling up bases and straightening leaning walls. Especially the upper parts – towers and roofs of galleries – were scattered across the site, and little buildings which are now nicely distinct were muddled with their neighbours in the debris of fallen stone.

Big red seedpods tapping you on the head or rainwater caught in inaccessible basins high on one of the artificial mountains can rank among the best moments at Angkor. The feeling that the presence of the local species and weather conditions were almost as important as the human constructions in the whole effect must have played a part in inspiring the French to leave one important temple group in its natural state, with cascades of stone blocking doorways and aggressive local trees enveloping stone pavilions in their roots before zooming higher. I thought it was quite a sophisticated idea to have a wilderness in the midst of what is mostly a more tended kind of garden, but Ta Prohm has always been popular, and has consequently picked up a nickname, the Tree Temple. In 2001 it appeared in *Lara Croft: Tomb Raider*, a film based on a video game, and its popularity surged.

At about the same time the Archaeological Survey of India, which had got a bad name in the 1980s for damage they had done, with the best intentions, to Angkor Wat, were given permission to restore

Ta Prohm, until then the last bastion of undisturbed ruin. They set about clearing low vegetation, re-erecting fallen galleries and installing wooden walkways for safety and order, but held off at first from taking down large parasitic trees, some of which are famous because they appear in paintings, a more acceptable fame than the connection with a film about non-existent tombs, we catch ourselves thinking.

The naturalness of Ta Prohm, now violated by archaeologists' obsessions (all sites should be studied as thoroughly as possible, even if it kills them) and tourist excursions: everyone wants to go everywhere, briefly – that old naturalness was already a construct. If the vegetation were not aggressively managed, you couldn't get anywhere near the temples, and the road system that passes within a few hundred yards of each complex has been continuously improved and extended. The system is so well-planned that you don't see or hear vehicles when visiting the temples, but everything will change as numbers increase. Now there are traffic jams, especially at certain times of day and at well-known traffic hot spots. There is talk of timed entry and prescribed routes through the sites. Judging from photos on the internet, this has already come to Ta Prohm, which has gone from the wildest to the most regulated ruin practically overnight.

Someone in *King Lear* says don't ever say that this is the worst, worse will come. Besides, Angkor has been identified as the world's largest pre-industrial city: this was formerly a more crowded place. Some experts think those wonderful empty spaces in the outermost precincts of each complex were formerly packed with inhabitants. It seems that we have resurrected only a hollow shell of the original reality, and have now set ourselves the problem of how to avoid running into lots of copies of ourselves who interfere with the lonely contemplation we imagine appropriate to this place.

At Angkor the jungle can be relied on to undo details of the restorers' improvements. Lichen covers many signs of the over-ordering instincts of archaeologists. But the battle between scientists and enthusiasts isn't likely to end. For too many reasons to count, the Parthenon in Athens is one of the most contested sites. Manolis Korres, the leading restorer in the 1990s, studied the monument more intensively and learned more surprising things about it than anyone

Ta Prohm, Angkor, Cambodia 'in the old days', when it was the only temple complex deliberately preserved in semi-overgrown state.

had before, but he seemed driven by the atavistic craving to complete a puzzle. He went through the rubble heaps surrounding the building more meticulously and more knowledgeably than previous sleuths and discovered hundreds of new fragments that belong to the Parthenon. His overriding goal was to get as many of them as possible back into place on the building.

The results are now visible in the nearly complete north colonnade. Under his and his successors' indescribably careful ministrations the building is getting further and further from an ancient building, and closer to a postmodern monument. The ruin-field of minced fragments on the Acropolis has its own authenticity. The present state of the north colonnade (in June 2014) has even made me wonder if the explosion of 1687 caused by a Venetian shell, the greatest single cause of damage to the Parthenon, isn't a historical event with its own validity whose effects we might even consider preserving. Doubtless this is going too far. But the restoration is already headed down another branch of that path: his successors will continue Korres's plan to put back the portal of the Ottoman mosque, which blocked the interior of the Parthenon for several hundred years, and some of the Byzantine pulpit from the period when the building was a church, thus partially reversing the purifications of the 1830s.

There's an intriguing parallel case in recent American archaeology. In 1968 a professor of history at Pratt College identified four run-down houses in an obscure part of Brooklyn as the best surviving examples of a type of house built in Northern cities for escaped slaves from the South. These were still being lived in but were recognized as such important fragments of the material history of African-Americans that they were quickly declared National Landmarks, emptied of inhabitants and turned into open-air museums. In studying their history researchers found that the houses had all undergone various modifications, porches added, cellars dug and, most incongruous of all, a garage squeezed in for an upwardly mobile family's automobile.

On the same theory that operated on the Acropolis in Athens in the 1830s all the later encrustations were stripped away to present the houses in the earliest, most primitive purity. Before many years had passed, though, different ideas about which historical traces were most meaningful demanded a fresh look. Now the additions and modifications which had been destroyed were carefully rebuilt from photographs so that the houses could tell the whole story of the intervening years.

No one had noticed the Hunterfly Road houses for the longest time, until the professor brought his exceedingly specific knowledge

Hunterfly houses, Weeksville, Brooklyn: unique survival of escaped slaves' houses, discovered from the air in 1968, and subjected to cycles of restoration and de-restoration since then.

to bear on them. Perhaps to recognize their importance we had to give them an overly precise name, and to see our new concept clearly we had to clear away later accretions, not just mentally but physically. Soon the time came when more richness and less simplicity was wanted; the idea of time attached to the houses had evolved into something more intricate, and the absurd project of rebuilding the unwanted appendages was the only way to satisfy the new craving.

For a long time a great widening has been taking place in conceptions of what the Angkor site really consists of, conceptions that only acquired physical form with the construction of comprehensive archaeological maps in 1999 and 2007. Bernard-Philippe Groslier first called Angkor a hydraulic city in the 1950s, a notion that took on an uncomfortable colonialist tinge in the 1960s and had to beat a retreat. But in the 1990s an Australian, Cambodian and French team began a longterm project to give the idea substance. By a mixture of methods including airborne radar imaging they began to find canals, causeways and roads, moated village temples and household ponds which filled in much of the empty space around the temple groups, until the latest plotting of this connected system of settlement, water distribution and communication looks like the Milky Way, a dense, speckled cloud or band in a wide diagonal stripe running from northwest to southeast, covering 1,000 square kilometres and putting more flesh on the claim that this was the largest pre-industrial urban development in the world.

The scale and density of the Angkor conurbation went unnoticed for so long because it was (and remains) largely imperceptible. Roads and canals are decayed and unused. Ponds seem too insignificant to be part of anything and village temples don't look venerable. So far no one is proposing to make the wider Angkor more evident by clearing, digging or rebuilding. The new conception will remain on the page and in the head, but it leaves the temples less isolated and the landscape even more numinous, concealing as it does a carpet of ruin diffused over such a large area it will never be uncovered.

The impulse to fill in the blank spaces in this venerable historical landscape comes rather late in the day, like the feeling that a real history of any place would look at the nobodies of that place, not the king and his ministers. But the little dots on the map are validated by their location in the magnetic field of the big temples, and the boy at the court of King Arthur, whose story is more interesting to ten-year-old us than the king's, only comes into focus because his life lies at a tangent to the court.

Vernacular buildings become interesting to scholars because they are sub- or pre-architectural, an escape from architecture into a deeper authenticity before the self-conscious artist goes to work on the materials of human shelter. This does not take long to become a sophisticated game. If we think much about it, we find ourselves viewing these artless structures aesthetically. That brings us to the paradox of a folk museum, a comparative collection of innocent productions that can now be classified in various ways and finally displayed in historical or regional series.

Folk museums and your grandparents

The most compelling exhibits in these museums are groups of buildings which try to disguise the fact that they have all been brought here from somewhere else. It isn't a secret that this one came from Harome and that one from Helmsley and this other one from Hutton-le-Hole itself, which is where we are, but from a different part of it. In this case (the Ryedale Folk Museum) the main exhibits all satisfy a strict definition of the Local, and yet, what they don't particularly want to you to notice, they have all been taken apart, moved a certain number of miles and reassembled again in someone's idea of a sympathetic location among the other uprooted buildings. So this is anastylosis with a twist; it's the price these buildings pay for surviving at all, rescued from ruin into a refuge where they are put back in working order and made to represent themselves when they were functioning properly, which could be a time fairly far back in their history. They now embody Cruck House or Victorian Cottage or Elizabethan Manor House, types they probably weren't aware of in their previous lives.

It was never an option to present them as ruins. They weren't imagined as aesthetic objects but as working models which would illustrate something as completely as possible. Yet the old photos can be very compelling. The manor house for instance looks much less grand and more vulnerable with its thatch coming to pieces and subsiding into the interior and its walls wobbling uncertainly. In the rescued form it seems pure reconstruction; its masonry is new. To a certain extent the slippage of its stones was the building's antiquity, which has been taken away. Was it a reluctant sacrifice, thought to be worth the price? Perhaps not, for in a certain perspective, ruin has nothing to recommend it.

Most magical at Ryedale is how meticulously lives are summoned up, first of all in a little row of shops and workshops. Part of their charm is that they're tremendously compacted, more like a series of cubbyholes than full-scale shoemaker, chemist and all-purpose village shop. The profusion of different tools, of half-finished boots and shoes, of little bottles and packages with worn but originally lurid labels of products long superseded, the profusion is overwhelming, but still we think we might be able to look at everything, reminded of habits just over the threshold of disuse, of others we can't claim to remember, of brand names known to someone who was a child in Britain but not to us. Strange how fascinating these memories we just missed out on are. We seem to be defining our position in time more precisely than there's ever been any chance to do until now. And then we wonder if this is just another form of shopping, and of finding that life boils down to a lot of insignificant detritus that held out a promise of vividness it couldn't fulfil.

Undoubtedly the fifteenth-century Cruck House is more of a rarity, is historically more significant and offers something more deeply strange, but the Victorian Cottage carries the strongest charge for me, probably because I can imagine my grandparents, my most immediate ancestors, living in it and owning all these slightly cumbersome, mostly ugly things. Perhaps this is just the furthest-back moment in time that I've actually inhabited, but even that is a fantasy, because my grandmother was born the same year as James Joyce, 1882. So she had a Victorian childhood maybe, but not more. Does it have anything to do with the beginnings of American literature in the nineteenth century? For some reason a scene in one of Cooper's novels of skating at night on a frozen lake comes into my head, and dark engravings of cutting ice and riding in sleighs from unwieldy Victorian periodicals we happened to have. All this by way of explaining the strong pull of these mocked-up environments stuffed so full of quilts, doilies, washbasins, fringes, Bibles, pictures with long legends attached – all of which we know have been imported here, not really native to the space, but filling it most convincingly because more fully than any actual dwelling could tolerate. Why is it such a pleasure to imagine oneself trapped in a narrow life where every inch of space is filled up and every possibility laid out already on the bed, the dresser, or the windowsill?

The Hida Folk Village on the outskirts of Takayama in Japan is not a collection or a hodgepodge but a consistent group of 30 rural buildings moved here to escape inundation when the Mibori dam was built in the late 1950s. It's a village in the sense that the buildings form a homogeneous group of weathered wood and thick thatch, but they are scattered too artfully on a gentle slope to feel like an actual village bound by the harsh realities of this infertile mountain region. They seem rather to obey the constraints of the Picturesque, as if this relaxed layout is an offshoot of the English landscape garden. It looks down on its reflection in a large tranquil pond, which is fenced and ringed by a wide concrete path. There are token rice fields – a particularly beautiful one planted in a concentric pattern right at the beginning of the circuit – but this doesn't pretend to be a working village.

The prize exhibits are the *gassho-zukuri* houses, large multi-storey structures with steep saddleback roofs. Their ground floors are rustic variants on traditional Japanese interiors, low, unobstructed spaces with beaten earth floors in the working areas and raised platforms in the living spaces. But the best part is the cavernous triangular space under the roof, a complex frame of straight trunks and branches all tied together with ropes and twines made from various natural substances, the whole construction made more venerable by black deposits of the smoke from decades of unvented fires.

Such huge interiors were devised to accommodate silk production, often the only way farmers in this impoverished region could make ends meet. The middle floors (of five) were turned over to large baskets of mulberry leaves on which the silkworms fed. The leftover spaces at the top, smokiest and least desirable, were where most of the family slept, without room divisions or privacy. As well as the silkworms, the monumental architecture of the *gassho* house was worked out to cope with unusual social structures of the district, formed from extended families of 20 to 30 members living under one roof. Each family was built around a head man. Only the head man and his oldest son were allowed to marry. Girls could leave the household only to marry the head man of another household; otherwise they bore children to outsiders who did not stay with them. These children remained in the family, while any children fathered by their brothers stayed in the families of the mothers. The head man and his wife and children slept on the more spacious lower floors; everyone else found space under the eaves. They were paid with three meals a day, a new set of clothes in the spring and a day off once a month to cultivate their own patch for a little extra to spend on themselves and their children. An encyclopaedic novel is needed to bring these harsh conditions to life. Perhaps Ema Shu's gigantic *Mountain Folk*, the story of a peasant rebellion in the district in 1869 is what we're looking for, but it remains untranslated.

Reconstructed houses in the folk village are beautifully pure and scrupulously maintained. The domestic architecture favoured by courtiers of the seventeenth century drew its inspiration from rural vernacular; the Hida museum has partially repeated this process by presenting farmhouses in purified form. But one could say that a kind of subliminal formalism is the whole point of such reconstructions.

It happens that there are revealing comparisons close at hand. First, in the rare dilapidated wooden buildings of Takayama itself, known for its wealth of traditional buildings. The poorer houses in the town are, as you'd expect, both more unspoiled, retaining archaic features because they can't afford to update them, and more unsightly, patching decayed bits of wood or thatch with salvaged chunks of corrugated metal or plastic sheeting that don't quite fit and end in rough edges. So we imagine an earlier state for the buildings in the museum when they looked cobbled together or sported makeshift extensions.

The second comparison is a couple of villages nearby which haven't been moved to escape a deluge and are still in their original locations. They've suffered a more complicated fate, and become tourist villages, whose inhabitants let out beds to visitors, turn their front rooms into gift shops or make parking lots of fields. At some point the flood became too much for the villages to support, so cars were banned in

Traditional Japanese house in Takayama, semi-derelict and boasting makeshift repairs but perhaps more authentic than museum specimens with all their flaws removed.

the centre, and a motorway was built to lead visitors to parking on the edge. Already before these villages gained World Heritage status from UNESCO the motorway was proving inadequate, and since then the tourist flood has swelled from 500,000 to 1.5 million annually. But YouTube is still full of comments on how much livelier and realer the 'actual' villages are than the dead museum. There are still indigenes to be seen, who park their cars outside their historic dwellings and leave junk in their yards. Here no one is pretending that they have slipped back into the pre-industrial past.

Immortality in Bangkok

There's a huge, crazily ambitious architectural park not far from Bangkok which administers a tremendous send-up to the whole idea of knowing what's authentically ancient, what's replacement and what bears little relation to anything old at all, a rebuke to the very idea of knowing exactly where you are with restorations and hence of your location in history at any moment. Surprising liberties have been taken with us before: even Austrian archaeologists make up a library square in Ephesus with carefully resurrected buildings, which were never there at the same time in the past, bumping against each other now.

But Muang Boran ('Ancient City') goes much further. It combines scholarly reconstructions of important buildings destroyed long ago, scaled-down replicas of key monuments in Thai architectural history, monastery buildings moved here from all over Thailand, public halls likewise, whole villages of old dwellings on stilts arranged in new configurations and modern architectural fantasias based on particular historical structures or whole regional or ethnic styles. You can visit the Old Royal Palace in Bangkok scaled down to 5/8, without the crowds, but with uncanny recreations of its intricate murals and glass mosaics. Or the important Khmer temples along the royal road from Angkor, saving long journeys and enjoying the sensation of scaled-down roofs of galleries grazing your head.

'Ancient City', which isn't a city but a scattering of 109 highlights in a generously scaled park, has a history too, which you're on your own in trying to discover. The detailed guidebook (5th edition, 1999) doesn't say a word about when anything was brought here or put up or where the craftsmen – to paint all the murals, carve the sculpture-mountains or detail all the stone and wood – came from. Lots of them are busy on all sides, adding inexplicable new features and repairing old ones. Not only architecture but Thai literature is here too, in the form of untraditional sculptural tableaux that liven up the spaces between buildings.

Kitsch and pastiche are words without much meaning here. The half-size replica of the imposing Khmer complex at Preah Vihear (now in Cambodia) sits on a fake promontory that is one-tenth the size of the actual outcropping. This is one of the cruder mock-ups and must be an early effort. Phimai, reputedly the most impressive Khmer structure in Thailand, is a more successful recreation in rose-tinted laterite convincingly weathered. As recently as 1936 the French archaeologists who reconstructed Ashram Maha Rosei in a tricky Vietnamese jungle location resorted to a solution of Chinese ink to make fresh-cut stones tone in with the old ones. I don't imagine the current taboo against harmonizing old and new this way operates at Muang Boran either.

We naturally want to know the history of this sizeable historical enterprise planted on a 200-acre site in the shape of Thailand near a famous crocodile farm. Maybe it helps to learn that the original idea was a golf course with miniature versions of Thai buildings dotted around it. The idea grew in seriousness as the projector, Lek Viriyaphant, learned about the parlous state of some of the buildings he wanted to shrink and decided to rescue the originals and add larger replicas to them. He also came to feel he needed expert advice and got the National Museum involved in the project. Viriyaphant also devised a three-storey museum of his collections inside a gigantic sculpture of a three-headed elephant. One of the most charming exhibits at Muang Boran is a large wax model of an impossibly intricate Thai temple looking slightly lopsided from the melting of the wax. Judging from photographs, I think the original of the model may be one of Viriyaphant's other projects, the Sanctuary of Truth, which contains an enormous collection of Buddhist and Hindu devotional sculpture.

Just as the golf course has disappeared as the ancestor of the Ancient City, the source of Lek Viriyaphant's wealth no longer seems to have a name. The disappearance or absence of detail about exactly when and how the various elements of Muang Boran got there may have a more interesting explanation. I wonder if reincarnation is perhaps the undeclared ruling idea here, the spirit of a place reappearing mysteriously intact somewhere else. A similar superstition might even be hiding beneath the surface in much Western historical study, or at least might be propelling those who find themselves hanging around ruins, which are less tainted by later lives than buildings still in use.

Invisible dwellings in Amsterdam

If the German persecutors of the Jews of Amsterdam had realized that the nondescript building on Prinsengracht, where they arrested eight Jews and two of their helpers on 4 August 1944, would eventually become a shrine to their victims' memory they would probably have torn it down. Certainly they would not have left the pages of a fifteen-year-old girl's diary scattered on the floor to be collected and hidden away by another of the helpers whom they left behind. After the capture the house went back to being a workplace until 1957, when it was threatened with demolition, then rescued by concerned citizens and finally opened as a museum in 1960, fifteen years after the end of the War. This is when it became the Anne Frank House, after her name had become widely known through the book published in the

Phimai, the most impressive Khmer remains in Thailand, reproduced at ⅝ their
original size in Muang Boran architectural park.

original Dutch in 1947 and finally in English in 1952 after earlier
rejection by a dozen U.S. publishers. And it was only in the 1990s that
the front parts of the building, offices and warehouse that provided
crucial camouflage for the Secret Annexe where the fugitives lived were
returned to a lifelike imitation of their state in the 1940s. Interest in
Anne Frank grew and grew, spread into the outlying parts of the
building until it could no longer be satisfied with photographs but
demanded life-size mock-ups, authentically 1940s kitchen and office
equipment, packing labels, empty bottles and invoices – for underneath the secret quarters the workmen had gone on manufacturing
the pectin and spice mixtures used in making jam, which was Otto
Frank's business from the time he arrived in Amsterdam in the 1930s.

The result is the oddest of all writer's-house museums, spaces
never meant for living in until these particular inhabitants needed to
become invisible. During the time they lived there none of them went
outdoors, so the diary has some of the quality of a prison notebook,
but the group of eight were so diverse, and so unsuited to living on
top of one another, that the young would-be novelist had quite an
overheated story to tell. The diary generates our curiosity about the
spaces, and in fleshing them out in such minute detail we are following the same instinct that made George Stevens and the others produce

Pieter Bruegel, *The Procession to Calvary*, 1564, in 2011 'reconstructed' in Lech Majewski's film *The Mill and the Cross*, which detects bitter references to contemporary politics in the painting.

the film of 1959, using models of the building constructed on a lot in Hollywood.

There are other hiding-places in Amsterdam which have also been turned into museums. Clandestine Catholic churches were common in Dutch cities in the sixteenth and seventeenth centuries, but Ons' Lieve Heer op Solder (Our Dear Lord in the Attic) doesn't strike most visitors as one of a tribe, but something secret and unknown. It takes up a position like the Secret Annexe's, at the back and the top, in a grand merchant's house. Our way of getting there, up narrow stairs and past secret cupboards containing confessionals, makes our progress feel precarious and conspiratorial. The melodrama is mostly our own contribution, though: worshippers here weren't taking big risks. Nonetheless, there's the tension and even threat of being outsiders, awkwardly digested by the wider society outside the hidden burrow where we are safe for the time being.

We don't need to invent melodramatic narratives in Anne Frank's house. The diary provides a more than adequate scaffolding on which every physical detail can hang. There can be few other spaces so intensely realized in words. It is still very uncomfortable to reflect

Still from Lech Majewski, *The Mill and the Cross* (2011): the aftermath of the Crucifixion, with the landscape of the painting stripped bare of the dense incident invented by Bruegel.

that the story would be less powerful if what we have spent the whole book hoping for had actually happened and she had survived.

For the most part the blacksmith at the forge or the waitress in petticoats does not make a historical reconstruction more evocative of its time. The furnished room that has everything in it but its people is the best stimulus to the imagination trying to enter the past. We know we're in the realm of the dead, and are happy to have it that way; living bodies are obviously fake, put there to catch the attention of bored children or those frightened by ghosts. Without the people, however well-equipped, these spaces are ruins; with them, nothing but kitsch. Maybe all reconstruction is a kind of theatre, but it works better if you don't think so.

And yet, there's a long tradition of recapturing moments lost in the past with paint, cardboard and plaster, in bird's-eye views and in models, which shrink whole landscapes onto tabletops. Pieter Bruegel's renderings of biblical events like *The Procession to Calvary* are among the greatest Western achievements but they're not strictly speaking historical, let alone archaeological, compositions. Lech Majewski's strange reconstruction of this painting, which lasts 96 minutes in the form of a feature film set in Poland, capitalizes on the freak survival of relics of old forms of Flemish from Bruegel's time (or near enough) in a forgotten part of rural Poland, and on the archaic skills of Polish seamstresses in other backward regions, capitalizes on them in the wonderfully regressive project of undoing Bruegel's achievement of condensation and spreading the painting across a landscape and 500 lives, each of which has some kind of warrant on the canvas. Perhaps *The Mill and the Cross* is just a longish way of showing how much there is in this painting, which it illuminates by turning it into a religious tract set in Bruegel's own, not biblical, time.

The Bruegel of the 1950s

It isn't at all certain that Alan Sorrell, the great painter of archaeological reconstructions in postwar Britain, was inspired by Bruegel or famous models of archaeological sites, like early nineteenth-century mock-ups of Pompeii, or Italo Gismondi's huge Imperial Rome of 1937, or the tiny paper cities inside miniature fortifications made for the old French generals to work out their strategies from.

Sorrell won a Prix de Rome, which let him spend 1928–30 there, and he returned in 1937 when he could have seen the Gismondi model, but he also had experience nearer home as a war artist, time spent on airfields and depicting bases from the air. In 1944 he refused to work on air campaigns against 'cities of irreplaceable artistic importance', and was diverted to enemy shipping. In 1948 he lost his job at the Royal College of Art at about the same time that the Ministry of Works decided that site models were too expensive, so they would have to make do with elaborate drawn renderings instead.

English Heritage rarely finds a place for Sorrell's drawings in brochures any more, though there must be hundreds of them in its files. They've become unfashionable for the very elements that make them special, the weather and the shadow. In Sorrell's world a storm is always brewing or dusk has fallen early, as in Bruegel's *Dark Day*. This weather and this depth of shadow seem to work best in black and white; the cheap colour printing of the 1950s can make his drawings look sickly or slightly out of register.

Sorrell is best at bringing rubble to life in the towns of Roman Britain, taking a ruin that's little more than foundations sketched out on the ground and putting tiles on the roofs, traffic in the streets, shopkeepers, travellers, donkeys and dogs. These are more thrilling than the most atmospheric interiors, because even when focused on a single building, like the Roman theatre at St Albans, they manage to include the embracing geometry of the Roman presence. The familiar bird's-eye perspective is less anachronistic in a Roman setting than in earlier or later centuries, for this is a civilization that really does see its settlements in the long, sloping view that is Sorrell's way of creating spatial grandeur.

Alan Sorrell's imaginative reconstruction of a street in Roman London, looking west towards Newgate, 1961.

He was unusually scrupulous, passing his sketches back to the archaeologists repeatedly for further refinements and revisions. The results don't and weren't meant to stand alone as independent works of art. They need photographs of the site and plans most of all (rarely provided in popular publications) to clarify his own achievement. His drawings are a healthier, more strictly imaginative substitute for actual reconstruction. What a place to end, only pictures, only fictions, letting a novelist take over from the scientists! But Sorrell's drawings tell us something important about the whole subject of ruins. Reconstructions in the flimsiest, most whimsical form give the clearest view of what the whole process is all about. They turn the ruin into a story, or a whole pack of them, and one that still has a long way to run.

Epilogue
Remembering and Forgetting

HOW MANY OF THOSE who flock to Saiho-ji, the famous moss-garden in Kyoto, realize they are looking at a ruin? Of course there is something unearthly about so much moss shrouding the forms beneath, making them indistinct as in a failing memory. Some ripples of moss form miniature mountain ranges seen from a height, some look like ripples on a pond, some are clearly just logs half-digested and thus still recognizable. Trees that happened to fall into the irregular lake (which started in the shape of the Chinese character for 'heart') become oddly shaped islands with 'populations' made from bushier species of moss. Some 137 different varieties have been counted here, have perhaps latterly been cultivated.

How many visitors see Saiho-ji as one big burial site, a natural graveyard with a long, naturally obscure history? Moss has collected that meaning, at least in the West, being associated with age and torpor, energies winding down if not yet entirely snuffed out. Moss at Saiho-ji tells an even sadder story than the general one of vegetable decay. It appears that this started out as a rock garden, but when the monastery fell on hard times that lasted centuries it became overgrown and finally unrecognizable, a picture of decline. At some point someone gave up on the idea of repair and decided to leave it that way, an unusable, almost un-enterable memorial.

By now it must be constantly and inconspicuously nurtured, until we are hard pressed to say what is accident and what design. By now it is clearly a treasured ruin. Recently I have woken up to half-disinhabited council estates, the ones at the bottom of the heap like Heygate and Ferrier, as the most poignant current ruins. It took an exhibition in a museum to get me to see this and my view still hasn't got over its aesthetized origins. An inhabited ruin is an uncomfortable idea, and makes you think something needs to be done. What's done at the moment is likely to be turfing out the occupants, replacing the slum with luxury flats and shifting the balance even further toward a London in which most people cannot afford to live.

Being forced to leave a second home can't compare with real dispossession, yet it's given me at least some insight into how it feels to have all your arrangements, built up over years, all your gear, assembled from here and there, become obsolete and superfluous in an instant, all your ties to lanes, fields, sloping high streets, all these to be ruined overnight and slipping rapidly into non-existence.

More than once I have read that forgetting is just as useful, just as necessary as remembering. Our elaborate plan for what would happen to every one of these pieces of our lives was a big exercise in un-remembering if not exactly forgetting. One by one furnishings that were on the point of turning into junk were rescued and reassigned to friends, charity shops, an auction house, or it must be admitted, the local dump. This meant that most of them received a decent burial rather than being thrown carelessly on a heap, a burial that in lots of cases was a new lease of life, for them if not for us.

I'm finding forgetting hard. It is too much like a rehearsal for death. My memories of Yorkshire are in ruins and give me no satisfaction at all, not even the aching kind I get from remembering our dog, buried in the ex-garden at Hill Top, her grave desecrated by the sheep who got in and ate the lady's mantle I put her under.

Forgetting apparently can't be forced, but if I'm such a lover of ruins, why can't I bask in or at least analyse and study the ruins of those years? There is a stage of ruin that is pure bewilderment and loss. I can imagine loss from which you would not recover, but this isn't it. My bewilderment carried on this long has become an attitude, like someone posing for the camera. There's a film which might help, *Memento*, in which a trauma of some kind has destroyed a man's memory. At this moment of all times he has decided to enact a complicated revenge for a crime that he, of course, cannot remember. The film is presented in the most scrambled order, as if to say that not-remembering can actually alter the structure of reality. The DVD even includes a retelling in which the scrambled bits are put back in normal order, a bewitching but also disheartening idea, because the ruin of this man's consciousness is the main interest of the film.

I have also turned for relief to that maddening Portuguese writer Pessoa, apparently pronounced so the word practically disappears: *p'soa*. This is the poet who divided or dissolved himself into 80-plus selves or fragments. They each have names, many have careers, quite a few have published poems, essays or books. The so-called *Book of Disquiet* is the best place to try to understand how someone reaches such an advanced stage of ruin or dispersion, which entails horrible alienation from ordinary closeness or connectedness.

What is left for the non-person *p'soa?* A hair-raising but thrilling immersion in weather, especially impending storms that in Lisbon blow over without happening more often than not, or in rain just before or just after it really takes place. The people who populate this narrative are errand boys, barbers and tobacconists, in other words the most anonymous denizens of the city. Much of the time *p'soa* is watching them in the street below from his third floor windows. He wakes up when he finds that the errand 'boy' has reached retirement, or that the barber who always worked at the next chair died just the day before, leaving an empty space. Pessoa is led to reflect that he too will one day no longer walk the familiar streets and that someone will notice him most feelingly in the gap he leaves behind.

Notes

p. 11 Pergamon frieze – see Andrew Stewart, *Greek Sculpture: An Exploration* (New Haven, CT, 1990), vol. I, pp. 209–13 for a stimulating interpretation of the political and aesthetic context of the frieze of the Great Altar and its relation to other Pergamene works like the *Dying Gaul*. For good online images of the complete frieze, see www.secondpage.de.

p. 12 German engineer – tuberculosis took Karl Humann to Anatolia in the first place, then road and railroad building. After success at Pergamon he became a full-time archaeologist, conducting a series of important digs, never gave up his house in Smyrna and died there in 1896. See Suzanne L. Marchand, *Down from Olympus: Archaeology and Philhellenism in Germany, 1750–1970* (Princeton, NJ, 1996).

p. 13 Mr Straw's House – see The National Trust guidebook (1993, and frequent reprints). The front cover shows a close-up of shoes stuffed with newspaper; the back, a general view of the lumber room with toppling piles of paper and boxes.

p. 14 The story of its travails – Denys Haynes, 'The Worksop Relief', *Jahrbuch der Berliner Museen*, 5 (1963), pp. 1–13, tells the story of the rediscovery and tracks the fate of the last remnants of Arundel's collection, unwanted by his sons and grandson, dumped in waste ground at Kennington, buried under rubble, refound by workmen and finally shipped off to Worksop to get rid of them.

p. 15 Seat of Satan – Satan's Seat in Revelation 2:12.

p. 15 inspired Russian novelists – A Russian novel inspired in part by the frieze's stay in Leningrad is Vasily Aksyonov, *The Burn* (first published in Italy, 1980), couched in a flamboyant hipster style under various Western influences. This novel precipitated the writer's exile or escape to the USA. One of its central characters is a sculptor obsessed by the battle between the Gods and Giants, which evidently has a special coded significance. Both Aksyonov's parents had been arrested in 1937 and exiled to the

Gulag. His mother, Yevgenia Ginzburg, wrote a powerfully truthful memoir about her prison experience, *Journey into the Whirlwind* (begun 1949, finished 1967), first published in Italy and Germany.

p. 16 Peter Weiss, *Die Aesthetik des Widerstands* (Frankfurt, vol. I, 1975; vol. II, 1978; vol. III, 1981). Volume I translated by Joachim Neugroschel in 2005. No further volumes of the English translation have appeared. The translator died in 2011. The temples and sculptures of Angkor occupy a parallel position at the end of volume III to that of Pergamon in volume I.

p. 16 Jacob Burckhardt – his enthusiasm for the Pergamon frieze was expressed in letters written from his hotel room in Berlin, where he had gone expressly to see it for himself in August 1882, and thereafter in lectures.

p. 18 Guaman Poma – an indigenous provincial noble who wrote mainly in Spanish with plentiful *quechua* words. He made a mistake in the title of his chronicle, calling it *Coronica* (as it is now always called) instead of *Chronica*. He drew its 398 full-page illustrations himself. The manuscript has been in Copenhagen since at least the 1660s but was only brought to public notice in 1908. Since 2001 a facsimile has been available online at www.kb.dk. The full translation of Guaman Poma, *The First New Chronicle and Good Government: On the History of the World and the Incas up to 1615*, is available at: https://muse.jhu.edu.

p. 18 Sahagún's *Historia* – Since 2012 the World Digital Library has had all 2,500 pages of the Florentine Codex of Sahagún's *General History of the Things of New Spain* on its website in high-resolution images. www.wdl.org/en/item/10096. A description of the fullest English translation of the Codex is available in Norman A. McQuown's review of Bernardino de Sahagún, 'The General History of the Things of New Spain', in *The Hispanic American Historical Review*, XXXVIII/2 (1958), pp. 235–8.

p. 19 Loeb – *Aeschylus*, vol. III: *Fragments* (LCL 505), ed. Alan Sommerstein (Cambridge, MA, 2008).

p. 20 Aeschylus – Peter Hall's adaptation of the *Oresteia* is available in a poor-quality video on YouTube. Copyright issues (the National Theatre?) apparently prevent the appearance of a DVD.

p. 21 *The Trackers of Oxyrhynchus* – performances are no longer available online, just an Open University paper on how important this play is in Harrison's work: Adrian Poole, 'Tony Harrison's Poetry, Drama and Film: The Classical Dimension', Open Colloquium (1999), www2.open.ac.uk; and Harrison reading the Marsyas section, crucial in what the play means but not powerful as drama at www.youtube.com.

p. 22 transmogrifications – Tony Harrison's *Prometheus*, his most ambitious film, shown many years ago on Channel 4; see Edith Hall,

'Tony Harrison's "Prometheus": A View from the Left', in *Arion: A Journal of Humanities and the Classics*, 3rd Series, x/1 (2002), pp. 129–40.

p. 23 Jardim Gramacho – *Waste Land* (2010), directed by Lucy Walker. An artist turns garbage pickers into stars by making waste from the dump into saleable art.

p. 23 Monte Testaccio in Rome – the largest rubbish dump surviving from antiquity was adorned in the Middle Ages with a *via crucis* and a cross at the top, the scene of a kind of sacred theatre. Near the Protestant cemetery where Keats is buried and the Pyramid of Cestius, formerly green fields, now bedraggled slums.

p. 23 papyrus fragment – all the Oxyrhynchus literary papyri are available in high-resolution images at www.papyrology.ox.ac.uk.

p. 24 Ruskin on Torcello – in *The Stones of Venice*, vol II: *The Sea Stories*, the chapter on the early basilica at Torcello begins with the arrival across a desolate marsh, a climb up a tower whose door hangs loose on its hinges and a survey of an empty vista from the top, all of which leaves a powerful impression before any architectural details are mentioned.

p. 24 Sassettas – without actually mentioning Sassetta, Nicholas Penny's review of Sarah Walden's *The Ravished Image: How to Ruin Masterpieces by Restoration* in *The London Review of Books* (4 July 1985) supplies an informed corrective to my view expressed in the text, a view based on no special expertise but on close amateur inspection of the paintings.

p. 25 Wang Bing – *West of the Tracks* (*Tie Xi Qu*) (2003), 545 minutes. Film Festival Rotterdam has issued this as four DVDs through Swiss distributors Trigon-film, including an interview with Wang. Excerpts can be found at www.youtube.com. His later work includes *Crude Oil* (2008), fourteen hours long, which follows oil workers in the Gobi Desert, and *The Ditch* (2010), about a forced labour camp *c*. 1960.

p. 29 Bill Douglas – his film trilogy about growing up (1972–8): British Film Institute (BFI) Blu-ray (2009), with much supplementary material. At the same time an elaborate BFI release of *Comrades* (1987), 182 minutes, Douglas's historical drama about the Tolpuddle Martyrs, early nineteenth-century agricultural workers in Dorset.

p. 32 James Agee – Robert Fitzgerald and Dwight Macdonald wrote memoirs of Agee. There is also Laurence Bergreen's *James Agee: A Life* (1984). A *New Yorker* piece by David Denby (9 January 2006) treats Agee's relation to the various magazines he wrote for, including *Fortune*. Dale Maharidge and Michael Williamson, *And Their Children after Them* (New York, 1990), goes back to Alabama 50 years after Agee and Evans; another remarkable book comes out of the later journey.

p. 36 Laban Centre, Deptford – competition 1997, project 1998–9, realization 2000–2003. The Herzog & de Meuron website gives a brief, evocative version of their intentions. Plans and sections at http://designenaction.gatech.edu/?p=78771.

p. 36 Seth Siegelaub – *The Stuff That Matters: Textiles Collected by Seth Siegelaub for the Centre for Social Research on Old Textiles*, a publication designed by 6a architects for the exhibition of textile fragments (London, 2012), with diagrams of the layout in flat glass cases and close-ups of the textiles, back sides the most startling. Available from Raven Row, 56 Artillery Lane, London E1 7LS, whose website has Siegelaub's texts about his collection.

p. 37 Dimitris Pikionis – paving around the Acropolis and Philopappou hill, 1951–7, paving of a children's playground in the suburb of Filothei, 1961–4. Kenneth Frampton's memoir of Pikionis as well as many Greek tributes available at www.eikastikon.gr. Good website on Pikionis sites in Athens with good photos of Filothei (17, Leof. El. Venizelou, Pl. Pikioni) at http://athenswalker.blogspot.co.uk.

p. 39 reconstructors of the Parthenon – well-illustrated presentation of the programme under Manolis Korres in the 1990s in *Die Arbeiten des Komitees zur Erhaltung der Akropolismonumente auf der Athener Akropolis* (2002).

p. 39 Jaywick Sands – Karen Guthrie and Nina Pope's *Jaywick Escapes*, a 48-minute documentary, appeared in 2012. A *Daily Mail* piece of 3 April 2013 headed 'Welcome to Misery-by-Sea' contains good photos and predictable rabble-rousing comment: www.dailymail.co.uk. The Wikipedia entry on Jaywick is a mine of assorted strange facts.

p. 41 Dziga Vertov – *Man with a Movie Camera*: exceptionally good audio commentary on the film by Yuri Tsivian on an old BFI DVD with inferior images. The later BFI version with Michael Nyman's music looks much better but lacks the commentary. Fascinating assemblage of Vertov material in *The Vertov Collection at the Austrian Film Museum* (Vienna, 2006), with parallel texts in German and English throughout. Graham Roberts, *The Man with the Movie Camera* (London, 2000), does a frame-by-frame analysis which performs the quixotic task of stopping the film's movement in its tracks.

p. 44 *Ulysses* – A 'critical and synoptic' edition of *Ulysses* edited by Hans Walter Gabler in 3 volumes appeared in 1984. Gabler explains his method – a form of Continental genetic criticism – in the afterword to the Penguin reprint of his 'corrected' text (a reading text without all the apparatus) of 1986. It has provoked controversy: see the special issue on editing *Ulysses*, in *Studies in the Novel*, XXII/2 (Summer 1990); For line-by-line commentary see Don Gifford, *Ulysses Annotated: Notes for James Joyce's Ulysses,* revised edition (Berkeley and Los Angeles, CA, 2008). There are rudimentary beginnings of an online commentary at http://en.wikibooks.org.

p. 46 *Battleship Potemkin* – subtitled *From the Series 'The Year 1905',* but no further parts ever appeared. *Battleship Potemkin*, Kino Blu-ray (2010), 71 minutes.

p. 48 Vertov's *Enthusiasm* – in Peter Kubelka's restoration it was meticulously presented as the first issue in the Edition filmmuseum series in 2010, which went on to do more Vertov and early Soviet film. The DVD includes an hour-long documentary of 2005 about the restoration (in 1972) by Kubelka, an interesting experimental filmmaker in his own right. The disc also contains the unrestored version of *Enthusiasm*.

p. 50 *Arcades Project* – the most puzzling of unfinishable works which defeats consecutive reading. The first comprehensive editing of the scraps and fragments Benjamin left behind appeared in German 40 years after his death and in English almost 60. In 1981 Giorgio Agamben discovered a missing Benjamin manuscript in the Bibliothèque Nationale, an assemblage of his notes on Baudelaire which Benjamin had said was a model in miniature of the larger *Arcades* project. This was finally published in 2013, in Italian (927 pages) and French. Is it part of the larger work, rearranged according to different principles, or a concentrated reduction of it, or a lopsided elaboration of limited aspects of it? Understanding Benjamin's prose forms isn't getting easier.

p. 51 'The Work of Art in the Age of Mechanical Reproduction' – Though written in 1936 for the *Zeitschrift für Sozialforschung,* journal of the Frankfurt School, it appeared first in French, published in Paris, when the Institute for Social Research had already moved to New York. The essay was ahead of its time in grasping how thoroughly technology would overwhelm the traditional processes of art. It first appeared in English in 1968 in a collection of Benjamin's pieces edited by Hannah Arendt. Neither the overwhelming nor the essay's influence has ended.

p. 52 Hashish – between 1927 and 1934 Benjamin experimented repeatedly with hashish, opium and mescaline, and wrote out his impressions with clinical care. These experiences profoundly influenced his ideas about human perception. Twelve short texts 'On Hashish' by Benjamin are available at www.wbenjamin.org.

p. 55 *The Waste Land* – a facsimile of the draft typescript of the poem with annotations by Pound and revisions by Eliot was published by Faber in 1971, edited by Valerie Eliot, and changed many readers' view of the poem. The early versions had been thought lost, until the New York Public Library revealed in 1968 that it had bought them privately some years before.

p. 58 *The Blue Cliff Record* – translated by Thomas Cleary and J. C. Cleary (Boston, MA, 2005). An earlier translation of 1961, said to be the first in English, is about half as long as the later one, and most of the time the two barely correspond. I owe a debt to the old one though, for its confusions pushed me to find the new one.

p. 60 *Late Spring* – directed by Yasujiro Ozu in 1949. As well as the dry garden at Ryoan-ji, this film includes a key scene at a Nōh performance which stands out from the otherwise heavily Westernized lives of the characters. Western critics sometimes find signs of deep but hidden Buddhist attitudes in Ozu.

p. 62 John Cage – in the 1980s Cage made a series of drawings inspired by the stones at Ryoan-ji, and based on chance operations. Concurrently or later (he doesn't remember which) he turned the drawings of rocks into musical compositions where curves on the page became glissandi played on an oboe. Some lines proved impossible to play so tape recordings were superimposed on performance by live instruments. Cage's drawings were mounted at Kettle's Yard, Cambridge, in 2010, in seemingly random patterns on the walls that resemble the disposition of the stones in Kyoto. Some of the drawings veer nearer than others to the appearance of music on the page, see 'On being uncagey about john, UK tour of cage exhibition' at http://notesfromafruitstore.net.

p. 64 Museo Bardini – a well-illustrated guide to the museum with text in Italian and English was published for the museum's reopening in 2011.

p. 66 Four antiquarian dealers' museums in Florence – two, the Museo Horne and Fondazione Salvatore Romano, have guides in the same Polistampa series as the Bardini (see above). Volpi's collection at Palazzo Davanzati is the only one of the four left out.

p. 66 The Cloisters – the complicated history of this project is well told by Timothy B. Husband in *Creating the Cloisters* (2013), a reprint from the Metropolitan's *Bulletin* (Spring 2013). Collectors, dealers, artists and curators are confusingly mixed in the story. Some, like the sculptor George Grey Barnard, play more than one part. The patron of Williamsburg, John D. Rockefeller, Jr, bought and landscaped the huge plot, paid for the lavish building and contributed much of the contents.

p. 68 'sculpture' leaves its pedestal / 'Buildings' split, teeter or divide – for example, Tatlin's *Corner Counter-relief* of 1914–15, Melnikov's Soviet Pavilion for the 1925 Paris Exposition.

p. 69 Le Corbusier's *Journey to the East* – his travel journal of a trip in 1911 through the Balkans to Istanbul and back via Athens was published in English by MIT Press (*c.* 1987), including his drawings (but not his photographs) of buildings on the Acropolis. When he used these drawings in *Vers une Architecture*, he matched them with photographs of the Parthenon by Frédéric Boissonnas, sometimes cropped to bring them closer to the configuration of his drawing.

p. 69 Villa Savoye – Poissy is a short train ride from the Gare St Lazare and the villa is open to the public. The catalogue of the Arts Council exhibition of 1987, *Le Corbusier: Architect of the Century*, is a good place to begin a study of this architect.

p. 70 Bernard Tschumi – in the essay 'Architecture and Transgression', *Oppositions*, VII (1976).

p. 70 Junichiro Tanizaki – primarily a novelist, most of whose work has been translated into English. He devoted much time to translations of the eleventh-century *Tale of Genji* into modern Japanese. *In Praise of Shadows*, which is only 60 pages long, appeared in Japan in 1933, and was translated into English by Thomas J. Harper and Edward G. Seidensticker in 1977.

p. 71 dry Zen gardens – *karesansui* carries the sense 'dried out', according to François Berthier, *Reading Zen in the Rocks* (Chicago, IL, 2000), p. 135.

p. 71 Skara Brae – the excavator was V. Gordon Childe.

p. 73 Derek Jarman – *Derek Jarman's Garden* is the title of the last book he wrote, published in 1995. Images are plentiful on the web and the garden is unfenced and easy to inspect without actually entering it.

p. 74 sound mirrors – on islands in a flooded gravel pit not far inland from Romney Sands station on the little Dymchurch Railway that runs between Hythe and Dungeness. They are easily viewable at all times, but if you want to enter the site, consult tour listings on the web. Map reference TR 077216.

p. 74 Yale Art and Architecture Building – the extension/addition in 2008 to the Art and Architecture building by Gwathmey Siegel took on the difficult task of harmonizing with Brutalism without imitation. It does this well, yet inevitably it detracts from the grandeur of Paul Rudolph's idea just by being there. Although I'm assured that nothing has been tidied up, only brought back nearer to the original intentions, interior surfaces in the old building look brighter and less threatening after Gwathmey's restoration.

p. 75 Boston City Hall by Kallmann, McKinnell & Knowles, 1961–8, is still locked in battle with dissatisfied users. The double- or triple-height atrium is the best interior space; corridors and most offices are undeniably grim. The most exciting external space, a wide passageway in brick which twists and climbs through a mixed forest of columns to dead-end in an enclosed courtyard, is now blocked off because it attracted vagrants. Another large Brutalist-style government complex – the State Health,

Education and Welfare Service Center built in 1970 by Paul Rudolph –
lies a short distance northwest of Boston City Hall.

p. 76 Southbank Centre – had as its starting point Festival Hall by
Robert Matthew, Leslie Martin and others, 1948–51, practically the only
visible remnant of the 1951 Festival of Britain. Further concert halls,
exhibition spaces and a film theatre came later (1956–68) and in different
materials, locked or threaded into a system of decks like a scaled-down
version of 'streets in air'. Nikolaus Pevsner made his last contribution
to the *Buildings of England* describing this complex, and his response is
powerfully conflicted: *London 2: South* (London, 1983), pp. 345–55.
Numerous plans to redevelop the site for more intensive use have come
and gone. Richard Rogers, Rick Mather and Feilden Clegg Bradley have
been among the proposers (latest scheme 2013).

p. 77 Robin Hood Gardens – designed and completed between 1966 and
1972, much later than the first formulation of the ideas on which it was
based. A fight over proposed demolition seems to have gone against the
buildings' survival. A concise negative appraisal in Bridget Cherry, Charles
O'Brien and Nikolaus Pevsner, *Buildings of England, London 5: East*
(London and New Haven, CT, 2005), pp. 647–8.

p. 77 Barbican development – Chamberlain, Powell & Bon, plans from
1955, construction 1963–82. Its lavishness sets it decisively apart from
public housing like Robin Hood Gardens. Simon Bradley and Nikolaus
Pevsner, *Buildings of England, London 1: The City of London* (London,
1997), pp. 281–6.

p. 78 Economist towers (St James Street, SW1), 1962–4. Simon Bradley
and Nikolaus Pevsner, *Buildings of England, London 6: Westminster*
(London and New Haven, CT, 2003), pp. 636–7.

p. 78 St Peter's Seminary, 1959–67. See Frank Arneil Walker, *Buildings of
Scotland: Argyll and Bute* (London and New Haven, CT, 2000), pp. 169–74,
for details of commissioning and construction. Recent minimalist plans
to stabilize the ruin can be found in *To Have and To Hold: Future
of a Contested Landscape*, ed. Gerrie van Noord (Edinburgh, 2011):
a maddeningly unfocused production that 'aims to dismantle the notion
of "ruin"'.

p. 79 Sir John Soane considered ox skulls 'puerile and disgusting'
decorations, in a publication of his designs for country houses, *Plans,
Elevations and Sections of Buildings* (1788).

p. 80 Philipp Otto Runge – quasi-religious imagery derived from plant
forms in four bilaterally symmetrical drawings and prints, the *Times
of Day* (1803, 1805). Runge left clear plant species behind and became
more mystical in the larger painted version of 'Morning' (1809).

p. 80 Balthasar Neumann – overlap of Rococo and Neoclassicism at Neresheim Abbey in Baden-Württemberg, and even in the stairhall at Würzburg in Bavaria in the zone below the frescoes.

p. 81 nineteenth-century French draughtsmen – French Beaux-Arts recolouring of ancient buildings, especially Benoit Louviot's Parthenon, 1879–81, in *Paris–Rome–Athenes: Le voyage en Grèce des architectes français aux XIXe et XXe siècles* (Paris, 1982).

p. 81 George Hersey – superstition in *The Lost Meaning of Classical Architecture: Speculations on Ornament from Vitruvius to Venturi* (Boston, MA, 1988).

p. 81 Pasolini's *Medea*, 1969, starring Maria Callas, who was Greek like the heroine, but not comfortable on screen. Perhaps Pasolini found a kind of authenticity in this, like using non-professionals, which he did repeatedly: it was shot partly in ruined early Christian churches in Cappadocia (another exciting mismatch?).

p. 81 *Cabeza de Vaca* – based on Álvar Núñez Cabeza de Vaca's journal, *La Relación* (1542), later known as *Naufragios: The Shipwreck* (the 2002 Penguin edition, called *Chronicle of the Narváez Expedition*, is a revision of a translation that first appeared in 1905).

p. 82 Carlo Scarpa – *Carlo Scarpa and the Castelvecchio*, by Richard Murphy (London, 1990), a wonderfully full treatment of this project of 1956–64.

p. 84 Alte Pinakothek – Erich Altenhöfer, 'Hans Döllgast and the Alte Pinakothek, Designs, Projects and Reconstructions 1946–73', in *9H*, no. 9, *On Continuity*, ed. Rosamund Diamond and Wilfred Wang (1995), a painstaking restoration of this neglected architect.

p. 86 bombed church in Munich – Döllgast's restoration of a bombed church is S. Bonifaz, Munich, 1949–50; his cemetery is the Ostfriedhof, St-Martins-Platz 1. Further complicated instances of Döllgast fighting off attempts to replicate the pre-war state of buildings is told by Gavriel D. Rosenfeld in *Munich and Memory: Architecture, Monuments, and the Legacy of the Third Reich* (Berkeley and Los Angeles, CA, 2000).

p. 86 David Chipperfield – Neues Museum, Berlin. The museum's website includes interactive panoramic videos for practically every internal space ('virtual architectural tour'): www.smb.museum/en/museums-and-institutions/neues-museum/home.html. The interesting clips with Chipperfield explaining his intentions are no longer available on the museum website.

p. 88 architectural replicas – Munich restorations and memorials after the Second World War in Rosenfeld, *Munich and Memory*.

p. 89 Rococo interior – I didn't realize that the Catholic monastery, St Anna im Lehel in Munich, had been almost completely reconstructed after bombing. According to Dehio, *Handbuch Bayern* IV: *München und Oberbayern* (Munich and Berlin, 1990), pp. 685–6, the building was largely destroyed, so it got a 'neubarocke Fassade von Erwin Schleich' (meaning a modern imitation of Baroque I think) and the internal restoration was done in stages. Most of the paintings and sculptures had survived, but the painted ceilings by Cosmas Damian Asam had completely disappeared and were only approximated by Karl Manninger in 1967–76. I must have arrived very soon after he finished his long labour.

p. 90 Astley Castle – near Nuneaton, Warwickshire. After watching a video on the Landmark Trust website with the architects explaining their intentions, I have changed my mind about this conversion. The ruin is held in place by the insertion, which is more like a huge piece of built-in furniture than a building. Seen this way, it becomes intellectually more satisfying.

p. 92 Lutyens – at Lindisfarne Castle, 1903, Castle Drogo, 1910–30 and Liverpool Catholic cathedral, 1929–58. See the exhibition catalogue, *Lutyens*, Hayward Gallery (London, 1981).

p. 93 Sigurd Lewerentz – late churches in Sweden at Björkhagen 1956–60 and Klippan 1963–6; see *Sigurd Lewerentz, 1885–1975: The Dilemma of Classicism* (London, 1988). For Lewerentz's photographs (negatives preserved in Arkitekturmuseet, Stockholm) see Luis Moreno García-Mansilla, 'Beyond the Wall of Hadrian's Villa, Parrhasius' Veil: Lewerentz' Journey to Italy', in *9H*, no. 9 *On Continuity*, ed. Rosamund Diamond and Wilfred Wang (1995), which reproduces seventeen of Lewerentz's Italian photographs.

p. 94 Elizabeth Bishop's poem – 'The Fish', written in the winter of 1939. Her letters from around this time and her Key West notebooks kept at Vassar College, Poughkeepsie, New York, contain many references to fishing expeditions.

p. 95 Khadambi Asalache house, 575 Wandsworth Road, London SW8. From his Wikipedia entry I learn that the young Khadambi read Shakespeare while herding cattle. He died in 2006 and left his house to the National Trust, which now runs tours. There are good images on their website of the amazing fretwork that began as a disguise for damp patches on the walls. Khadambi was inspired by the mosque at Cordoba and wooden houses in Istanbul among others.

p. 96 'Kubla Khan', written by Coleridge in 1797, published 1816. On the back of an autograph manuscript of the poem, which turned up in 1934, is a different account of the poem's genesis: 'This fragment with a good deal more, not recoverable, composed, in a sort of Reverie brought on by two grains of Opium taken to check a dysentry, at a Farm House between Porlock & Linton, a quarter of a mile from Culbone Church, in the fall of the year, 1797.'

p. 97 greatest of all critics of Shakespeare – Coleridge on Shakespeare collected in 2 volumes edited by T. M. Raysor (1960), now superseded in part by volume 5 in the *Collected Works*.

p. 98 Coleridge *Marginalia*, ed. George Whalley and H. J. Jackson, 6 vols (New York and Princeton, NJ, 1980–2001). Whalley's 'Foreword', 'Notes on Editorial Practice' and 'Introduction' fill 170 pages in volume 1 and are a fascinating guide to a scholarly obsession. He began work on the project in 1946. When Whalley died in 1983, Jackson took over; her brisker approach, explained succinctly in volume III, was crucial in order to see the project through to conclusion in a normal lifetime.

p. 101 Étienne de La Boétie – his friendship with Montaigne described in Book 1, chapter 28 of the Essays, *De l'amitié*, which M. A. Screech translates as 'On affectionate relationships' rather than 'On friendship' (London, 1991).

p. 102 Surinam toad – a creature that fascinated Coleridge, which he turns into a metaphor for the imagination and refers to in widely scattered places (this one in a letter to a friend, *Letters* III, pp. 94–5).

p. 102 Sara Hutchinson – the woman Coleridge was in love with was the sister of Wordsworth's fiancée.

p. 105 Joe Orton's defaced library books are now part of the Islington Local History Centre collection, and Islington Museum exhibits a few of them. They can also be found online.

p. 106 'Joyce's personal library' – details are not presently available on the University website.

p. 107 the 'disciple left in charge' of notes and drafts for *Opus Maximum* was Joseph Henry Green, a surgeon and student of German literature who had known Coleridge for many years when he became his literary executor. He later studied Hebrew and Sanskrit with a view to synthesizing Coleridge's notes.

p. 107 Coleridge's plagiarism continues to generate controversy. Norman Fruman's *Coleridge: The Damaged Archangel* (New York, 1971) is the strongest negative voice; Richard Holmes, Coleridge's biographer (see the second volume particularly), is one of the most temperate defenders. Most lovers of Coleridge probably recognize that he is a perplexing mixture of originality and dependency in thought and feeling, and have even wondered if his emotional weaknesses do not make the paths of his thinking more intensely interesting.

p. 107 genetic criticism of *Finnegans Wake*. Genetic criticism is a French (and German) invention, applied to classic French texts in *Genetic Criticism:*

Texts and Avant-textes (Philadelphia, PA, 2004). It is a set of techniques that could have been dreamed up just for *Finnegans Wake*, as demonstrated in *How Joyce Wrote Finnegans Wake*, ed. Luca Crispi and Sam Slote (Madison, WI, 2007).

p. 108 hoarding – tackled by a psychologist and a social worker in Randy O. Frost and Gail Steketee, *Stuff: Compulsive Hoarding and the Meaning of Things* (Boston, MA, 2010).

p. 108 Metropolitan Museum of Art and panelling from Gwydir Castle in North Wales. The story is recounted by the woman who rescued this building with her art historian husband, in Judy Corbett, *Castles in the Air* (London, 2004).

p. 111 nineteenth-century German scholar – Jacob Feis, writing in 1884, taken from Frances Yates, *John Florio: The Life of an Italian in Shakespeare's England* (Cambridge, 1934), the translator of Montaigne into English.

p. 112 in Purgatory on the Confines of Hell – *Marginalia*, vol IV, pp. 161–3, annotation in poems by Barry Cornwall, pseudonym of Bryan Waller Proctor.

p. 113 Kafka, diagnosed with tuberculosis in August 1917, moves to the rural village of Zurau, produces short pieces on separate sheets. The Zurau aphorisms as they are called, 109 of them chosen by Brod in 1931, are available (posted in reverse order) with the German text, two different translations and commentary by Michael Cisco at http://zurauaphorisms. blogspot.co.uk.

p. 114 Indians from the New World – Montaigne's talk with an Indian from the New World occurs in 'On the Cannibals', Book 1, chapter 31.

p. 116 Pontano – or Pontanus, Giovanni or Jovianus (Burton uses both forms) was a fifteenth-century Italian poet and humanist, three volumes of whose poems and dialogues appear in the I Tatti Renaissance Library in Latin with facing English translations. Not to be confused with Isaacus Pontanus, seventeenth-century Danish antiquary, another of Burton's sources.

p. 118 amateur edition – of 1927 by a pair of non-scholars: *The Anatomy of Melancholy*, ed. Floyd Dell and Paul Jordan-Smith (Farrar & Rinehart, 1927, reprinted Tudor Publishing; New York, 1955).

p. 118 scholarly edition of Robert Burton, *The Anatomy of Melancholy*, 6 vols (Oxford, 1989–2000). Three volumes of text and three of commentary.

p. 120 nine kinds of demon – in Part 1, Section 2, Member 1, Subsection 2 (vol. 1, p 181 in Oxford edition). Pinpointing locations in Burton is a nightmare.

p. 123 Captain Zisca in Montaigne and Burton. In Montaigne in Book 1, Chapter 3: *our affections get carried outside us*, where Zisca appears as Jean Vischa who brought insurrection to Bohemia in defence of the errors of Wyclif; and in Burton in *Democritus to the Reader*, where he is 'that great Captain Zisca'. It is thought that Burton probably took the reference from Florio's Montaigne.

p. 125 Shklovsky – his essay on *Tristram Shandy* carries further the ideas of *Art as Technique* (1917). It was published separately as Viktor Shklovsky, *Sterne's 'Tristram Shandy' and the Theory of the Novel* (Petrograd, 1921). On the first page it is renamed *Sterne's 'Tristram Shandy': Stylistic Commentary*. For Shklovsky the distinction between story and plot was crucial – story was the natural order of cause and effect, plot was a defamiliarized order of events dislodged from simple chronology by the choices of the author. Sterne's book was the supreme violator of narrative continuity, hence the most purely novel-like of all novels. This statement remains paradoxical, but isn't just a thoughtless upending of common sense.

p. 127 Theodore Baird, 'The Time-scheme of "Tristram Shandy" and a Source', PMLA, LI/3 (1936), pp. 803–20.

p. 128 film based on *Tristram Shandy – A Cock and Bull Story*, directed by Michael Winterbottom (2005), 94 minutes.

p. 130 marbled pages – these were conceived (and exist in copies of the first printing) as hand-painted sheets, so that every side and every set of pages would be different. This conception has provoked comparison with Marcel Duchamp and his attempt to insert unrepeatable difference into mechanical process and cheaply printed imagery.

p. 130 Martin Rowson's graphic novel adaptation of *Tristram Shandy*, published in 1996, followed his rendering of T. S. Eliot's *The Waste Land* as a comic book six years earlier. It is amazingly faithful to the novel, though it introduces extra characters, the clergyman Cicerone (Sterne himself? An older, more effete Tristram?) and the cartoonist and his dog Pete. It runs for an astonishing 161 large pages, all jammed with drawn detail. See interview with Rowson, 'Books: "The Life and Opinions of Tristram Shandy"', *The Independent* (1 September 1996), www.independent.co.uk.

p. 137 Samuel Beckett – on Joyce; see *Dante . . . Bruno. Vico . . . Joyce*, an essay published in 1929, which was Beckett's first published work and his contribution to *Our Exagmination round his Factification for Incamination of Work in Progress* – a strange tribute to Joyce from twelve friends and admirers (and two 'enemies'), put together at a time when Joyce had published nothing but scraps since *Ulysses* seven years before.

p. 137 Vico – now a cliché in connection with Joyce, ever since he noticed a resemblance between Vico's theory of historical cycles and his own sense that things repeat themselves. For Joyce, Vico supplied a bit of needed stiffening to loose narrative structures; others took the parallel more seriously.

p. 138 Anthony Burgess on the wealth of jokes in *Finnegans Wake*: it is interesting to read, though, that Burgess worked on a shortened version of *Finnegans Wake* and thought of doing the same for *Ulysses*.

p. 138 Joyce's commentary is conveyed mainly in letters to Harriet Shaw Weaver (who supported him financially from 1914 onward and arranged the first publication of *Ulysses*) and in books or pieces by collaborators to which Joyce contributed: Letters to HSW, explicating page 3 of *Finnegans Wake* (15 November 1926); explicating page 23 (13 May 1927); explicating page 196 (7 March 1924); explicating pages 213–15, notes on ALP published by C. K. Ogden; further letter to HSW explicating page 219ff (22 November 1930); explicating page 260, letter to Frank Budgen (end of July 1939); explicating page 403, HSW (24 May 24); explicating pages 414–17, HSW (26 March 1928); explicating pages 449–52, Stuart Gilbert, *Prolegomena to Work in Progress* on which Joyce collaborated; explicating page 470, HSW (8 August 1928). These all taken from Roland McHugh, *Annotations to 'Finnegans Wake'*, 3rd edition (Baltimore, MD, 2006). They are only a drop in the bucket, but a crucial one.

p. 139 notebooks and drafts of *Finnegans Wake* are now mainly in Buffalo, New York, and have been published in meticulous editions by Vincent Deane, Daniel Ferrer and Geert Lernout.

p. 139 wonderful resources – see the Bibliography pages of *fweet* website, www.fweet.org. A comprehensive commentary is not unworkable, just impossible for any single reader to make full use of all of it.

p. 139 *fweet* – Raphael Slepon's website contains the most complete line by line commentary on *Finnegans Wake*, and a host of other resources, like a searchable concordance to the book, a list of Joyce's sources, a list of the 9,000 improvements made in the 'restored' 2012 edition (this list is still in progress). Slepon is presently a firmware engineer in California.

p. 140 earlier ending – concludes Book I of *Finnegans Wake*, on pp. 196–216, one of the sections partially explicated by Joyce.

p. 145 restored *Finnegans Wake* – this project first appeared in an expensive private printing in 2010, then in a relatively expensive Penguin in 2012. It boasts over 9,000 'corrections' but is unsatisfactory in two main ways: it departs from the established pagination of all previous editions, which means you cannot conveniently use it with existing commentaries, and a list of the 9,000 changes is not provided. Maddening and inexplicable. The most convenient list of important mistakes and omissions in current editions of *Finnegans Wake* is provided by the book's Dutch translators in the back pages of their Oxford World's Classics edition: *Finnegans Wake*, ed. Robbert-Jan Henkes and Erik Bindervoet (Oxford, 2012).

p. 149 persuasive advocate – Thomas A. Vogler in 'Wonder did he wrote it himself: Meditations on Editing "Finnegans Wake" in the "Gabler era"', *Studies in the Novel*, xxii/2 (1990), pp. 192–215.

p. 151 *Les Demoiselles d'Avignon* now in the Museum of Modern Art, New York. It was painted in the summer of 1907 after a long gestation and shown to a few friends but not exhibited. It was exhibited for two weeks in 1916, then rolled up in Picasso's studio until he sold it in 1924 to designer Jacques Doucet. So this painting, which is now considered to mark the beginning of Cubism, was not generally known in the crucial Cubist years.

p. 152 *Fan, Saltbox and Melon* – Picasso (1909), Cleveland Museum of Art. Where do these titles come from? Perhaps mainly from dealers, who have a special need to keep similar paintings from getting confused with each other.

p. 154 Kurt Schwitters – his collages in Karin Orchard and Isabel Schulz, *Kurt Schwitters: Catalogue Raisonné*, 3 vols, Sprengel Museum Hannover (2000–2006). Schwitters' late work in *Schwitters in Britain*, exh. cat., ed. Emma Chambers and Karin Orchard, Tate Britain (London, 2013).

p. 157 *Merzbau* – it evolved slowly from 1923 and began to take over whole rooms from 1930. Because it exists now only in black-and-white photographs it is hard to be sure of the layout, but eventually it included two rooms in Schwitters's parents' flat and an adjoining balcony, as well as spaces in the cellar and the attic. Schwitters left it behind when he fled Germany in 1937, and it was completely destroyed by an Allied bombing raid in 1943. He began other *Baus* in Norway and the Lake District, the first of which was destroyed in a fire; fragments of two others will eventually be mounted in museums in Molde, Norway and Newcastle, England. A replica of the first room of the Hannover *Merzbau* based on three photos of 1933 was made by the theatre designer Peter Bissegger in 1981–3 for the Sprengel Museum in Hannover. A second travelling replica was also produced. There's a good video of its erection at Berkeley accessible on www.youtube.com, titled 'MERZbau reconstruction', 29 July 2011.

p. 158 Gordon Matta-Clark – films of some of his best works under construction and/or destruction: *Conical Intersect*, *c.* 18 minutes, at http://vimeo.com/10617205; *Office Baroque*, a patchy film and *Splitting*, *c.* 7 minutes, can be viewed at www.youtube.com.

p. 163 'Crude Hints towards an History of my House in L.I.F' – Soane's *Crude Hints* was published for the first time in Sir John Soane's Museum, *Visions of Ruin: Architectural Fantasies & Designs for Garden Follies* (London,

1999), pp. 53–78. This publication also has full details of the fake ruins at Ealing (entries 25–31 in the catalogue).

p. 165 Tower of Babel – Bruegel's two paintings in Rotterdam and Vienna are the best and best known. There's a strange stepped pyramid version by Marten van Valckenborch at Towneley Hall, Burnley, Lancashire, a large number by Tobias Verhaecht including examples in Norwich and Antwerp, Joos de Momper II, Lucas van Valckenborch, Abel Grimmer and lots of unidentified artists. The subject exercised a fascination we can't entirely fathom. Kafka's Babel sketches are all short, four of them in *Parables and Paradoxes*. The Great Wall of China attracted him for similar reasons, two of those included in *Parables and Paradoxes*.

p. 167 surviving remnants of Norse poetry – the *Poetic Edda*, or as it is called in the 2011 Penguin translation by Andy Orchard, *Elder Edda: A Book of Viking Lore*, which is the best easily available version (for its notes and apparatus, and its appreciation of the poems' fragmentariness and diversity, and for not smoothing over difficulties).

p. 168 *Prose Edda* – the only easily available complete version is the Everyman, called simply *Edda*, trans. and ed. Anthony Faulkes (1987). Text summaries at the back are surprisingly useful, as is the full index.

p. 168 Norse kennings – kennings draw glancingly on a common fund of stories and act something like metaphors that do not need to be elaborated, only named. Brief explications below of the stories behind kennings for gold. To fill out these names properly, the whole story should be told, or the whole poem read. The Everyman *Edda* and Penguin *Elder Edda* both index all occurrences of the names in the surviving texts.

> Glasir's foliage: *glasir* means *gleaming* – Glasir is either a tree (the most beautiful in the world) or a glade with gold leaves, outside Valhalla.
>
> Sif's hair: Loki steals her hair and is obliged to get black elves to make a new head of hair from gold, which will grow even though it is metal.
>
> Fulla's snood: her forehead is so bright it casts light.
>
> Freyia's weeping, or her tears, or rain from her eyes: her tears are made into the gold inlay of an axe-head.
>
> Voice and words of giants: counted as gold because they are powerful?
>
> Dripping from Draupnir, rain or shower from Draupnir: draupnir = dripper, Draupnir is a gold ring which every night drips eight more rings whose weight adds up to its own. The

same word occurs in the list of dwarves' names in *Völuspá*, the
opening poem of the *Poetic Edda*.

Otter-payment, Aesir's forced payment: Loki kills an otter who
turns out to be a son of the man who is Loki's host later that day.
To pay for this he must fill the otter's skin with gold to the top.

Seed of Fyri plains: Hrolf Kraki diverts Swedish pursuers by
emptying a horn of gold on the ground which they stop to
pick up.

Holgi's mound-roof: a king whose pile of sacrifices is finished off
with a layer of gold.

Fire of all kinds, of waters and of the arm: gold is fire because it is
red, silver is snow, ice or frost because it is white; fire of the
arm is gold jewellery.

Stones, rocks or gleam of the arm: more names for gold jewellery.

p. 169 *Beowulf* – the poem is set in Scandinavia but generally thought
to have been written in England. Some of the controversy about the
Iliad is repeated over *Beowulf*: is it the product of an oral or a literate
culture? How close is it in time to the events it describes? Dates
suggested for its composition have ranged from the sixth to the eleventh
century (the last is the date of the only surviving manuscript). For some,
including me, it's a work of pagan imagination with a Christian overlay;
for others it's a Christian poem with antiquarian trimmings of archaic
pagan lore. The manuscript is first mentioned in the late seventeenth
century and only begins to inspire much interest in the early nineteenth
century, a fascinating example of neglect and of catching up with
the past only after long delay. The manuscript is a nice example of
ruin, which almost disappeared in a library fire in the eighteenth
century, and lost parts of itself when being bound for safekeeping.
Some of these bits at the edges have recently been retrieved by fibre-
optic backlighting.

p. 170 ruins and epic poems – following the Austrian classicist Albin Lesky,
Martin Mueller thinks no heroic poem occurs without ruins to set it off:
'the mere ruins in the Troad were a sufficient factual irritant to produce in
time the pearl of the *Iliad*', in Martin Mueller, *The Iliad* (Bristol, 1986).

p. 170 Morris and Wagner – Morris learned a little Icelandic from Eirikr
Magnusson who then provided him with cribs that he used to produce his
own translations of the sagas from 1869 onward. He made two journeys
to Iceland in 1871 and 1873 during which he kept notable journals. After
this he produced his own version of the Norse material, *Sigurd the Volsung
and the Fall of the Niblungs*, which came out in 1876, the same year as the

first *Ring* at Bayreuth, which Morris thought a perversion of the material. Already in 1848 Wagner is deep in the *Volsunga saga* in German translation from Old Norse, Wilhelm Grimm on heroic saga, in Eddic poetry and Snorri's compilation, which became the principal sources for *The Ring*.

p. 170 William Barnes – for Barnes's linguistic purism, see Jonathan Roper, 'English Purisms', *Victoriographies*, ii/1 (2012). Roper puts Barnes in a wider context with other purifiers of language.

p. 171 Norse placenames in Britain – the Key to English Place-names site at Nottingham University lets you pick out Norse names county by county. You can eliminate names from different source languages leaving only the language you want to trace. For the North Riding of Yorkshire, for instance, this process gives a graphic demonstration that almost all names are Norse in origin. But name-formation isn't as simple as this makes it sound. Askrigg and Skipton are two names that were 'norsified'. The Old English names were converted to something more familiar to Norse ears, distorting what their names formerly conveyed. The name for York has been through at least four languages. Brittonic *Eborakon* (perhaps 'place of the yew trees') became Roman *Eboracum*, then Anglo-Saxon *Eoforwic* ('Boar-town'), then Old Norse *Jorvik* ('Horse-bay'), then modern English *York*.

p. 171 Indian names in the U.S. – the most comprehensive work on this subject is William Bright, *Native American Placenames of the United States* (Norman, OK, 2004) at 608 pages. It includes 11,000 names, among them many created by non-natives with only rudimentary grasp of native languages, names that look European but are distortions of native words, and others purely invented which are meant to look Indian.

p. 172 Norse words in English – an interesting but unsourced piece by Edward Sproston (2011) at http://germanic.zxq.net/ON-Engloans.html; and a book I have not seen by a lecturer at the University of York: Matthew Townend, *Language and History in Viking Age England: Linguistic Relations between Speakers of Old Norse and Old English* (Turnhout, 2005), which argues that the two languages were mutually intelligible.

p. 175 Byzantine iconoclasm – contemporary texts from both periods of iconoclasm and the restoration that came between them, in Cyril Mango, ed., *The Art of the Byzantine Empire, 312–1453: Sources and Documents* (Toronto, 1986).

p. 176 Byzantine churches converted to mosques – for photographs of reoriented spaces and early twentieth-century exterior conditions, see Thomas F. Mathews, *Byzantine Churches of Istanbul: A Photographic Survey* (University Park, PA, 1976). See W. Mueller-Wiener, *Bildlexikon zur Topographie Istanbuls* (Tübingen, 1977), for help in locating the more obscure examples (and for good plans of them).

p. 176 *Paradise Lost* – for pagan gods in Milton's epic: the devils rise in a great swarm at line 331 of Book 1, and after general jokes at their expense are treated individually, Moloch from 1. 392, Chemos ('Peor his other name') from 1. 406, Baalim and Ashtaroth from 1. 422, Astoreth, called Astarte from 1. 438, Thammuz from 1. 446, Dagon from 1. 462, Rimmon from 1. 467, Osiris, Isis and Orus all in a pack from 1. 478, Belial last from 1. 490. It is Milton at his most garish and gorgeous.

p. 176 St Catherine in the Sinai – K. Weitzmann, *Monastery of St. Catherine at Mount Sinai: From the Sixth to the Tenth Century*, 1: *The Icons* (Princeton, NJ, 1992).

p. 178 William Dowsing – Trevor Cooper, ed., *The Journal of William Dowsing: Iconoclasm in East Anglia during the English Civil War* (Suffolk, 2001).

p. 180 Soviet posters – in David King's remarkable album of graphic art and photographs from his collection, *Red Star over Russia: A Visual History of the Soviet Union from 1917 to the Death of Stalin*, Tate (London, *c.* 2009).

p. 180 tearing down the colossal statue – in Eisenstein's *October* (1927–8).

p. 181 graffiti – for a compact and well-illustrated history see Anna Waclawek, *Graffiti and Street Art* (London, 2011).

p. 185 *The Wire*, a reality-based TV drama by former *Sun* reporter David Simon about drugs, politics and corruption in Baltimore, Maryland, much of which is seen from inside the city's police department. It lasted five seasons on HBO from 2002 to 2008.

p. 185 graffiti films – all of those mentioned and others besides are available on www.youtube.com.

p. 187 Tony Harrison's poem 'V' – in his *Selected Poems* (London, 1984); and read by him on www.youtube.com.

p. 187 *Iliad*: the most interesting English translations, in chronological order: George Chapman's translation of 1598–1611, in spite of awkward rhythms and twisted syntax, is worth sticking with for its continual linguistic invention; Alexander Pope, 1715–20, has a contrary failing – the heroic couplet can digest anything; I. A. Richards (not exactly a translation), 1950, for remarkable clarifications; Richmond Lattimore, 1951, seems too fluent and too flowery now; Robert Fitzgerald, 1974, the most consistently pleasing complete translation since Pope; Christopher Logue (books 1–4, 16–19), 1967–2005, mostly brilliant, but riffs on the poem rather than faithful in detail; Robert Fagles, 1990, consciously modern, tending toward jazzy.

p. 188 corpses in the *Iliad* – a recent rendering of the poem, *Memorial: An Excavation of the Iliad* by Alice Oswald (London, 2011), concentrates on corpses and landscape, to the exclusion of almost everything else. One effect of this strange procedure is to bring all the names of the dead into sharp focus.

p. 188 Ulrich von Wilamowitz-Moellendorff (1848–1931) was a legendary German classical philologist of 'terrifying erudition' and astonishing memory, who learned all the extant tragedies by heart as a teenager. He rejected large parts of the *Iliad* as inauthentic, keeping only material from Books 1 and 2, 3–6, 11, 12–15, 16–22.

p. 189 ramparts near the Greek ships – in Book 12 of the *Iliad*.

p. 190 Achilles surprising his victim in an orchard – the encounter with Lycaon, one of Priam's sons, occurs early in Book 21.

p. 191 ruin-words in the *Iliad* – 'There are also quite a few etymologically opaque adjectives that occur in highly restricted contexts, modifying one noun or a few semantically similar nouns. We do not really know what these words mean, but it is quite likely that Homer did not know, either, and the contexts in which such words appear do little to specify their meaning': Martin Mueller, *The Iliad* (Bristol, 1984 and 2009), available online at www.stoa.org/hopper.

p. 192 I. A. Richards on enjoying the foreknowledge of death, in *The Wrath of Achilles: The Iliad of Homer, shortened and in a new translation* (London, 1951), p. 6, at the end of a characteristically provocative summary of why we read the poem.

p. 192 David Jones, *In Parenthesis* (London, 1937), his memoir of his time as an infantryman in the First World War.

p. 192 Flandriad – from Flanders, by analogy with *Iliad* from Ilion, an old name for Troy.

p. 193 Rachel Bespaloff – 'On the Iliad', in *War and the Iliad* (New York, 2005). First published in French in 1943, this short piece is one of the high points of recent writing about Homer, followed here by reflections on Bespalloff by Hermann Broch.

p. 193 *The Dying Gaul* – a geometrical diagram has been discovered on the base of this sculpture which is thought to show how it fitted into a kind of constellation of other defeated figures on the Acropolis at Pergamon; see Filippo Coarelli, *Da Pergamo a Roma: i Galati nella citta degli Attalidi* (Rome, 1995), with an appendix by Myriam Fincker, 'Il diagramma inciso sul plinto del Galata morente'.

p. 194 Seamus Heaney's 'The Grauballe Man' in *North* (1975), one of four poems about bog burials.

p. 194 English translations of the *Iliad* – George Steiner, ed., *Homer in English* (London, 1996), an anthology of short selections from over a hundred Homeric translations (including a few poems more vaguely

Homeric) with an introduction and brief headnotes for each selection by George Steiner.

p. 194 Simone Weil – 'The Iliad, or the Poem of Force', in *War and the Iliad* (New York, 2005). First published in French in 1940 in a periodical based in Marseille. This is more obviously a response to the war than Bespaloff's contemporary piece (see above), the war that drove both of them to New York soon after.

p. 194 *Hamlet* – in Act II, scene 2 Hamlet recites twelve lines he remembers from a play about Pyrrhus roaming the burning city, then prods one of the visiting players to carry on where he's left off, into the scene of gruesome vengeance on the old Priam (*Hamlet* II, ii, 388–458). By this time the player is in tears, which is picked up in Hamlet's subsequent soliloquy, 'What's Hecuba to him, or he to her, / That he should weep for her?'

p. 194 Plenty of ruined cities – there's a strange genre of rubble-models that represent German cities after bombing. In his contribution to *Ruins of Modernity*, ed. Julia Hell and Andreas Schönle (Durham, NC, 2010), Helmut Puff discusses twelve of these, from the earliest, Frankfurt, dating from 1945, to the latest, Pforzheim, still under construction as he wrote, and including Heilbronn, Bielefeld, Wurzburg, Dresden, Kassel, Hannover, Munster, Schwetzingen, Munich and Hamburg.

p. 195 Studs Terkel – *Working: People Talk about What they Do all Day and How they Feel about What they Do* (New York, 1974). A remarkable range of experience, 129 different people, from 120 different occupations.

p. 195 *God's Own Junkyard: The Planned Deterioration of America's Landscape* by Peter Blake (New York, 1964), mainly black-and-white photographs from the 1950s and '60s.

p. 196 *Requiem for Detroit?*, a film by Julien Temple (2010), 76 minutes.

p. 197 *Amazon: The Truth Behind the Click*, BBC Panorama, 30 minutes, first shown 25 November 2013, a picture of working conditions in an Amazon warehouse somewhere in Wales.

p. 197 investment bankers' pay revealed on the front page of the *London Evening Standard* in November 2013.

p. 198 Ruskin drawings – *S. Michele, Lucca*, Ashmolean Museum, Oxford; *St Sauveur, Caen*, Ruskin Library, Lancaster University. A modern photograph of the carving Ruskin drew is available at www.victorianweb.org/art/architecture/gothic/ruskin/caenstsauveur.

p. 201 anti-restorers – formed the Society for the Protection of Ancient Buildings in 1877, which included William Morris, Philip Webb, W. R. Lethaby, Ernest and Sydney Barnsley.

p. 201 Shakespeare's Globe – for the building see *Rebuilding Shakespeare's Globe*, by Andrew Gurr with John Orrell (London, 1989); for performance theory see Christie Carson and Farah Karim-Cooper, *Shakespeare's Globe: A Theatrical Experiment* (Cambridge, 2008).

p. 202 Ludwig Tieck – now known to have disguised his daughter Dorothea's translations as his own.

p. 205 Williamsburg – the very long Wikipedia entry for Colonial Williamsburg airs recent controversies and chronicles the decline of Williamsburg as a paying attraction; see also Suzanne E. Coffman and Michael Olmert, *Official Guide to Colonial Williamsburg* (Williamsburg, VA, 2000).

p. 205 Colonial Parkway – part of a wider plan to keep the twentieth century from intruding on the experience of the eighteenth century. Five-hundred, mostly nineteenth-century, buildings were removed from the 'historic area', leaving 80 eighteenth-century structures standing. Later efforts to rearrange roads and keep traffic at bay have been extremely complex. Financial pressures have caused Colonial Williamsburg to sacrifice some of its seclusion by selling adjoining land for development. Paradoxes multiply here like Surinam toads.

p. 206 original pronunciation – David Crystal and his son Ben deliver famous Shakespearean passages in original pronunciation, explaining where our ideas of it came from: in an Open University talk available at www.youtube.com.

p. 206 Warsaw – pre-war photographs in a touching album published by a Polish army unit interned in Switzerland: *Warszawa Varsovie Warsaw Warschau 1945* (Basel, 1945). An album of 200 photos, evenly divided between restored Old Town and new buildings of the Soviet period: *Warszawa 1960* (1960). See aerial video of the destroyed city at www.youtube.com/watch?v=twDouTqS4c8, which seems to be made by panning over still images to give the impression of flying over the ruins.

p. 207 *Bernardo Bellotto: A Venetian Painter in Warsaw* (Milan, 2004) accompanied an exhibition of 23 of Bellotto's paintings of Warsaw at the Louvre and reproduces them all with lots of details. The relation between the paintings and the reconstruction is more complex than non-readers of Polish can easily discover. The paintings were reputedly used as much to recreate the overall perspective and sense of space as to reproduce details of facades, roofs and railings. Apparently Bellotto's colours and textures influenced reconstructions in parts of the city he never painted, so in more than one way Warsaw is more Bellotto-like than it was in the nineteenth century.

p. 208 Fredric Jameson – in 1995 at a conference in Bucharest, Jameson judged that the reconstruction of Warsaw's Old Town was a 'Disney-related operation'. The comment appeared later in his essay 'History Lessons' (from Ella Chmielewska, 'The Cultural Logic of Reconstruction: Critical history lessons in/of the post-socialist city', conference paper, Edinburgh, 2009).

p. 208 W. G. Sebald on bombing – see *On the Natural History of Destruction* (London, 2003).

p. 209 *Ephesus: The New Guide*, ed. Peter Scherrer (2000).

p. 211 Angkor – an M.Phil. thesis from the Asian Studies department of Australian National University includes valuable articles from early French investigations at Angkor as appendices, including Marchal's report on his visit to Java in 1930, two papers by Marchal on reconstruction at Banteay Srei, 1935, Mauger's account of anastylosis of a small Vietnamese shrine in 1936 and Malleret on restoration and its problems at Angkor, 1959: J. V. Crocker, 'Imagined Pasts: Anastylosis and the Creation of the Thai National Past (volume 2 appendices). Maurice Glaize's classic guidebook, *Angkor: A Guide to the Angkor Monuments* (1944), an atmospheric period piece, is downloadable at www.theangkorguide.com. Bruno Dagens gives a good summary of early activity at the site, in *Angkor: Heart of an Asian Empire* (London, 1995).

p. 214 Parthenon as a contested site – the website of the Acropolis Restoration Service is exemplary: a mine of information and extremely good recent photography. There is a virtual tour of the entire Acropolis giving high-resolution close-ups of almost any detail. Yearly newsletters focus on problems and challenges in painstaking detail. In the latest issue (2012) an article is devoted to a single crumbling capital: www.ysma.gr/en.

p. 216 Brooklyn's Hunterfly houses – see Pamela Jerome, 'An Introduction to Authenticity in Preservation', *APT Bulletin*, XXXIX/2–3 (2008), pp. 3–7.

p. 217 comprehensive archaeological map of Angkor region, 2007 – Damian Evans et al., 'A Comprehensive Archaeological Map of the World's Largest Preindustrial Settlement Complex at Angkor, Cambodia', *PNAS*, CIV/36 (2007), available at www.pnas.org.

p. 218 Vernacular buildings – Paul Oliver, *Encyclopedia of Vernacular Architecture of the World*, 3 vols (Cambridge, 1997); and Bernard Rudofsky, *Architecture without Architects: A Short Introduction to Non-pedigreed Architecture* (New York, 1965), and later reprints. If any single work set off the recent enthusiasm for vernacular, this was it.

p. 218 Ryedale Folk Museum, Hutton-le-Hole, North Yorkshire (founded 1964), tour guide and souvenir brochure, 4th edition (2001), has some detail about its donors and their collections, the history of its buildings and a bibliography.

p. 220 Hida folk village in Takayama – there are no museum publications in English, but good plans, sections and exploded structural drawings in its Japanese guidebook. For detail of villagers' lives, see Matthias Eder, 'The Folk Customs Museum in Takayama (Hida, Gifu Prefecture)', *Asian Folklore Studies*, XXXI/2 (1972), pp. 141–8.

p. 221 Ema Shu, *Mountain Folk* (*Yama no tami*), 2 vols (1949).

p. 221 villages nearby – two districts with *gassho-zukuri*: Shirakawa and Gokayama, the first easier to get to and more developed. Ogimachi is the largest village and main attraction of Shirakawa-go; many of its farmhouses are now restaurants, museums or *minshuku* for overnight stays. Gokayama is more remote: Suganuma village and Gokayama no Sato are connected to each other by a tunnel, which also connects via elevator to the parking lot overlooking the village. Ainokura is the largest and most remote of the Gokayama villages; many of the houses are still lived in. See www.japanguide.com for more information.

p. 224 *Anne Frank House: A Museum with a Story* (Amsterdam, 2001).

p. 226 Ons' Lieve Heer op Solder – see Frederik F. Barends, *Geloven in de Schaduw, Schuilkerken in Amsterdam* (Ghent, 1997), which lists 30 clandestine churches in Amsterdam and focuses on several of the surviving ones at length.

p. 227 *The Procession to Calvary* – Pieter Bruegel, 1564, Kunsthistorisches Museum, Vienna. Lech Majewski, *The Mill and the Cross* (2011), 96 minutes.

p. 228 Alan Sorrell – see Sacha Llewellyn and Richard Sorrell, eds, *Alan Sorrell: The Life and Works of an English Neo-Romantic Artist* (Bristol, 2013).

p. 231 Saiho-ji – the so-called moss temple, historically crucial for features no longer perceptible. It was redesigned by the monk Muso Soseki in the fourteenth century who devised the first promenade garden and the first dry landscape (a waterfall made of rocks recycled from prehistoric tombs). The whole is formed of two worlds in tension, the paradise of the pure land on the flat, which was open to the public, and the mountainous defiled world, open only to the monks. It sounds paradoxical and is now hard to revisualize. Two texts that help are found in François Berthier, *Reading Zen in the Rocks: The Japanese Dry Landscape Garden,* translated and with a philosophical essay by Graham Parkes (Chicago, 2000).

p. 231 Heygate Estate in Elephant & Castle, London, designed by Tim Tinker and completed in 1974, now being gradually demolished to be replaced by luxury flats. The Ferrier Estate, Kidbrooke, Greenwich, of similar date and neo-Brutalist design: twelve-storey towers and long horizontal blocks connected by elevated walkways. Well-rendered by Laura Oldfield Ford in highly detailed pencil drawings. Now entirely demolished and replaced by peak-roofed maisonettes in oatmeal brick, built by private developers using Lifschutz Davidson for design. Similar stories of misinformation and broken promises, all aimed at replacing poor tenants with well-heeled homeowners.

p. 232 second home – for seventeen years on a sheep farm in Spaunton, North Yorkshire.

p. 232 Christopher Nolan, *Memento* (2010), 113 minutes.

p. 233 Fernando Pessoa, *The Book of Disquiet*, trans. Richard Zenith (London, 2001; Portuguese edition, 1998). This book, if it is a book, has a strange history. Pessoa died in 1935. He left behind thousands of unsorted pieces, many in a notorious trunk. The present work is impossibly fragmentary, much of it written or typed on scraps of reused paper. No one had the temerity to hazard a form for all these fragments until 1982, and it was soon clear that there was more to include. Various subsequent versions picked up more parts, until there were 481 separate pieces in Zenith's edition. Four English versions of widely different length, each purporting to be complete, came out in the same year, 1991.

Acknowledgements

In fragmentary form, in lieu of a bare list of names:

Christobel Kent for her hospitality in Florence, Kelly Zinkowski and Livia Signorini for their hospitality in Rome, Philip and Nelly Trevelyan for providing a peaceful workplace over many years and for many happy evenings, Adam Caruso for his house in Swan Yard, Niall Hobhouse for the trip to Astley Castle, Ernie Hankamer for the chance to live in Munich, Eric Streiff for bike tours in Boston, my brother Craig for the trip to New Haven and the days in Amsterdam, my parents for the first trip to Williamsburg, Greg Ripley-Duggan for conversations about and tickets to Shakespeare's Globe, Roger Sale and Robert M. Adams for their example, ASD at London Metropolitan University for research trips to Thailand, Cambodia and Japan, students at ASD for discussions of Eliot, Agee, Stevens, Benjamin and much else, Colin Davies and the MA and first-year students for some memorable trips to Dungeness, Venice, Istanbul and other destinations, Charlie Chambers for a memorable trip to Greece, the helpful librarians of Worksop, the helpful staff of the London Library, Carla Marchesan for Chapman's Homer, Artis Bernard for the Book of Disquiet, Howard Davies for *p'soa* and advice on difficult pages, Tom Emerson for the lecture on incompleteness, Matthias Sauerbruch and Louisa Hutton for hospitality in Berlin, Hector Arkomanis and Andy Kelleher for excursions in Deptford and elsewhere, Andrew Mead for telling me about Cardross, Ellis Woodman for the chance to write about film, the charity shop in Kirbymoorside North Yorkshire for the Blue Cliff Record (which must stand for many other unexpected finds), Julia Sorrell for help with her father's work, Hélène Binet for the Lewerentz photograph, Vivian Constantinopoulos for much help and great patience, Robert Williams for the care and intelligence with which he read the text, Harry Gilonis for help with pictures, Michael Leaman for crucial support, and last and most of all Esther Whitby for encouragement and support of every imaginable kind.

Photo Acknowledgements

The author and publishers wish to express their thanks to the below sources of illustrative material and/or permission to reproduce it.

Photo Anonitect at the wikipedia project: p. 216; Ashmolean Museum, Oxford: p. 199; photos author: pp. 12, 37, 38, 40, 72, 73, 91, 177, 193, 215, 222, 225; photo Hélène Binet, reproduced courtesy of the photographer: p. 93; from Jakob Böhme, 'Aurora: the Day-spring, or, Dawning of the Day in the EAST', from *The Works of Jacob Behmen* [sic], *the Teutonic Theosopher*, vol. 1 (London, 1764): p. 99; British Museum, London (photo © The Trustees of the British Museum): p. 174; photo © DACS 2015: p. 156; photo Der Scutt: p. 75; Kunsthistorisches Museum, Vienna: p. 226; Kurt und Ernst Schwitters Stiftung, Hannover, on loan to the Sprengel Museum Hannover: p. 156; Library of Congress, Washington, DC (Prints and Photographs Division: pp. 34 (from 'Pictures of the house and family of an Alabama cotton sharecropper/ photographs by Walker Evans', vol. 1), 75; Museum of Fine Arts, Houston, Texas/ The Allan Chasanoff Photographic Collection/ Bridgeman Images: p. 162; from Martin Rowson, *The Life and Opinions of Tristram Shandy, Gentleman* (1996), copyright Martin Rowson; reproduced by kind permission of the artist: p. 131; Ruskin Library, Lancaster University (Ruskin Foundation collection): p. 200; The Sackler Library, Bodleian Libraries, Oxford: p. 19; photo Sipa Press/ Rex Features: p. 183; Sir John Soane's Museum, London: p. 164; photo © Riccardo Sala/ Alamy Images: p. 83; reproduced by kind permission of the Alan Sorrell Estate (www.alansorrellarchive.org.uk): p. 229; from Laurence Sterne, *The Life and Opinions of Tristram Shandy, Gentleman*, vol. VI (London, 1762): pp. 132–3; Towneley Hall Art Gallery & Museum, Burnley, Lancs: p. 165.

Tony Hisgett, the copyright holder of the images on pp. 181 and 203, and Humberto Moreno, the copyright holder of the image on p. 206, have

Index